HISTORIC TORRANCE

A Pictorial History of Torrance, California

This is
Copy Number
4579
of 5,000 copies
printed.

HISTORIC TORRANCE

A Pictorial History of Torrance, California

Written by Dennis F. Shanahan and Charles Elliott, Jr.
Designed by Wm. Fridrich

Legends Press, Redondo Beach, California

For Lady Lee —
and for 25 years of collaboration.
Time really flies when you're havin' fun! — *Denny*

To Charles —
who deserves a chance to grow up in a peaceful world, though history is against that.
And to those who — in different ways at different times during this long project —
encouraged me when I hesitated, got me up when I was down and made me believe
that together we really could make history. — *Chuck*

HISTORIC TORRANCE
A Pictorial History of Torrance, California

Published by
Legends Press
Post Office Box 10304
Torrance, California 90505

Printed in the United States of America by
Lithographix, Inc.

Page Design by Marsha McKee.
Typography by Ellen Jaklitsch.

First Edition.

Library of Congress Catalogue Card Number 84-81716.
ISBN 0-9608808-1-X.

Design by Wm. Fridrich.

Table of Contents

Foreword

As this book was going forward, the Torrance Historical Society launched another exciting project. They will place plaques at historical buildings and sites in Torrance. They began, appropriately enough, with the Society's own headquarters at the Torrance Historical Museum, 1345 Post Avenue, at Cravens.

Seen here are Mayor Jim Armstrong and Society president Georgean Griswold at the February, 1984 unveiling. Armstrong played an important role in getting the old Public Works Administration-built library for the museum, as did Claire Crane, a library commissioner and one of the founders of the Torrance Historical Society. The structure, a splendid example of the "federal architecture" of the 1930s, became available when the new Main Library opened in the new Civic Center in 1971.

Another plaque has already been placed (June, 1984) at Torrance High School, which is now enrolled in the National Register of Historic Buildings. Others are planned for the Marcelina Street post office and at the site of the old Hollywood Riviera Club.

A word now, if we may, about the philosophy which directed the authors' efforts as we wrote *Historic Torrance.*

We believe that men and women DO make a difference. They affect history; they are not its pawns or victims. So we spent considerable time with Manuel Dominguez, Sidney Torrance and Judge George W. Post; with Isabel Henderson and Dorothy Jamieson; with Albert Isen, Ken Miller and Jim Armstrong.

We subscribe to the new school of historiography, which suggests that the details of everyday life — prices, social events, slogans, street names — are invaluable for making a distant time come alive for us today.

Finally, we like to picture *Historic Torrance* in 2034 A.D. — a half century from now — especially in the hands of a woman then in her eighties, who bought it and will read it with her family here in Torrance when they ask about "the old days." Or *Historic Torrance* may be a proud possession of her son, 50, or her granddaughter, 25.

For them, the Torrance of 1950 or even 1984 will be "history." For the son, born in 1980, the Torrance of 1950 will seem a quaintly distant place belonging to people who drove funny cars, had strange haircuts and wore odd clothing. And for that granddaughter, born in 2009 A.D., the Torrance you and we know today will truly be "history."

It is with that thought, both humbling and exciting, that we include information and photographs about our recent past in Chapters 10 and 11.

The Authors

Seeing *Historic Torrance* in print marks the most noteworthy single event for our Torrance Historical Society. Preserving local history has been the general overall goal of the Society since its beginnings shortly over ten years ago. Aside from developing and maintaining a museum and placing bronze plaques on sites of local historic significance, the appearance in print of a hard-bound text illustrating and explaining the birth and growth of our fine city has been an exciting and most provocative undertaking.

Jared Sidney Torrance was well into his mature years when he ventured west from upstate New York and settled in the Pasadena area. His efforts toward realizing his dream of establishing a fully planned community of "industrial opportunity," along with the accomplishments of so many others who contributed to the well-planned growth of this community during its formative years, are beautifully preserved in this outstanding book. I am confident that all who are interested in contemporary history in general, and the city of Torrance in particular, will enjoy *Historic Torrance* for many, many years.

On behalf of the entire membership of the Torrance Historical Society, it is with a deep sense of pride and sincere pleasure that we place a copy of Legends Press' *Historic Torrance* by William Fridrich, Chuck Elliott and Denny Shanahan in your hands.

James M. Weyant, President 1984-85
Torrance Historical Society

Torrance is a unique city. Planned with an industrial, agricultural and residential balance, the quiet town of oil derricks, steel mills, and vegetable, fruit and flower fields has grown into a city with major national and international significance. And yet, we remain a community of caring residents, proud of our Indian and Spanish history and proud of the metropolitan area we have become.

The citizens of Torrance share a bond of love and loyalty for their city and a determination to maintain a balanced community. Whether born here or adopted residents like myself, it is truly "home." We raise our children, fight furiously to preserve the last wetland area of our natural heritage, and enthusiastically continue to support community traditions, like Rose Parade floats and military parades, traditions that bind us together and to our past, and set us apart as a community unafraid to continue to be the leader.

I am pleased that Legends Press and the Torrance Historical Society have chosen this time to gather and publish this story of our city in a permanent collection. A time when some of our city's first citizens can still contribute their experience, yet ironically, also a time when we see our last agricultural fields disappear and our original industrial area begin to recycle.

This book captures Torrance — what was and what is — preserving a heritage rich and exciting for all future generations.

Georgean Griswold, President 1983-84
Torrance Historical Society

It was a memorable day two years ago when I received a telephone call from Stanley Remelmeyer, immediate past president of the Torrance Historical Society, suggesting that we meet with Dennis Shanahan, a public relations expert, regarding publishing a Torrance historical book similar to the one that had just been published by Redondo Beach, written by him and William Fridrich.

Present at this meeting were Stanley Remelmeyer, Dennis Shanahan, and Chuck Elliott, a columnist for the *Daily Breeze* and later co-author with Dennis Shanahan for the Torrance historical book.

It was decided that the Torrance book could be as successful for Torrance as the Redondo Beach book was for Redondo Beach. A presentation was made to the Torrance Historical Society board of directors, who enthusiastically accepted it and voted to go ahead with publishing the book.

Thus, the Torrance historical book was born, and I am happy to say is now completed.

The book has been the work of three Torrance Historical Society administrations. We are proud to present this book to you, and we are sure it will become "a collector's item" in the future.

William A. Henderson, President 1982-83
Torrance Historical Society

7

The first inhabitants of the South Bay

The Chowigna Indians and some fascinating examples of how very much like us they were; their forgotten accomplishments and their sad and undeserved fate — 10,000 B.C.-1769 A.D.

Five centuries ago, before Europeans arrived to change the face and the fate of North America, there was life and there was culture here in what is now the city of Torrance.

Indeed, this part of the Southern California coastal plain was vivid with life, with plants, flowers, trees, with birds, fish and game and with an

imperial policy in this lonely and neglected corner of the ramshackle world empire that was Spain, thought the Chowigna had neither culture nor religion. They were determined to give them religion, and to teach them how to lead useful lives around Mission San Gabriel. ("Useful for whom?" we would now ask.) In the process, they destroyed most evidences of a frail culture that

Chumash Indians building a canoe, conceivably in the marshy and shifting estuary of the South Bay, 300 or so years ago. This model was created by Elizabeth Mason in 1929 for the Southwest Museum. Jared Sidney Torrance was a close friend of Charles Lummis who founded the museum. He donated the prominent bell tower there and served many years on the museum's board of directors. The "Tomol" or Canoe Brotherhood was an important factor in Chumash life, cutting across clan lines. The Channel Island Indians regularly crossed miles of open water in canoes like these, which may have contributed to mainland belief that the islanders were all-powerful wizards.
COURTESY OF SOUTHWEST MUSEUM, LOS ANGELES

impressively large, varied, complex and prosperous human population: the American Indians of the Shoshonean family whom we call variously the Chumash, or the Chowigna lodge, or to use, reluctantly, a Spanish name, the Gabrielino.

Let us look at how life was for them here, where in centuries since, two European cultures have successively supplanted them. To do so, we must go to the prehistorians.

They can tell us about cultures and people that flourished before the written word, even cultures whose oral records are scarcely available, because they were either suppressed or disregarded by their conquerors.

The Franciscan friars who dictated

might otherwise have survived.

The first confirmed human incursion into California was by the ancestors of the Chumash. Our best evidence points toward their arrival from Asia, via a land bridge across the Bering Strait, perhaps 12 to 15 thousand years ago.

Other Indians, already in North America, came to California from northern Mexico about the same time. Those from the East may well have been fleeing harsh winters, a practice which still flourishes 12,000 years later among members of the majority culture. As the centuries passed, the native American population of California grew to about 250,000.

Now, this is not very many people — less than twice the present-day

Grinding acorn for meal was the first and foremost order of business for an Indian family of the old South Bay.
FROM THE COLLECTION OF WILLIAM DEANE

PUBLISHED EVERY SUNDAY AND THURSDAY MOR▮
—the ONLY Newspaper Published AND PRINTED in Torrance. ▮

TORRANCE H▮

Entered as second class matter Jan. 30, 1914, at post office Torrance, California,

—and Torrance Herald Shopper reach

40th Year—No. 35   TORRANCE, CALIFORNIA, SUNDAY, MAY 2, 19▮

(Herald Photo)

FROM THE PAST . . . Clemente Barajas (left), and John Montoya examine the cache of Indian relics which they dug up while grading around new homes near 215th and Normandie Ave. Wednesday. Included in the collection are stone bowls, grinding stones on which acorns, not corn, were ground because the Indians had no agriculture; mortars, pestles, and stone cups. The discovery may be dated to pre-Spanish days—1760 and before.

(Herald Photo)

EXPERT OPINION . . . R. M. Ariss, curator of anthropology at the Los Angeles County Museum, looks at some of the stone artifacts discovered in a field near Torrance Wednesday. He pronounced the objects well-preserved remnants of an Indian civilization which flourished here in pre-Spanish days. A check of the site was to be conducted to get a more accurate date on when the relics were used as kitchenware by Shoshonean speaking Indians. If Spanish relics are found in the same place, that would mean the Spaniards were already here and would place the date after 1760. If Spanish remains are not found, the artifacts are probably pre-Spanish and therefore can not be pinned down to a definite date, Ariss stated.

Museum Official Says Find May Be Prior to 1760s

Stone kitchenware which may date back as far as the pre-Spanish days was discovered in a field near 215th St. and Normandie Ave. Wednesday by Clemente Barajas, 1552 W. Carson St. and John Montoya, 18545 Roslin Ave.

Barajas and Montoya were grading in a tract around some new homes in the area preparatory to landscaping when they began to turn up strange looking stone cups, grinding stones, and mortars and pestles made of rock about three feet below surface.

When they realized what they had discovered, the men began to set aside all of the artifacts which they unearthed. They came up with quite a collection.

R. M. Ariss, curator of Anthropology at the Los Angeles County Museum, examined the find Friday morning and said that it contains some very good examples of utensils used by the Shoshonean speaking Indians in pre-Spanish California days—before the 1760s.

To Examine Site

Ariss was to examine the site of the discovery to see if Spanish tools and utensils can be found at the same level as the stone instruments. If so, this would date the Barajas find as in the Spanish era of early California history. If no Spanish remnants can be found, the pots and pestles could very well be from pre-Spanish days and undateable.

Lack Records

Ariss explained that it is extremely difficult to trace human life back to its beginnings in this part of California because of lack of adequate records. Speculating, he said that the Indians may have come here up to 3000 years ago.

The stoneware is mostly soapstone, a soft material, and volcanic rock. Both of these varieties of stone were probably gathered while moist or warm and thus were easily shaped into pots and cups by the Shoshonean speaking Indian tribes, Ariss said.

The rarest things about the Barajas—Montoya discovery, the Anthropologist said, are some examples of pottery, with designs on the outside, which are seldom found in this area. This
▮ pottery was made in

This clipping tells of an exciting find made near here 30 years ago. It is the hope of similar finds that keeps archeologists and amateur diggers so young in spirit. Just this year, the tomb of a Mayan noble, probably from about 800 A.D., reminded us again that the past is not yet a completely open book.

FROM THE COLLECTION OF WILLIAM DEANE

★ ★ ★ ★
OVERED
TRACT

"Twice Weekly Is Twice
As Well Read"

10¢

Per Copy

Every Sunday and Thursday
Home Delivered by Carrier
30 Cents Per Month
(Average 9 Issues per Month)

ONE FAirfax 8-4000 ◄═══► 12   12 PAGES

population of Torrance — spread out across 160,000 square miles. On the other hand, it was about 15 percent of the native American population at the time. It seems that the Indians, with a choice of all 48 continental states to call home, were the first, but not the last, Americans to opt for California.

The Coastal Indians, like most in California, were hunters, gatherers and fishers, not farmers. They ground acorns and mesquite pods into a meal which nutritionists tell us was healthful and high in calories.

The ocean teemed for them. They may even have hunted the whales in their annual migrations, though probably with infrequent success. They may only have learned to hunt the whale from the Russians and the Aleuts, when they began coming south to Fort Ross and beyond in the eighteenth century.

We do know that the Chumash made excellent plank canoes and that one of their most important organizations, after the family and the lodge, was the Canoe Brotherhood or Tomol.

Chumash basketweaving was stunningly beautiful, both in design and function. The Russians fancied it greatly. Through Alaska and Siberia, many fine specimens were carried in the eighteenth and nineteenth centuries to Moscow and St. Petersburg. It was so good, in fact, that it thwarted any creative instincts the Chumash might otherwise have expressed in pottery.

This was because other Indians, especially those of the San Bernardino Mountains, appreciated Chumash basketware so much that they came regularly to such natural meeting places as the salt lake, in what became Redondo, to trade for it. What they traded was all the pottery the Chumash needed.

This also gave the Chumash the chance to trade their carvings, including pipes made from steatite, the white-green talc or "soapstone" found in the Channel Islands. Since abalone shells, prized for their iridescence, were a medium of exchange among Southern California Indians, the Indians of the South Bay were in a favorable position among their Indian brethren. They had easy access to salt, steatite, abalone shells and basketware, all things much in demand inland.

Such economic realities doubtless led to sporadic warfare, conducted with simple and relatively ineffective bows and arrows, spears and clubs. But since the territorial imperative was largely absent, the Chumash did not find that much to fight about. The weak usually moved away from the strong. Indeed, that was the first reaction of many Chumash when the Spanish came.

All of these details paint a picture of the Chumash as a simple Stone Age society. This could lead to the error of regarding them as not just primitive, but also stupid. Certainly the Spanish friars began with the presumption that they were childlike, though they softened that attitude with a genuine desire to teach them agricultural arts and husbandry, and to "save their souls."

In fact, too late to be effective, the Mexican governors of California did try to make landowners out of the Mission Indians, an effort doomed by Mexican corruption and inertia, and brought to an end by the American conquest.

That conquest, of course, brought into play an attitude toward the Indians which was even harsher in its effects than the Spanish had been. Those whom disease had spared, and these were only about 20,000 of the 80,000 or so gathered around the missions between 1780 and 1850, were now to be ignored, used or dispatched by the new rulers of California.

Here is a revealing paragraph from a Los Angeles newspaper in 1869: "For years past it had been the practice of those engaged in the cultivation of the soil, to hang around the Mayor's court on Monday morning and give the degraded Indian a few dollars with which to pay his nominal fine for having been dragged through the streets to the station house in a state of beastly intoxication and on Saturday night after

deducting the sum advanced, pay him a couple of dollars, should he not lose his miserable life in a drunken brawl before that time — and thus the process goes on."

The Gabrielino, who had largely lost their wild skills after two generations under mission rule, were ill-equipped to survive in the increasingly complex economy of Southern California. The California Desert Indians — the Agua Caliente and the Borrego, for example — have survived. Thanks to the vagaries of Palm Springs real estate, some even prospered, though in most cases only briefly. The last full-blooded Gabrielino died in 1950.

□ □ □

Before we settle for an assessment of these first settlers of Torrance as primitive, let us take note of how well they did what their environment required them to do. The more we learn of them, the more we realize how sophisticated, how in harmony with their environment they were.

They had a great deal of star lore, for example. Their shamans knew how to anticipate eclipses. When they occurred, the shamans would rally the people to sing songs "to help the moon get well." (On the other hand, they probably didn't have a Deluge Myth. Earlier stories that they did, probably reflect the desire of Christian explorers to find, wherever they looked, such endorsement of Genesis.)

Some of their customs were tenacious, surviving with their sadly few descendants into the twentieth century. One such was their belief in "charm stones" and the belief that these small, round, flat objects were actually live animals that could burrow into the earth when it suited them. In 1928, a rancher who thought he had found one, offered it to an Indian friend who recoiled in horror, crying, "Be careful! It might not be dead."

The South Bay Gabrielinos had a wide variety of pleasures to help soften the edges of what was already a pleasant succession of seasons in the sun.

They gambled, though not with the excessive zeal of the Mayans far to the south, where a loss at handball could mean disgrace and total ruin. They let their humor show in their everyday life and language; their name for December, a month after the harvest, meant "when

11

you get padded out with fat all over your body."

In the nineteenth century, when Gabrielinos felt they could trust a white man, they would let him witness their devastating parodies and imitations of their Caucasian overlords. The tiny wrinkles of suppressed laughter around the mouth of a Gabrielino absorbing a tongue lashing for his "incompetence" often came because, at night, in secret and among his comrades, he would play Rich Little and have his revenge.

Much will be forever denied us. Because the archeological record has been plundered by "pot hunters," little is being found today.

As Bernice Eastman Johnston says (*California Gabrielino Indians*, Southwest Museum, 1962, p. 75): "Along the ocean shores of their own homeland the Gabrielino villages teemed with well-fed fishermen and their thriving families. Kitchen-middens, or ancient refuse heaps, mark these remains, deep, darkened with innumerable bits of charcoal from old fires, and with a telltale oiliness that adds its own evidence to the myriads of fishbones and broken shells.

"Most such middens, as well as the burial grounds, have long since been robbed of their mortars and pestles, of their fine chert and obsidian arrow points and knives, of their exquisitely shaped fish hooks of haliotis shell, by casual or commercial souvenir hunters."

In an elegiac tribute, Johnston sums up the Gabrielinos' view of the world from which they were so abruptly torn two hundred years ago. "We have John Peabody Harrington to thank for the preservation of a phrase which sounds

as though it might have been the first tenet in a Gabrielino's statement of his faith: TAVI HETEKRINUJ ATAVIN TUVANGNAR — God has placed the whole world."

□ □ □

In 1769, it was still a world of their own, except for the legends of Viscaino's, Cabrillo's and Drake's hasty visits generations before. Since then, only the stories of a few Channel Islanders and coastal headland dwellers every generation or so, insisted that they had glimpsed great ships with huge sails far at sea. (The Manila galleon, bound for Acapulco every year, would make its landfall off California and run before the wind to Mexico.) Such reports must have been greeted with the scepticism we now afford UFO stories.

And then in 1769, the legends became real as Gaspar de Portola and Junipero Serra led their little band into the South Bay of Southern California. Those visitors arrived with preconceived notions and prejudices which would hurt the Indians greatly.

At times, the lust for gold led Spanish explorers to cling against all reason to the belief that they would find whole cities festooned with that metal. When the reality fell short of that golden dream, the reaction was to hold the Indians they did find in unwarranted contempt. They scorned their "indolence," not asking what need there was for frantic industry in the California that was, before their arrival. They made an issue of nakedness, blissfully unaware that a few hundred years later, highly civilized Californians of European ancestry would become world-famous for aesthetically pleasing seminudity.

They made no effort to understand the

Indians' spiritual scheme, built on a complex relationship between man and animals, the land and the sea, and the winds and the rain. They settled down instead to teach the Indians a set of values derived from Palestine a millenium and a half earlier, and even then disputed by Protestants and Catholics in their European homeland.

With these observations in mind, let us look again at those who moved about in the great South Bay, through the gently rolling grasslands which were to become Torrance.

The whole question of names for peoples, tribes, cultures and languages is a weighty one. Indeed, it is a safe rule to assume that the names for past peoples which we use today are not those which they themselves or their contemporaries used.

Perhaps as good a clarification as we need is in Bernice Johnston's treatise: "A Hokan-speaking people whom we call the Chumash. Long separated from the tribes of the southern border counties and those other Hokans, the Yuma and Mojave bands, the Chumash had made, in later periods, a striking development along technological lines."

In 1769, Father Crespi, diarist of the Portola expedition, wrote of them: "They are of good figure, active and industrious and inventive. They have surprising skill and ability in the construction of their canoes, which are of good pine planks, well joined and of a graceful shape with two prows. They handle them with equal skill. Three or four men go out into the open sea in them to fish, and they hold as many as ten men. They use long oars with two blades, and row with indescribable lightness and speed."

Do Crespi's oarsmen bear any resemblance to the "Diggers" that American writers were making fun of a century later?

From the collection of William Deane, a lifelong student of the Indian cultures of the South Bay, especially these found in his home town of Torrance. Studies in North American prehistory are still exciting. Serious scholars believe they will find proof that the great woolly mammoth survived into the very dawn of historic times in the Rocky Mountains.

FROM THE COLLECTION OF WILLIAM DEANE

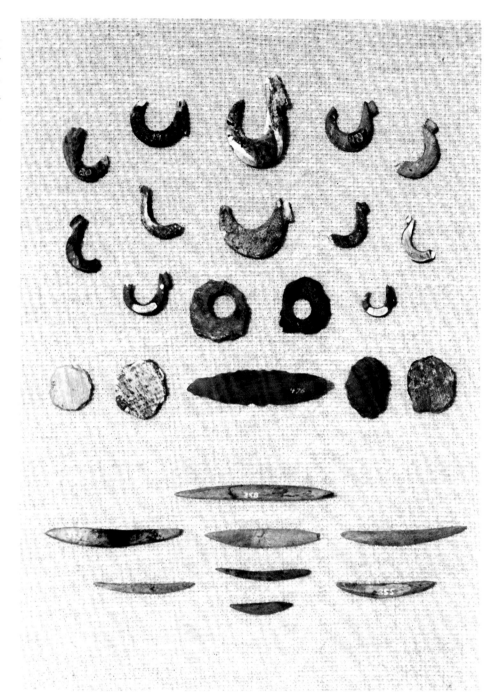

If what has survived of South Bay Indian cultures seems primitive, we must remember that all their wooden and other vegetable creations have inevitably disappeared. Many of those — canoes, ceremonial gear and weapons — were, of course, more sophisticated. These painstakingly channelled-out stones were doubtless intended as ax heads.

FROM THE COLLECTION OF WILLIAM DEANE

So important were such canoes and other items originated by these inventive people that they were copied by many of the Shoshoneans. The result was that the material culture of these tribes, for an indefinite distance down the coast and on the Channel Islands, was practically one and the same.

As a rough guide to linguistic separation, we know that Malibu was Chumash, while Topanga was Gabrielino. The baptismal register and other records at Mission San Fernando show that three languages — Chumash, Serrano and Gabrielino — were spoken around it. The impression is of fluidity and mobility, much like present-day California.

Overall, there is also the clear impression of what can only be called a busy, even crowded, scene along the coast. Listen to Sebastian Viscaino's diarist, writing of his experience in 1602, when the Spaniards were the guests of the Channel Island Gabrielinos: "We anchored and the admiral ... with some soldiers went ashore. Many Indians were on the beach, and the women treated us to roasted sardines and small fruit-like sweet potatoes.

"The general gave them beads and they gave him prickly pears and a grain like the gofio of the Canary Islands, in some wicker baskets very well-made, and water in vessels resembling flasks which were like rattan inside and very thickly varnished outside. They had acorns, and some very heavy fur, which they used for blankets."

13

The Channel Islanders were so highly regarded by their mainland cousins that they were reputed to have the fiercest and most able shamans. Most of the poetic and inspiring elements of coastal religion came from the Islands, as did steatite carvings of dolphins and whales, for example, which delight us today.

Much of what we know about the vanished Gabrielino nation, their Chumash cousins and the Canelino culture which they created is due to the diligence of the Southwest Museum and the zeal of its founder, Charles Fletcher Lummis.

It is good to know that one of the earliest and most substantial benefactors of the museum was Jared Sidney Torrance, who was president of the museum board for the last four years of his life.

☐ ☐ ☐

In our zeal to redeem the California Coastal Indians from their undeserved reputation as stupid brutes, we must not go to another extreme and paint them as well-adjusted natural philosophers — dwellers in Arcadia.

Like all primitive peoples, their lives were excessively governed by taboos and a strict ritual for every aspect of birth, sexual maturity, marriage, illness and death. We say "excessive"; Ramadan, kosher food and indulgences remind us that the three great monotheistic religions also have "taboos" and rituals which, to a Martian visitor, might seem pointless.

One of the Chumash ritual indulgences, their equivalent of "getting stoned," was the *totoache* cult when the juice of the jimson weed was decocted and drunk, or the weed itself burned and its fumes inhaled, to induce stupor and visions.

They had other means of expressing an ecstatic communion with nature and all its forces — ground paintings, music created with deer bone flutes and ritual branding of themselves.

Even in the San Bernardino Mountains and beyond Cajon Pass, where their legends taught them that their Shoshonean ancestors first came into the country "when the earth was still soft," ritual songs were in "the ocean language," the tongue spoken by the valued and revered sorcerers of the

Every nation under heaven has a special skill, some difficult and demanding art at which it excels all others. The Vikings had their longboats, the Mayans their calendar, the ancient Greeks their sculpture — and the Chumash had their basketware. European museums prize their examples of it; the inland neighbors of the Chumash appreciated it so much that they traveled from the San Bernardino Mountains all the way to the salt lake at Redondo to trade for it.

A Chowigna basketmaker, about 1900, surrounded by evidences or recreations of tribal culture and economy. Chumash and Canelino basketware was so magnificently done that, carried home by the Russians, it attracted the admiration of all Europe, and examples can still be found in museums there. This woman's parents probably encountered Fray Junipero Serra in the late eighteenth century; their resettlement under the walls of Mission San Gabriel may have been carried out by Juan Dominguez, acting under orders from Gaspar de Portola.

Channel Islands. Think of this as their equivalent to Church Latin!

Their shamans were not altogether free to ride roughshod over the clan, group or tribe. In the nineteenth century, an inland shaman, a Cahuillo, was killed by his people, led by his own daughter. He was apparently too powerful. His talents, as the Gabrielinos put it: "He could catch bullets in his hand, pull tobacco from the ground and see the child in the sun."

The Gabrielinos had some customs which seem different from ours — until we tilt our perspective a quarter turn and look at them anew. For example, when they reached puberty, Gabrielino girls were baked for several days in a pit. But there is evidence that, to reduce expenses, some clans would delay the ceremony for some girls and hurry it for others, so that they could have a "bakeoff" with half a dozen or more at once. It sounds like Las Madrinas.

Here are some more tantalizing details of Chumash and Gabrielino life. They may help us, across the blur of the

centuries, to see them as real people.

Like the Northwest Indians, they practiced "potlatch" or the duty of the prosperous to impoverish themselves by feast and gift-giving. Their chiefs, clearly as a reward for their added responsibilities, were given the privilege of practicing polygamy.

Their warfare was sometimes bloody; just as often it was tongue-in-cheek or downright hypocritical. They practiced verbal slanging matches, where enemies massed near each other and shouted maledictions and insults in song and poetry. Nowadays, the practice in our urban areas is called "ringing the changes" or "signifying." Johnny Carson regularly practices variations on it: "May the bluebird of happiness commit a *faux pas* on your toupee."

They loved steambaths and they loved to lay about for hours, basking in the California sunshine. They were obsessive about the need to bathe every day, preferably in running water. In other words, they would have been right at home in a typical Torrance condo complex in 1984!

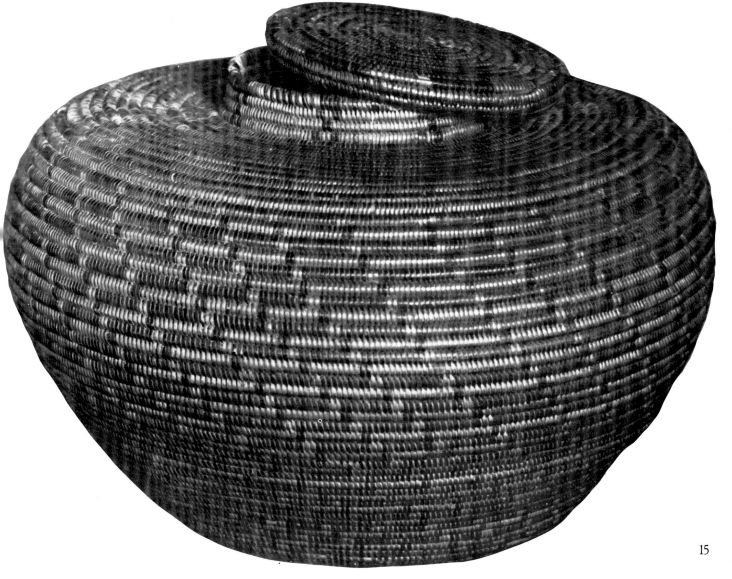

Some things which they did well we are just now learning about. A recent show, "Skywatchers of Ancient California," mounted by D. Travis Hudson of Santa Barbara Museum of Natural History, is a vivid demonstration of this.

We see, for example, recreations of Chumash observing sites, where a particular alignment of rocks and rock markings points to a spot on a distant hill where the sun rose at the winter solstice. In one case, the "observatory" was set up so that the sun shone through a hole in a rock at solstice rising, and at no other time.

On Cowles Mountain in San Diego County, rituals involving rocks and a bisected circle took place at the winter solstice. The bisection still clearly points directly to solstice sunrising.

Perhaps we might try this experiment in empathizing. Imagine a dark and stormy South Bay night, like those in January of 1983. Suddenly, there is a glitch in the warp and woof of time. You are carried back five hundred years. The walls of your home have dissolved around you, your Rolex has disappeared from your wrist and your Levis have vanished, as have your La Coste shirt and your Adidas shoes.

The Porsche is not in the garage; in fact, the garage is gone too. Looking toward Del Amo Fashion Center for succor, all you see is marshland and only the Palos Verdes hills beyond to assure you that though you may have been carried back in time, you have not been transported elsewhere in space.

You see before you a man, slight of build, clad at most in a loincloth. He is carrying a spear, a dead rabbit, and a collection of nuts and herbs. Up ahead is a woman with small children, peering out of a thatch hut. But it does look warm and dry, and smoke indicates a blessed fire.

The man beckons tentatively, cautiously. But he seems willing to be friendly. You hope so. You realize that you are terribly ill-prepared for life in fifteenth century California and that there is much he can teach you.

Much of this vivid prehistoric life took place within the present-day boundaries of Torrance, of course.

We noted in our previous book, *Old Redondo*, some settled sites which amateur archeologist John Bradley, himself of Comanche, Creek and Irish extraction, had described for us. One site was along the Torrance/Redondo border, especially near the coast; another was around the Hollywood Riviera and south from it. Ax heads have been found near Torrance and Prospect. Indeed, this may have been a focus for ceremonials.

One of the most interesting finds came in the mid-fifties, when Torrance's rapid growth led to home construction and site excavation on an unprecedented scale. On May 2, 1954, the *Torrance Herald* called attention to an exciting archeological find in a field near 215th Street and Normandie.

R.M. Ariss, curator of anthropology at the Los Angeles County Museum, determined that most of the stoneware was soapstone, likely from the Channel

Those who would like to know more about the South Bay Indian way of life are urged to visit the Southwest Museum. Torrance residents can take pride in the role Jared Sidney Torrance played in helping this valuable repository achieve its respected position. We need such places to remind us of those who came before us. By 1930, only 30 people in Southern California claimed Shoshonean ancestry in the census; by 1950, the last full-blooded Gabrielino had died.

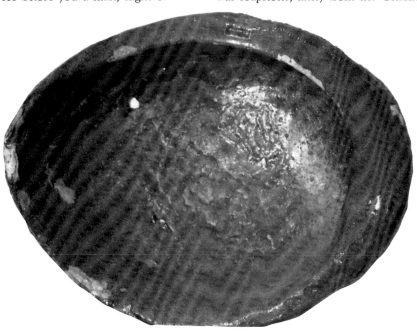

The ocean gave up its treasures for the Channel Islanders and the Chumash or Gabrielino Indians of the South Bay mainland. This abalone shell was a plate, a cup and a ladle for a contented family in the Palos Verdes hills long before Gaspar de Portola and Junipero Serra arrived in 1769.

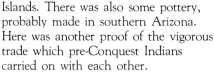

Islands. There was also some pottery, probably made in southern Arizona. Here was another proof of the vigorous trade which pre-Conquest Indians carried on with each other.

Some of the most worthwhile local archeological work has been done by dedicated amateurs. As one put it in a recent letter: "Digging for Indian relics is against the law ... in the 1930s, Malaga Cove was private property but was open land with no posted 'keep out' signs or fences. Lots of people would dig there and I don't know of anyone ever being run off. So ... I will just say I picked my relics up after strong winds had moved the sand and exposed them."

William Deane, a long-time resident of Torrance whose father was the first postal employee to carry mail on foot in Torrance (1924), recalls finding large stone mortars, about 1951, north of 215th Street and Normandie. He found another near the corner of Hickory and Maricopa, north of Torrance Boulevard, when the land was still being farmed.

Perhaps the most thorough and exciting excavations here were those done by the University of Southern California in 1936-37 in the sand dune on the bluff above Malaga Cove. Edwin Francis Walker directed the work on a stretch of coastal cliff owned by Clifford F. Reid, the developer of Hollywood Riviera.

Stratified sites, where erosion and the action of wind and weather on an isolated area have allowed artifacts to be covered over in clearly defined layers, are rare in Southern California. This one promised such finds that a call went out for volunteers. These labored on weekends and during their summer vacations. What these dedicated amateurs accomplished almost fifty years ago was remarkable.

The cliff itself rose 223 feet above the

ocean, the first 165 feet of it being solid Pleistocene uplift. Atop that was 25 feet of terraced detritus like fine salt, washed from low hills to the north. Above that was 33 feet of sand dune, the last eight of it wind-blown with no evidence of human occupancy. But in the top three feet of detritus and the lower 25 feet of sand, were the stratified evidences of four distinct occupancies, clearly separated in time and sophistication.

Level I, in the yellow detritus, was almost as hard as stone; "ice picks could penetrate it only an inch or two ... no one had worked this lowest level before." They found microliths, tiny chipped stone implements and worked shells there. Harpoon barbs were smoothed and polished. There was evidence that the people of this "shell village" hunted sea lions, seals, sea otters, deer and porpoises. No human bones were found, which could mean simply that the diggings were not where the cemetery was. David Banks Rogers, a respected prehistorian who visited the site, said that Level I was the oldest culture he had ever seen unearthed.

The Level II site, at the base of the sand dune, was much larger. Human burial and ceremonial reburial were both much in evidence. Manos and metates, the stones used for grinding and milling seeds, acorns and roots, abounded. There were only a few animal and bird bones; hunting was not important in this people's economy. Every evidence is that they brought their culture with them, fully developed. They may have been separated in time from the Level I people by more than 1,000 years. After a while, the Level II people disappeared from the cove, perhaps moving inland because of earthquakes or storms. (There is plenty of evidence, in this and other sites, of earthquakes in prehistoric times.)

The Level III people who came next had large stone mortars and long stone pestles. They were successful hunters and fishermen. They may not have gone to sea after whales, though we know that the Indians farther up the coast did. But when wounded whales drifted ashore, they obviously took them. We have circumstantial evidence, in the form of beautifully made abalone fish hooks, that they had something like the board boat or "tomolo." This was like an outrigger canoe without the outrigger. The Indians of this area were using it when the Spaniards arrived.

Level IV showed the development of an ingenious basket hopper mortar, with the hopper being the rim of the basket fastened with asphaltum, preventing the escape of acorn meal or seed meal during the pounding.

Some artifacts not found at Malaga Cove, but which we know from excavations elsewhere that this culture possessed, were balsa boats of tule grass, wickiups, seagrass skirts and the boomerang-like rabbit stick.

They had an abundant supply of animal food. They enjoyed enough leisure that they left behind hundreds of elaborately painted gaming stones. And they buried their dead usually in the flexed position, knees drawn up to the torso. They rarely practiced cremation.

This occupancy clearly lasted into historic times; a few small Spanish trade beads are found at the very top. Chowigna was probably abandoned shortly after 1769 when the friars began gently, but oh so firmly, to gather the Indians of this area under the walls of Mission San Gabriel.*

*The authors are grateful to William Deane, a student of Indian lore, a long-time resident of Torrance and a member of the Torrance Historical Society, for much of this information.

A giant oak standing among acorns

Manuel Dominguez and the empire he inherited, nurtured and defended; his formidable daughters and their canny and loyal advisors — 1769-1882.

Life in the South Bay changed very much in 1769. In a last spasm of imperial energy, Spain decided to impose its writ upon Alta California in fact, as well as in name.

Viceroy General Jose de Galvez had spurred Madrid to this effort by dark warnings of a Russian threat. In fact, the Russians and their Aleut conscripts

from La Paz in Baja California. One officer, Manuel Costanso, wrote grandiloquently in his diary: "This enterprise desired for so many years, begun many times with great preparations and expenses, will undoubtedly be pleasing to the August Monarch of Spain."

We do not know how a rough-hewn

What would lovers of history not give if this ruined adobe, photographed in 1890, could have been preserved! It was the very home which the old soldier, Juan Jose Dominguez, great-uncle of Manuel Dominguez, built in 1784, when he took his discharge bonus on this distant frontier of imperial Spain. The home stood on the northwest slope of Dominguez Hill, near Del Amo and Alameda. A pious man who never married, he spent much of his time doing church work and socializing with the friars at Mission San Gabriel. In his final years, he was cared for at Mission San Juan Capistrano by his nephew, Cristobal, Manuel Dominguez' father, to whom Juan Jose left the vast rancho.

were fishing and whaling off the California coast and behaving badly in the Channel Islands.

There were also concerns about the British. They now had the commanding position in North America, accorded by the Treaty of Hubertusberg in 1763 ending the Seven Years' War. Spain reacted with a dramatic expansion on one of its many frontiers.

These were the secular considerations. The spiritual were left to the Franciscans, successors to the contentious Jesuits whom Spain was now expelling from Mexico. Junipero Serra had this matter in charge; Gaspar de Portola was the military chieftain.

The sea-borne element in the great expedition sailed on January 9, 1769,

sergeant in the land force, Juan Jose Dominguez, viewed the move north. Of his background we know only that his family was from the fierce, energetic province of Catalonia in northeast Spain. But he did his work well, we may conclude, as the Spaniards toiled their way to San Francisco Bay and back, and established, between 1769 and 1773, several missions.

One such, of importance to our story, was Mission San Gabriel, founded in 1771. It was there that the Chowigna, Chumash and Gabrielino Indians of the South Bay were gathered in by the Franciscans. They were to be taught Christianity and industriousness simultaneously. It does not surprise us that many of them found the combination unappealing, and fled for a few more years of freedom in the Palos

The pattern of a well-ordered and prosperous life. *History of Los Angeles County,* Thompson and West, Oakland, California, 1880, made available to us by Ken Bennett and Judson Grenier of CSUDH, tells that in 1858, Manuel Dominguez, while a rich man, only held property worth about 70 percent as much as his brother Nasario's. Confirmation of Manuel's title, which came the following year, increased the value of Rancho San Pedro dramatically.

Verdes hills, or even farther, to their distant kinsmen deep in the San Bernardino Mountains.

Juan Dominguez took his retirement here on the frontier in 1784. What a retirement bonus it was, even then. What it has become just two hundred years later!

It was nothing less than the 75,000-acre Rancho San Pedro (17 square leagues). It included present-day Torrance, Palos Verdes, Lomita, Wilmington, Gardena, Compton, Carson, the Dominguez area, western Long Beach, San Pedro, Terminal Island and Redondo Beach.

Juan Dominguez ran cattle on his ranch, never married and spent his time socializing at Mission San Gabriel. When he died in 1809, he left the rancho to his nephew, Sergeant Jose Cristobal Dominguez, stationed in San Diego.

According to *Time and the Terraced Land*, Cristobal was so appalled at the debts his uncle had left that he was quite content to let his uncle's major domo pay them off and then assume the style of the owner of the grant. This man, named Gutierrez, was from a

prominent Spanish family and was related to the Sepulvedas, to whom he confirmed permission to graze cattle on the Palos Verdes peninsula, thus lending credibility to their later successful claim to adverse possession. Gutierrez even became for many years "Judge of the Plains," the arbiter during the annual chaotic cattle roundup and branding in which all the ranchers shared and socialized.

Jose Cristobal Dominguez never thought enough about his wild northern holdings to even visit them. But when he died in 1825, his son, Manuel Dominguez, with more foresight, moved his mother here. He began buying out his brothers and sisters, and built a house on Dominguez Hill above Alameda Street. In 1827, he married Maria Engracia de Cota.

For the next 55 years, this extraordinary man prospered and was content. His was the first major California land grant. It was to be diminished only by the successful effort of the Sepulveda family to claim the 32,000 acres of the Palos Verdes hills because the Dominguez family never occupied or utilized the area. Unique among the old Spanish land grants, and largely due to the

Three documents which help to tell the Dominguez story. Left, the 1773 payroll records of the original *Compania de Cuera*, at Loreto in Baja California. Juan Dominguez' name is on them; his pay then was modest, but it was to be enhanced by his retirement bonus — the entire South Bay. Middle, title page of the decision which brought to a victorious conclusion Manuel Dominguez' thirty year battle to retain the vast Rancho Dominguez. The year was 1858 and the grant to 43,119 acres was now confirmed by President James Buchanan. The 30,000 acres of the Rancho Palos Verdes, part of Juan Dominguez' original grant, had been lost to the Sepulvedas by adverse possession. Right, Manuel Dominguez' signature on the California Constitution, signed in 1849. He was the leader of the seven Spanish-Californians among the 48 delegates. Even the victors in the recent war held him in high regard; one called him "a giant oak standing among acorns."

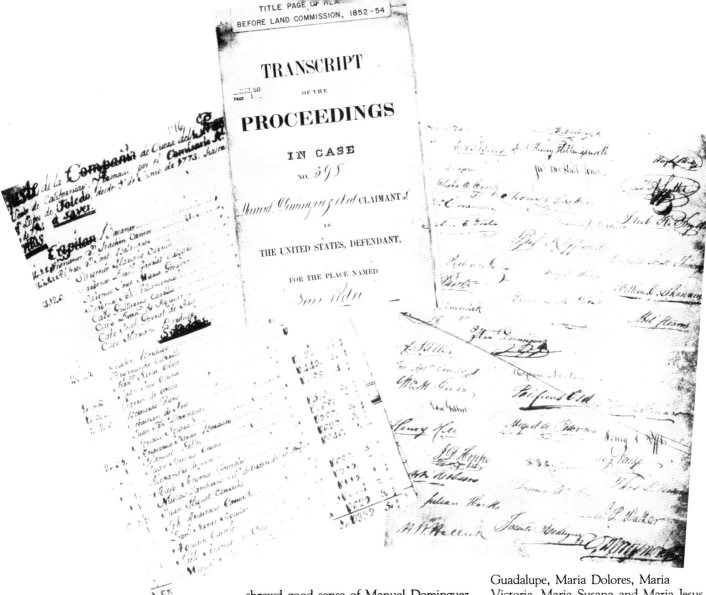

The Dominguez adobe sits on 17 acres of carefully tended land set off by ancient olive trees and hundreds of rose bushes. A California Historical Landmark, it is now essentially restored to what it was and became over the past two centuries. Four flags — Spain's, Mexico's, the Republic of California's and the American — have flown over it, and do so today in harmony. Father Patrick McPolin of the Claretians and the Dominguez family descendants are primarily responsible for the authenticity of the restoration. Dominguez heirs donated furniture for the bedrooms, living room, chapel and kitchen. The Victoria Carson room, for example, has been restored to reflect the solid serenity of the post-Civil War period when Manuel Dominguez, confirmed by President Buchanan (1859) in the possession of his fabulous empire, lived out his years with the respect and affection of his new neighbors. Victoria had married her father's trusted aide, George Carson, in 1857, when she was a strong-willed girl of 15. Speaking in 1972 to Judson Grenier, her 79-year-old grandson, John Victor Carson, still recalled her with awe and respect.

shrewd good sense of Manuel Dominguez from 1825 until his death in 1882, the family holdings survived and prospered.

Retaining the rancho against the legal wiles of the new Californians was no easy task. It took iron nerves and great steadiness of purpose. Witness a note Dominguez executed in 1855 to borrow $12,000 at three percent per month, with an undivided half interest in the entire ranch as security. He clearly needed the money desperately to fight his never-ending legal battles.

He served in positions of trust under the Spanish, Mexican and American flags. He was councilman, alcalde, prefect, a delegate in 1848 at the California Constitutional Convention and in 1852 was a Los Angeles County Supervisor.

Though his two sons died early, six of his eight daughters survived him; five of them married and three had children. The names are familiar to South Bay residents. (Streets in Redondo Beach and nearby cities were named for the ladies.) The sisters: Ana Josefa, Guadalupe, Maria Dolores, Maria Victoria, Maria Susana and Maria Jesus de los Reyes. Maria Victoria's husband: George Carson. (He was her father's principal assistant and ran the rancho until he died in 1901. Victoria and George Carson married in 1857, when she was only 15.) Susana's husband: Dr. Gregorio Del Amo. Maria Dolores' husband: James A. Watson. Maria Reyes' husband was John F. Francis.

There were, of course, some sales of Dominguez lands over the years. Don Manuel himself had sold the 214-acre Redondo salt lake to Henry Allanson and William Johnson in 1854 for five hundred dollars. In the same year, pressed for cash, he sold the 2,400 acres which is now the heart of Wilmington to Phineas Banning.

When Maria Dolores Watson, a widow for 55 years, died in the old ranch house in 1924, it was bequeathed to the church. It became a Claretian Seminary in 1927. The Claretians were founded in Spain in 1849 and members of the order first came to California in 1907. Completely and lovingly restored, it has been an official California State

Landmark since 1945. It is, in the words of Dr. Robert Gillingham, the official historian of the Rancho San Pedro, "a fitting monument to a distinguished pioneer family."

Maria de los Reyes Dominguez Francis became the richest of the family in 1922, because she was sole owner of the land on Dominguez Hill where oil was first discovered. For some years thereafter, she had the distinction of paying more income tax than any other woman in the country. When she died at 86 in 1933, a widow and childless, she left most of her wealth to the Dominguez Estate Company.

In fact, there is a connection between the discovery of oil in Torrance and elsewhere on the Rancho San Pedro in 1922 and the building of the large 60-year-old structure across the courtyard from the old Dominguez adobe.

Father Patrick McPolin studied at Dominguez Seminary soon after it opened, and then returned in 1965 to supervise the restoration of the old adobe. He says, "The property was signed over to us in 1922. And that was the same year — it was a few months later — that the Del Amos discovered oil in Dominguez Hill. The family, which had been kept broke by taxes until then, found their worries were over. Successively, each member of the family found oil on her property. So," Father McPolin says, "in gratitude to God for all His bounty, the family put up this building for us."

In 1892, George Carson and his principal advisor, Henry O'Melveny, decided $250,000 was a good price for a scrubby atoll named Rattlesnake Island after its only inhabitants. So they sold it to the Terminal Railroad Company, which obviously decided that changing the name was their first order of business. And in 1885, Daniel Freeman and Vail had bought 400 acres between the salt lake and Clifton which was eventually to become the nucleus of Redondo Beach.

The Dominguez Estate Company played a major role in the development of Torrance and the South Bay. It was formed in 1907 when the oldest of Manuel Dominguez' daughters, Ana Josefa Dominguez Guyer, died a widow and without children. The company was the device employed to transmit her valuable property to her five sisters. Her sister Guadalupe, who never married, died in 1913 and used the same technique. So did "Reyes," Mrs. Francis, twenty years later. The other sisters (Mrs. Del Amo, Mrs. Watson and Mrs. Carson) left separate estates of course.

John Victor Carson, Victoria's grandson, deprecated the conventional wisdom that the Dominguez Estate Company had been extremely profitable. (It was liquidated in 1970.) Until 1921, its income was mostly from dry farming, cattle and sheep grazing. "There was a time when income wasn't too plentiful."

Oil money began to flow in the 1920s and there were some profitable land sales. The bad floods (1889, 1893, 1913, '14, '15, '16) became a memory, the stuff of anecdotage, though there was one more bad one in 1937.

The distinguished attorney, Henry O'Melveny, one of the real "grey eminences" of early Southern California politics and finance, was the first administrator of the estate with Carson's father as the chief aide. It is clear that the entire family relied heavily on O'Melveny's shrewd judgment in those early, critical years when he was steering the family's fortunes through the shoals of boom and bust.

What was life on Rancho Dominguez really like in those supposedly halcyon times? There was a frontier reality to the Dominguez rancho in the nineteenth century; far different from the picture of guitar strumming rancheros and idle, overdressed senoritas which Hollywood has painted.

Under Spanish law, all the ranchero really had was a grazing permit. He had to use it to keep it, and he could still lose it if the missions claimed they needed it. When Mexico became independent in 1822, the permits were made grants. When the missions were secularized in 1833, the granting of ranchos accelerated.

It picked up even more in the final few years of Mexican rule. Many American contestors of rancho titles claimed that most of these last grants were highly suspect, like the federal judgeships

Maria de los Reyes Dominguez married banker John F. Francis in 1892. This picture was taken on their honeymoon at the Coronado Hotel and yes, the gentleman in the middle is a priest. "Reyes," as her sisters called her, was the youngest and most amiable of the six daughters of Manuel and Maria Dominguez. John Francis died in 1902; she lived until 1933, her affairs managed by Henry O'Melveny. Following his and her husband's advice, she always leased rather than sold her share of family land, so she benefited greatly when the discovery of oil on Dominguez Hill rescued the family fortunes.

One of the rooms in the lovingly restored Dominguez adobe in Compton. Manuel Dominguez built it in 1826 and brought his bride, Maria Engracia de Cota, granddaughter of the holder of Rancho los Nietos, here in 1827. As first built, the home was a one-story, L-shaped adobe with six large rooms. The walls were 24 inches thick, reinforced with heavy planks. The original flat roof was of hewn timbers, topped with tules from the nearby marshes, then tarred and sanded. The couple lived here for 55 years and died within a few months of each other in 1882, survived by six daughters, the last of whom died in 1933. The present configuration dates from 1907; the restored rooms from 1976 as a bicentennial commemoration. The adobe is open to the public several afternoons a month. Guided tours are arranged for groups of ten or more with advance reservation.

PHOTO BY WM. FRIDRICH

sometimes awarded by a President during his last days in office. Of 450 California ranchos, 400 were granted under Mexican rule. The Dominguez and Sepulveda grants were, of course, Spanish.

The Yankees took their land hunger into the courts. From 1848 through 1862, the titleholders — men wealthy in land and cattle, but with little in liquid assets — had to defend their patrimony through long trials and four levels of automatic appeal. They borrowed money at villainous rates. A two-year drought in 1862 forced most into sale or foreclosure.

Thus, Manuel Dominguez' accomplishment in securing clear title from President James Buchanan in 1859 is all the more impressive a feat when measured against the fate of so many of his peers. The unique regard in which Manuel Dominguez was held by his fellow Californians is indicated by an encomium delivered by Major Howard Bell in 1882, just before Dominguez died. Bell had a reputation for being a critical man, not given to compliments.

"Don Manuel Dominguez, as a representative Californian of the educated and intelligent class, deserves more than a passing mention. Nothing more is necessary to illustrate the sterling worth of this iron octogenarian than to say that through all the misfortunes that befell the landed proprietors of California, he, almost alone, stands as a sturdy oak midst the desolation around him, all of his contemporaries having bowed, bent and fallen before the storms of adversity."*

His wife, Dona Maria, died only four months later. She was, incidentally, a granddaughter of Manuel Nieto, whose vast Rancho los Nietos bordered Rancho San Pedro on the southeast. That she too was held in unusual contemporary regard is evident from this tribute in the magazine Land of Sunshine: "Don Manuel was the perfect type of the old California gentleman ... so his noble dame, Dona Maria Alta Gracia Cota, was the embodiment of all the virtues and graces which make of the Castilian maiden the most beautiful and wifely of matrons."

But the expansive life style of the Dominguez heirs was to continue, little diminished for another generation until another man of vision, Jared Sidney Torrance, was to put his stamp on the lands of the rancho.

*Quoted by Gillingham in The History of the Rancho San Pedro.

From rancho to townsites, from cattle to commerce

The seignorial days draw to an end as the great rolling plain between Los Angeles and San Pedro attracts the settler and the developer — 1882-1912.

In 1887, George Henry Carson and his wife, Victoria Dominguez Carson, built their new home on Dominguez Hill. It was close to the adobe where five years earlier her parents had died. Their oldest son, John Manuel, is seated in the middle. George Carson had married the strong-willed Victoria when she was only 15, in 1857. He had spent decades as Manuel Dominguez' major domo and most trusted aide. A city in the South Bay has been named after him; a beautiful regional park after her.

FROM THE LIBRARY COLLECTION, CALIFORNIA STATE UNIVERSITY DOMINGUEZ HILLS, CARSON, CALIFORNIA

This was the one-room Perry School classroom on October 3, 1911. One question on the blackboard behind the class: "Show how the Panama Canal will make it cheaper to ship freight from the East to the West by boat." Also pictured is the old Perry School bell, now in the lobby of the Torrance Historical Museum. Since it dates from 1905, it is one of our oldest artifacts. For some unfathomable reason, the school's World War Two honor roll separates the names of the Japanese-American graduates in military service from their classmates, though the gold stars in the flag are for Johnny Wallis, Leo Nielsen and Miyoto Nakatsu. An inscription dedicates the flag to those three and to "Laura Combs, the teacher who made this flag — who not only taught democracy — but lived it." The school on Prairie Avenue closed in 1981, one of the many rendered superfluous by the end of the baby boom.

PHOTO BY WM. FRIDRICH

An invaluable resource for a view of life on Rancho Dominguez as it adjusted to modern times is found in *Reminiscences of the Dominguez Ranch and the Carson Family,* an oral history by John Victor Carson.

In 1972, Carson was interviewed by Judson Grenier in Carson's office at the Dominguez Water Corporation in the city named after his pioneer family. Grenier is professor of history at California State University Dominguez Hills.

Almost 80 when he sat for this extensive interview, Carson was still a vivid raconteur. He radiated great affection and pride in his family and the Dominguez legend, and for what these remarkable people had accomplished here in the South Bay for two centuries. These invaluable conversations were set down just four years before John Victor Carson's death on February 9, 1976. He was the great-grandson of Manuel Dominguez, who died in 1882, 11 years before his birth, and the great-great-great-grandnephew of Juan Dominguez, founder of Rancho San Pedro.

He was born in the very new city of Redondo Beach in 1893, less than a year after Captains John C. Ainsworth and Robert R. Thompson had seen their dream begin to be realized with the incorporation of that city.

He was the oldest of the four children of John Manuel and Kate Smythe Carson. His father was the oldest son of George and Victoria Dominguez Carson, who married in 1857.

It was a different, a slower and in many ways a more spacious life here in the South Bay 80 years ago. When the Carson family decided to move from their ranch in Torrance to Normandie Avenue in 1902, they moved the house too. "It took 32 mules to pull it ... across fields; there were no fences, no roads. And in those days, there was no gas ... no electricity ... no indoor plumbing."

At Weston School — "one room, one teacher ... never more than 30 kids, from first to eighth grade" — the students tended to be unruly, Carson recalls almost proudly. "We didn't have women teachers, we had men. The kids at that school were pretty tough. It took a man to handle them. A pretty good

man too."

When they had their cattle roundups on the old Weston Ranch, the branding corral was near Pacific Coast Highway and Crenshaw Boulevard. Students at the Weston School could hear the thunder of hooves and the bawling of calves all day long. "Uncle Ben" Weston purchased his 3,000-acre holding in 1847. It ran from Madison Street to the Lomita line and from Sepulveda to the Palos Verdes foothills. It cost him $525.

Carson recalls his parents affectionately, but without sentimentality: "I think they were pretty average parents. We were brought up in the Catholic Church. My mother and father were both Catholics, and of course in the old days, they were what you would call devout. My mother was half Irish, half French. We had to drive to Redondo Beach to church on Sundays. My father wasn't around too much on Sunday morning; he didn't go like my mother did. She had to drag all of us. We went in a carriage. We had a coachman."

His recollections of the old Dominguez ranch are vivid. His grandparents lived on the ranch. "They always had a great many people around ... there were many children. My grandmother (Victoria Dominguez Carson) presided. She sat at the end of the table. My grandmother could speak English — she understood it, but she wouldn't speak it because she wanted her children to be able to speak two languages, and the

only way she could get them to, was to refuse to talk to them in anything but Spanish." Carson adds wistfully: "When I was eight years old, I could speak Spanish like nobody's business. Now I can't speak it at all."

The character of a formidable woman, "Donna Victoria" emerges: "She was a disciplinarian ... stern with the family ... very gracious to her grandchildren ... she would smile and be very happy when she was around them ... with her own sons and daughters she would unbend a little ... not very much. She had a great responsibility ... she had to ... lay down the law once in a while. She had three or four pretty wild sons, young fellows, that were in their twenties and they got around plenty. She had to keep them lined up, which she was able to do."

Even in Carson's youth, the old Carson house, where his grandmother lived until she died in 1916, had a feudal air about it. "They had servants ... the place was jumping with servants ... people who had been born and would die there."

When he was a boy, he used to go over to the nearly deserted Dominguez rancho to play. His great-aunt, Guadalupe, did not move back to the house until 1907; it had been largely uninhabited since 1885. "I played all through the ruins of that place, checking up on stuff; found all kinds of stuff there."

John Manuel Carson. His son, John Victor, recalls with regret how fluency in Spanish died out in the family in the course of three generations: "He (his grandfather) was a great old guy, a very nice fellow ... so funny, married that woman who wouldn't speak English to him ... when I was a kid, she'd shout Spanish to him ... he'd shake his head and talk to her in English. 'You can speak English just as well as I can, so why don't you do it?' She wouldn't even answer him ... she wanted her children to continue speaking Spanish ... thanks to my grandmother, my father (John Manuel) spoke perfect Spanish. I don't speak a word anymore."

Jerry-built shelters like this appeared and disappeared along the South Bay coast in the early twentieth century. This "Flotsam Castle" picture is variously attributed to 1905 and 1918. Fishermen, some serious, most perhaps temporarily escaping domesticity, camped there. Above this one, at Malaga Cove, excavations have uncovered detailed evidence of four distinct native American cultures, widely separated in time and sophistication. Clifford Reid, developer of Hollywood Riviera, was always generous with permission to dig. William Deane recalls that, as late as the 1930s, little of the private land was posted. Some diggers, he allows, were always ready to claim that whatever they found had been uncovered by the wind.

Road building in Torrance, circa 1912, on the Weston Ranch. The horsepower generated for these excavators is the real thing. It is worth noting that the motive power for the great armies which were to clash in Europe a few years later was still largely provided by horses and mules. The entire area south from Torrance to the Palos Verdes hills was still almost as pristine then as it had been 150 years earlier, just before the Canelino Indians of Chowigna and Suegna looked up from their timeless rounds to see Gaspar de Portola's band marching across the rolling countryside.

Cowboys in the Palos Verdes hills? Yes! This area was dotted with thriving ranchsites in the early years of the century. Such families as Kettler, Venable, Ellinwood, Quandt, Narbonne and Weston had purchased their acreage from the Dominguez holdings. Narbonne was a Basque sheepherder, whose name is commemorated both by Narbonne Avenue and the high school. The Quandt family played an important role in the development of Walteria and built the first waterworks there. Mrs. Evelyn Schooley of Torrance is a descendant of Charles Henry and Hanna Quandt who founded the ranch. Bernice Venable, a school teacher and realtor in Torrance, who died within recent memory, was the widow of Pierce Venable who put together that holding. Ben Weston's ranch was the largest and included all of what is now Torrance Airport.

The ranch property itself was still busy — there were cattle, wild and domesticated horses, and as many as 30,000 sheep grazing on old Dominguez Hill, or between there and Torrance, before the (1910) air show.

After a while, they replaced the horses with mules and the beef cattle with dairy cattle. "A mule did a lot more work than a horse and didn't get sick."

Dry farming was a gamble here then; droughts were frequent. On one or two occasions, Carson recalls, his grandfather herded his sheep up to Mount Whitney and back, a six-month round-trip. The sheep were grazed all the way up and back to keep them alive in the dry season.

The end of an era, 1913, when the last of the famous barbecues (250 people) was held on Rancho Dominguez. " ... down on the Pacific Electric from Los Angeles ... long picnic tables under the willow trees ... whole beeves ... chickens ... steer heads barbecued. The biggest facility was the bar." (J.V. Carson) "All the important people in Los Angeles attended these events over the years — mayors, famed attorney Earl Rogers, his even more famous daughter, writer Adela Rogers St. Johns, Sheriff Bill Traeger, Gene Biscailuz." Sixty years later, J.V. Carson was tough minded about the end of an era and a way of life: "Things change. It takes people some time, and me in particular, to learn that things can't stay static. You either have to go ahead or you just go backwards."

Carson paints an exciting picture of what young people in Torrance and the South Bay did for amusement. "We had these rodeos ... parties at night. Every place we went, we went on horseback. Picking up handkerchiefs off the ground (from horseback) you could get your neck broken ... but nobody young thinks of anything like that ... we used to have coyote hunts ... we patterned them after fox hunts."

About this time, in staid new Pasadena, Jared Sidney Torrance was a member of the Valley Hunt Club, where Anglophilia flourished so luxuriantly that they had had real fox hunts until 1892.

It was a life thoroughly worthy of a feudal lord. "My father had greyhounds; 23 of them. We had a eucalyptus grove over there on what is now 228th and Main. We'd take one of those cows or horses to the grove. So we always had a cadaver out there and the coyotes would come and feast. And then we'd ride in there with those dogs ... and go after them. The women would ride sidesaddle."

Carson remembers the old slough on the great central plain. "Prior to 1917, there were 3,000 acres or more under

water, running from Main Street clear over to Alameda. There was no Carson Street as such. ... After about 1910 or 1911, they started putting up fences."

He remembers what a wonderful place for sailing and duck hunting the slough was. It was drained and cleared in 1916 when the Dominguez Estate Co. cut a ditch from 213th Street southeast to 223rd and Wilmington.

Carson had vivid memories of the great floods of 1914 and 1916. "It was the overflow of the Los Angeles River out there ... the railroad tracks were still above water and that was the only thing that was." One year (1912), an ill-advised effort to dig a channel in the Los Angeles River ended when the floating dredge "ran off to sea" and "the channel that we cut disappeared ... they were never able to contain that channel until they cemented it."

He also recalls the great Dominguez Air Show in 1910. He was 17 then. People came out from Los Angeles to Dominguez Junction on the steam trains. "If you saw an automobile, you and your horse would both run away."

Farmers would get their buggies and meet the trains. "For two bits a ride,

It would be misleading to say that some of the greatest aviators and aerialists in the world were present atop Dominguez Hill in 1910. *Anyone* who flew in that dawn of flight was a great pioneer. This is the balloon spot-landing competition. Over 20,000 people attended, most arriving on the Pacific Electric or the Southern Pacific steam train from Los Angeles. Only those with grandstand seats paid; the Dominguez sisters had a box, of course. John Victor Carson, 17 and pleased with a chance to impress the young ladies, was able to bring them there. Louis Paulhan, in a French Farnham, set an altitude record at 5,000 feet. In fact, he flew out over soon-to-be Torrance, buzzed Redondo Beach and gave the South Bay, now a world renowned center of flight, its first view of air-borne man. Soon thereafter, there was a cross-country race from the field — all the way to Pasadena and back!

Guests at Dominguez-Larson Ranch, July 27, 1913. Prance Photo.

they'd go up the hill and two bits to come back." He gained esteem in the eyes of the young ladies because he had box seat tickets for the event which was held on family land.

He had wonderful recollections of his great-aunts, Manuel Dominguez' daughters; Mrs. Guyer, the oldest one: "When she'd see me — I was one of her favorites ... and, of course, I'd bring her that Christmas turkey — the first thing she'd do was go down in that little basket, a little Indian basket with a lid on it, and in that thing was Bull Durham tobacco to roll in cigarette papers. I was very adept at that. She would ask me to roll her a cigarette; I'd been doing it for quite a while. (He was 12 or 13 then.) Then she'd say to me — she could speak English, you know — 'Ah-ha, ah-ha, so you know how to do it at your age!' I said, 'Si.' So we'd sit and chat — she'd smoke a couple of cigarettes ... then ... down in this great big pocket and come up with a ten dollar gold piece and give it to me."

Carson recalls the barbecues at the Carson home on Dominguez Hill. As many as 250 people would attend, most coming down for the day on the Pacific Electric. "The fastest facility was the bar. And they had whole beeves barbecued.

They had chicken heads and steer heads barbecued."

Guests included "Earl Rogers ... the sheriff, Bill Traeger. And Gene Biscailuz — just ten years older than me to the day — and we both went to St. Vincent's."

The last great barbecue on the Dominguez ranch was held in 1913, except for one in 1922 when oil was discovered. Woodrow Wilson's son-in-law, William Gibbs McAdoo, a senator from California, attended that one.

Carson remembers the progress of drilling in this area as being first Signal Hill, then Santa Fe Springs, Huntington Beach and Torrance.

The first oil well on the Rancho San Pedro was located on Del Amo property in Torrance, north and west of the business district. A lease was signed on February 6, 1920 with the Chanslor-Canfield Midway Oil Co., a subsidiary of the Santa Fe Railroad. At 3,500 feet, the first well came in on June 7, 1922.

This marked the beginning of widespread activity from Torrance east to Dominguez Hill. The original well was in production until 1953.

But, of course, the South Bay was changing dramatically as John Victor Carson and the other great-grandchildren of Manuel Dominguez were growing up on the wonderful but anachronistic Rancho San Pedro.

The railroad had come, as had fast interurban transportation.

The film industry was gaining credibility. As early as 1913, a feature film was shot in Redondo Beach. Labor unions were growing in power; management fought back.

Out of all this came the thought that perhaps in a new industrial city, with a new industrial policy built around municipal cooperation and the defusing of industrial strife, a new departure could evolve.

John Victor Carson would see that dream realized before he died a few years ago, and he knew and dealt with the men most responsible for it — Jared Sidney Torrance and those unique architects of the human environment, the Olmstead family and Irving Gill.

John Victor Carson (1893-1976), great-grandson of Manuel Dominguez and great-great-great-grandnephew of that sturdy soldier Juan Dominguez, who, in 1784, accepted a retirement bonus and turned it into a private empire. For many year, Carson was a senior executive of the Dominguez Water Co. As a young man, he met and did business with Jared Sidney Torrance. A warm, outspoken man with a zest for life and a love of travel and sailing, he sat for a remarkable interview in 1972 with Judson O. Grenier, professor of history at CSUDH. He gave a rare insight into the South Bay in transition from rancho to townsite-studded modern times.

The incredible life and times of Jared Sidney Torrance

A small-town boy from western New York becomes a millionaire Southern California capitalist dreaming of a worker's paradise.

Jared Sidney Torrance, founder of the city of Torrance and a leader in the Greater Los Angeles business community during the last decade of the nineteenth century and the first two of the twentieth, was born in this house on August 3, 1852 in Gowanda, New York, a small town about 24 miles east of Buffalo in western New York State. The house was then opposite Gowanda's drinking establishment, the Eagle Tavern.

COURTESY OF GOWANDA HISTORICAL SOCIETY

This sketch of Jared Sidney Torrance seems to catch something of the genial, straightforward integrity of Torrance's founding father. With the straw hat he often wore and the bow tie fashionable in that period, he looks a little like Maurice Chevalier in *Gigi*. The city of Torrance has been consistently fortunate, not least in the character of the man who founded it. In an age of robber barons who took no heed of the public or the working man, he was an entrepreneurial capitalist of great probity who built Torrance, determined to improve the lifestyle of the town's ordinary citizens, the men who worked in the factories and shops, and their wives and children. There was tragedy but never a breath of scandal in his long life. He seemed as happy endowing hospitals, libraries, sanitoria and museums as he was making the money in real estate, oil and other ventures that made his philanthropies possible. In addition to his thriving namesake city, his legacy includes a host of other Southern California institutions.

At the age of 59, when most men concern themselves with plans for retirement, Jared Sidney Torrance of South Pasadena was planning his grandest project — a new industrial city on the flatlands between Los Angeles and the harbor at San Pedro. It was an immense undertaking, expected to take years to complete and to cost more than the then-magnificent sum of seven

million dollars. Announced to the public on March 16, 1912, the new city was a pioneering venture that literally would put Torrance's name on the map of Los Angeles County.

Torrance already was a millionaire financier; a tall man with sparkling eyes and a prosperous paunch who moved quietly behind the scenes in the most influential circles in Los Angeles and Pasadena society and — like many security-conscious millionaires today — was reluctant to be photographed.

He was more than a little experienced in the three major ways of making big money in Southern California in those early days: real estate, oil and cattle. He had learned accounting and bookkeeping in childhood, and had begun to manage family businesses as a

teenager. By 1912, he was a salesman with years of experience buying and selling real estate, a veteran at running a scenic railway and resort business, a member of the Los Angeles Stock Exchange well-versed in securities, and an oil company executive who knew how to organize, run, and finance corporate enterprises.

Jared Sidney Torrance also was a strong family man who never hesitated to do business with a relative or friend, or set one up in position to forward and profit from one of his enterprises. He was a friendly, charming, socially prominent civic leader and philanthropist, a Yale man born in Gowanda, New York, a small town in western New York State. His family was prosperous and he seemed to take *noblesse oblige* seriously and liked to support hospitals, sanitariums, and libraries almost as much as he enjoyed the hearty give-and-take of negotiating big business deals.

Torrance easily could have retired and lived comfortably on the fortune he'd accumulated during his first 25 years in Southern California, in the lovely South Pasadena mansion he'd moved into in 1910. That house, appraised at $75,000

in 1921 — a great amount of money in those days — still stands at 929 Buena Vista Street.

A circular drive sweeps grandly up to the three-story, 33-room English-style manor house with its substantial stone porches. Myriad mahogany chairs and tables, oil paintings, bronzes and other works of art were among the posh furnishings.

In the dining room, ten people could be served an elegant dinner at a long mahogany table set with expensive silver placesettings, two large silver candelabras, and two pairs of silver salt and pepper shakers. At tea time, an elegant five-piece silver tea set would be brought out. And whether it was simply a piece he liked, an indication of his cattle interests, some sly comment on bull-headedness or "shooting the bull," or even an expression of Torrance's own bullishness on every endeavor he undertook, a needlepoint depiction of a bull's head gazed from the wall above the diners.

Three bedrooms were set aside for the Torrances' live-in staff, which had a distinctly Scandinavian accent to it in 1917, when Miss Mary Larson was the cook and Miss Anna Lindsfors the housemaid.

Torrance's widowed mother, Mary Torrance, initially lived in her own home on South Orange Grove Avenue in Pasadena, but moved in with her son when he moved to the South Pasadena house. After Torrance, a widower, wed his second wife, however, Mary Torrance moved to a small flat at the Fremont Apartments on Fremont Avenue in South Pasadena, 11 blocks from her son's home.

The Torrances' neighbors on Buena Vista included prominent attorney Seward A. Simons and Republican State Senator Egbert G. Gates, who was in the cattle business, as was Torrance.

In 1916, four years after Jared Sidney Torrance founded the city of Torrance on the then-empty land between Los Angeles and San Pedro, he could still vividly recall the day he first set foot in the land of unlimited opportunity — Southern California; it was Independence Day, 1887.

His father, in ill health, had wintered in Southern California in 1886, Torrance recalled. "On his return in the spring of 1887, he gave such a glowing account of his trip, that in June following I made the journey to California via the Canadian Pacific and Coast routes, and arrived in Pasadena July 4, 1887."

It was a memorable day to arrive in Pasadena. A transcontinental railroad rate war was under way, brought on by the completion of the second transcontinental rail line to Los Angeles — the Santa Fe — in 1885. The rate

The Torrance family lived in three houses in Gowanda during Torrance's lifetime. The last, pictured here, was on a hill overlooking the town. Torrance was the second of six children born to Cyrenius Chapin Torrance and Mary (nee Curtis) Torrance. Torrance's father was an attorney, District Attorney of Erie County, New York and a businessman whose interests included lumber and grain mills. He sought to instill industriousness and basic business skills in his five sons and a daughter, so there were many chores for Torrance and his siblings. Due to an epidemic of diptheria after the Civil War, only Torrance, his sister Jennie, and his brother Lewis lived to adulthood. Even so, Torrance recalled a mostly happy childhood, marred only by his father's long and ultimately fatal struggle with tuberculosis.

COURTESY OF GOWANDA HISTORICAL SOCIETY

Already a young capitalist, Jared Sidney Torrance posed for this photo at the age of 11 in 1863. He was already selling fruits and vegetables throughout the nearby countryside from a horse-drawn wagon and was employed, in those days before copy machines, in his father's law office copying documents and at the county courthouse taking notes on testimony in criminal cases prosecuted by Torrance's father. He also learned bookkeeping as a boy and traveled the region near his home buying corn and wheat for his father's flour mill.

COURTESY OF GOWANDA HISTORICAL SOCIETY

About 1905, Torrance bought this house in Gowanda, New York, his hometown, and donated it to the city fathers for use as a public library. Torrance was a philanthropist whose major interests were libraries, museums and tuberculosis sanitaria. Torrance gathered 300 books from his own bookcase-lined living room and those of his friends and arranged for Isabel Henderson, his cousin, to open the first public library in the front room of her Torrance home. Torrance's will left money for libraries both in Torrance and Gowanda.

COURTESY OF GOWANDA HISTORICAL SOCIETY

war with the Southern Pacific — which established the first service to Los Angeles in 1876 — brought thousands of Easterners and Midwesterners into Southern California and started a frenzy of real estate sales that sent property values soaring and opened whole new towns, including Redondo Beach. July 4, 1887 was the first Independence Day celebrated in the newly incorporated city of Pasadena, and the city was determined to do the occasion up right. The Pasadena City Band played loudly, a cannon and other fireworks boomed, local dignitaries paraded in the streets, and a time-capsule cornerstone was laid at the Pasadena Public Library amid speeches about the great future of Southern California.

The *Pasadena Union* reported: "The day was ushered in at midnight of the third by the loud and startling report of an anvil battery and the bang of firecrackers, great and small. The sharp crack of revolvers continued until dawn when the music of ringing bells was added to the noisy but jubilant demonstrations."

After the band led a parade along Colorado Boulevard, a cornerstone was laid for the public library, and C.T. Hopkins, president of the Pasadena Library Society, made a speech in which he said: "With your aid this building will soon be the most striking ornament of our architecturally beautiful city, the

whitest and broadest mark of our civilization, the most distinctive of the many peculiar features that raise Pasadena above the average of Western settlements, and attract to us an immigration that for culture, intelligence and wealth has never yet so concentred in any new American town."

It is not certain from available records that Torrance was in the crowd that cheered Hopkins' remarks that day, but Hopkins' words certainly seem consistent with Torrance's later actions. He clearly was convinced of the importance of public libraries and in 1905 donated a house in which a library was established in Gowanda.

In 1913, he gathered three hundred books from his own private collection and those of his friends and stocked Torrance's first public library, which was run by a cousin, Isabel Henderson, in the front room of her Gramercy Street home. When Torrance died, his will offered a $25,000 bequest to the Gowanda city fathers if they would match that amount and use the $50,000 total to build a new library there. Despite that offer, it was not until the 1930s that Gowanda got a new library as a federal public works project, about the same time the Torrance library at 1345 Post Avenue — now the Torrance Historical Society Museum — was built, also as a federal project.

After looking around Southern California briefly during his first trip in 1887, Torrance later wrote, "I was not long in concluding to immediately dispose of my interests in the East, and make Pasadena my future home. Making a few real estate investments, I returned to Gowanda, and three months later became a Californian."

Not only was Torrance impressed by his first glimpse of California, but he had become less than satisfied with Gowanda. "I decided that a small village, with its lack of opportunity, and its over-supply of jealousies, was too narrow a field for my ambition," he said of his move to Pasadena, which listed only 1,072 residents in its city directory the year he arrived from Gowanda.

Torrance harbored a lingering fondness for Gowanda, however, "which was nestled in as smiling a valley as nature ever fashioned," he said. It was there that he chose to be buried in the family cemetery. It was in Gowanda, after all, that Torrance began to learn the attitudes and skills that would enable him to become a prominent millionaire, Southern California capitalist and philanthropist of broad-ranging interests, a man who would serve on more than 140 corporate boards of directors, helping to guide major companies dealing in oil, land, electricity, transportation, banking, securities, water, steel, industrial tools, construction and other goods and services. It was Southern

California, however, that provided him with the widest possible opportunities to exercise his full range of entrepreneurial talents.

Interestingly, Torrance's most-enjoyed business deal was not a major coup of adult acumen, but a boyhood experience buying and selling apples around Gowanda. The apple deal, he recalled in 1916, was the second business deal of his career. His first, at the age of 13 or 14, was buying a house and lot at a sheriff's sale for seven hundred dollars, fixing it up and selling it for a profit.

The apple purchase, though, he seemed to think, was more interesting. "Returning from Springville and other towns where I had been selling flour (from my father's mill), I passed the orchard and home of an old farmer named Tracy Burnap. He was big, corpulent and crafty, and disliked by everybody. His orchard hung with fine-looking, medium-sized red apples. It occurred to me that I could buy the fruit and have our team haul empty barrels up, on top of the barrels of flour — and packed apple barrels back — thus loading both ways.

"I closed a bargain with him, making a payment down and taking a receipt which recited the terms of the deal. I was a little dismayed, a few days later, when I learned that Burnap was bragging how he had worsted young Torrance in a deal by selling to him his

orchard of Grindstones (the name given to a hard, juiceless variety of apple which was rather despised by apple buyers) at a good round figure.

"But that season proved an unusual one. The apple crop was short — and red apples were red apples. The price ruled abnormally high, and I made a big profit on the deal, and I think Burnap never heard the last of the taunts of his neighbors at having let a little 15-year-old town boy get the better of him in trade."

Torrance was born on August 3, 1852 at Gowanda, a small town about 24 miles east of Buffalo in the foothills of the Allegheny Mountains, actually two townships astride the Erie and Cattaraugus county lines, divided by a creek running through the middle. The family home, at the time he was born, was on Buffalo Street in Gowanda, opposite the Eagle Tavern.

Torrance's great-grandfather was an Irish Protestant who emigrated from Ireland to a farm in Vermont about the middle of the eighteenth century. Torrance's grandfather was a woolen manufacturer.

Jared Sidney Torrance was the second son of Cyrenius Chapin Torrance and Mary (nee Curtis) Torrance, who were married October 21, 1851, when Cyrenius was 26 and Mary was 20. Though Mary Torrance had six children

Jared Sidney Torrance came to Southern California from New York in 1887. As director of the Rubio Canyon Land and Water Association, which provided the water supply necessary to develop Altadena, he had dealings with Professor Thaddeus S.C. Lowe, who founded the Mount Lowe Electric Railway Co. The railway ran up Rubio Canyon and thence to the top of Echo Mountain, where Lowe built the resort popularly known as Mount Lowe. Lowe's resort on Echo Mountain included Echo Mountain House, the Chalet Hotel, a giant searchlight and an observatory. Professor Lowe ran into financial difficulties despite the hoopla with which he ran the resort, and in 1897, a judge appointed Torrance the sole receiver in the bankruptcy of the resort. Torrance, seen on Echo Mountain in this photograph, spent two years there improving the line, obtaining Congressional legislation to clear up a legal tangle over property ownership, refinancing the company's long-term debt and converting Mount Lowe from a playground for the rich to an accessible, inexpensive place for family outings and picnics.

— five boys and a girl — rural life was hard and modern lifesaving medical techniques were then unknown. Only Jared Sidney, his younger brother Lewis Curtis Torrance and sister Jennie lived to adulthood. Lewis was born October 21, 1855, while Jennie was born June 1, 1866.

Another brother, Addison Torrance, was born on December 14, 1859 and died of croup — according to an 1865 census compiled by the state of New York — on November 5, 1864, before his sixth birthday. The eldest brother, Clarence, was born in early 1851 and died of diptheria on February 14, 1865 at the age of 14, during an epidemic that swept the nation at the close of the Civil War. Cyrenius Chapin Torrance was born on June 25, 1864 and was less than eight months old when he died five days after Clarence, on February 19, 1865, also of diptheria, according to that New York census. Though there was much death in his family — later Torrance's first wife and both his sons would die prematurely — the death of Clarence is the only one mentioned specifically in his 1916 reminiscences, perhaps an indication of how very hard the passing of his older brother hit him.

"We were a happy family — lived exceedingly well — were generally prosperous — our happiness being marred only by Father's ill health," Torrance recalled.

Torrance's father was an attorney who was elected District Attorney of Erie County during the Civil War years of 1861-64. He hired as his young assistant Grover Cleveland, who later became the only man to serve two nonconsecutive terms as President of the United States and thus is known as both the twenty-second and twenty-fourth President. Cyrenius Torrance later also made an unsuccessful bid for the New York State Senate on the Democratic ticket, and served as an Erie County Supervisor from Collins township — the Erie County half of Gowanda — from 1879 to 1881, though the voters of his township were predominately Republican.

The *History of Cattaraugus County*, published in 1893, describes Cyrenius Torrance as "a man of intense activity, great pertinacity and strength of will combined with keen intelligence, and in the practice of his profession ... a foeman whose steel was always to be dreaded. He was a tireless worker, a hard student, and thoroughly prepared all his cases."

In 1916, Jared Sidney Torrance wrote a brief autobiography focusing on his business career, but also touching upon more intimate aspects of his life. In that work, he remembered his father as a lawyer who, "in my early youth ... became interested in farming, and later in milling, lumber and real estate. He was naturally industrious, and always ambitious. He believed in the idea that

it was wise to cultivate the habit of industry in boys, and likewise, by loading them with responsibilities, to teach them self-reliance.

"The winter following my sixth birthday, I was made to care for and feed a flock of about an hundred sheep," Torrance recalled, and on weekends that same fall and winter, with his brother Clarence, "I hauled all our firewood from the Cattaraugus Indian Reservation, four miles or more away."

"Incidentally, also, I fed and cared for the pigs and poultry. Father always had one of the best vegetable gardens in the village, and we boys did the greater part of the work.

"In 1860 he purchased a home much larger, and more pretentious than the one we had previously occupied. There we boys raised vegetables for the market as well as for our family, and peddled fruits and peas and other truck over the country, going, with a faithful old horse and wagon, as far as Ellicottville — 26 miles over a hilly, rugged road. I was then only eight years old.

"We went regularly to school, but early and late we were given our regular and special tasks. Each season we placed in the cellar an hundred or more bushels of apples, a few barrels of cider, and quantities of winter vegetables.

"As a boy I excelled in penmanship.

Jared Sidney Torrance, a 59-year-old widower whose two sons had died in childhood, lived in this sprawling mansion in South Pasadena in 1911 when he began to plan his crowning achievement, the creation of the new industrial town of Torrance. The grand house, with a sweeping circular drive, an indoor swimming pool, quarters for three live-in servants and other amenities, was acquired by the Bishop of the Los Angeles Dioceses of the Episcopal Church after Torrance's death. It is popularly known to South Pasadenans as "the Bishop Stevens house." Many features of the house show Torrance's interests, including his years as an owner of the Pasadena Electric Co. and his fascination with the then-novel electrical equipment of his day, his appreciation for and active participation in water companies that served his hometown in New York, and opened to development such Southern California places as disparate as the San Fernando Valley, Altadena and Torrance itself, his close ties with his cousin, Isabel Henderson, and perhaps even his early role in the Pasadena Tournament of Roses.

PHOTO BY WM. FRIDRICH

That the Torrance house's exterior is virtually unchanged since this photograph was taken in about 1912 seems clear. Two chimneys seen in this picture were the major casualties the house suffered during the 1971 Sylmar earthquake. Ivy vines have climbed up to engulf the second story of the grand staircase area in the middle of the facade. But the house was well-built and reportedly has never even been reshingled on the sides, though the roof was resurfaced to keep out the ravages of nearly three quarters of a century of occasionally inclement weather.

Torrance's sister, Jennie Welch, is seen gathering blossoms in the extensive gardens that in 1912 stretched behind the house, alive with pink foxgloves and other flowers. The grounds behind the house have since been subdivided. Two additional large, stately, modern homes have been built below the Torrance mansion. The Pasadena Freeway passes just below those houses.

During school vacations, and especially on rainy days, I was sent to the law office and copied papers — typewriters then being unknown. I could write an hundred folios, or ten thousand words in a day. Partly, I suppose, because he had a partner in the law business, and partly to encourage me in thrift and saving, I was paid the regular price of two cents per folio for that work. We were given a certain percentage of our fruit and vegetable sales, and therefore in early childhood, we boys became capitalists."

While his father was Erie County District Attorney, Torrance recalled, he "occasionally accompanied" him to his office in Buffalo, less than 30 miles from Gowanda. "I frequently took the notes of testimony in criminal cases being prosecuted by Father and Mr. Cleveland."

But Torrance remembered his father's Buffalo headquarters as "a dark, dingy, ill-ventilated courtroom" and believed that "the long hours and arduous duties of his office in a polluted atmosphere cost my father his health."

Cyrenius Torrance suffered from respiratory problems for many years and died of tuberculosis on April 1, 1888 in Gowanda at the age of 62. Perhaps because this disease provided the main source of unhappiness in his family during his childhood, Jared Sidney Torrance later served on the boards of

two tuberculosis treatment facilities in the Greater Los Angeles area and made significant contributions to their coffers. Perhaps not coincidentally, his own death was attributed to a respiratory ailment — pneumonia.

At the end of the Civil War, Torrance recalled, his father and a business partner bought a flour mill in Gowanda, a sawmill and some timberland near Collins, New York, and opened a lumberyard in Gowanda.

Torrance, then only 13 or 14, traveled to Buffalo, Dunkirk and Toledo to buy corn and wheat for the flour mill. One grain dealer in particular, he recalled, was "quite surprised to have a boy of my years negotiate the purchase of grain" from him.

"I did practically all the buying, kept the books and paid the bills — out of school hours.

"That boys should acquire the ability to keep books was a hobby of my father and a legacy in his will gave the village school district (in Gowanda) a considerable sum of money, the interest upon which was to be given as a prize in books to scholars who excelled in certain studies, naming bookkeeping especially.

"Following the close of the Civil War," Torrance also recalled, "the price of dairy cheese was high, and the

dairymen farmers could feed their cows corn meal at a profit — and our sales over a certain period of the year would average well towards a thousand dollars a day."

Lest you think all teenaged runaways become ne'er-do-wells in later life; at 15, Torrance, too, ran away from home.

"In the latter part of 1868, I became restless and dissatisfied, and one day becoming displeased at some slight criticism from my father, I remarked that I was quite competent to support myself — gathered together my accumulations, a few hundred dollars — and left home. I had always wanted to see the West, and therefore purchased a ticket for Chicago."

There he found a job as a bookkeeper, though "times were dull and places (jobs) hard to find." He worked for Tribbals, Shirk & Whitehead, a wholesale stove firm. The boss was a "fine old gentleman with side whiskers — a Methodist who looked the part," who was surprised at how young Torrance was, but impressed with him all the more.

"Well, my boy, I like the way you talk," the old man told him during the pre-employment interview. "You write a good letter. It is not a crime to be young."

Finding the company's books "untidy," the young Torrance asked for and was allowed the privilege of opening new ones. "My books were models of neatness, accurately kept, encompassing a business of over a million dollars annually."

Within a few weeks, the old gentleman again remarked that "youth is not a crime," told Torrance he was doing a good job and gave him the then-princely salary of fifteen hundred dollars per year. Torrance continued to work for him until early 1870, when his mother and a family friend in Chicago "induced me to return home and complete my education."

After returning from Chicago, "I attended school at Suspension Bridge, during the spring term of 1870, but finding its military features distasteful, I prepared for college during the following school year at Homer Academy in Courtland County, New York."

He entered Sheffield Scientific School at Yale University in the fall of 1871 with

Torrance had extensive holdings and interests in developments in other communities, but for relaxation in a rural setting, he would visit his ranch in Chino. Family members are informally seated on the front steps of the modest ranch house in this photograph which was probably taken in late 1912 or early 1913. He was especially busy then, of course. His new industrial city in the South Bay was becoming a reality.

Elizabeth Winter, the present owner of Torrance's South Pasadena house, acquired it from her sister during the 1960s, and is only the third owner since Torrance lived there and died there 63 years ago. She is shown on the terrace of the house near the spot where Torrance was photographed in 1912, and is holding the original photo of him. Ms. Winter graciously opened her home to the authors.
PHOTO BY WM. FRIDRICH

Jared Sidney Torrance disliked being photographed, so this shot of him on the terrace of his South Pasadena home on Christmas Day, 1912, is a rare full-length portrait. The picture apparently was taken by his cousin, Isabel Henderson, who was a houseguest there at the time, and whose shadow intrudes into the late-afternoon scene. The Union Tool Co. plant in Torrance was already operational and the town of Torrance had begun to rise that Christmas.

the Class of 1874, and stayed with that class two years. He was a popular student, elected president of his class both years. He also was secretary and treasurer of the Sheffield Baseball Club during his first year and president of that club the second year. According to Yale records, he also was a member of the Sheffield Glee Club for two years.

In 1873, he withdrew from school for one year to return home and manage family business interests during a business panic and a severe phase of his father's continuing illness. But in 1874 he was able to return to Yale for his final year and served on the Senior Class Supper Committee of the Class of 1875. Torrance recalled in his autobiography: "I was graduated in (June) 1875 — without honors — I never took a prize in my life, but with the record of successfully passing every examination from entrance to exit — without a condition."

Torrance returned to Gowanda after graduation and tended his ailing father's businesses until early 1876. Then, with his father encouraging him to study law as he had done, Torrance heeded the call of the West again. He returned to Chicago, where he worked as a clerk and studied law with the legal firm of Clarkson & Van Schaack.

"My work was interesting, but so burdensome that I had to do my reading at night, with the result that in September, 1876, my own health was so impaired that I accepted an offer to go to Stralsund, Prussia, for a wealthy German family — and tutor their young boys who were there in school, my duties being, however, very light and very agreeable. I was glad, also, to

quit the law, as I found the task of fighting out other people's quarrels very distasteful.

"I remained in Stralsund, excepting for frequent intervals spent in travel, until early 1878, when I journeyed to Paris, saw the Exposition, and finally in June of the same year returned to Gowanda."

Torrance said his father bought a new house, with fifty acres of meadow, pasture and orchard overlooking Gowanda. The house had been owned by an unpopular man who became an extensive owner of farm properties in the vicinity by foreclosing on mortgages. There reportedly were no banks in Gowanda in those days, and in modern times an old secret passage has been discovered from the main bedroom in that house to a secret cellar under a nearby coach barn. Some investigators have speculated that the original owner may have hidden his wealth in that cellar, though it is not known if the Torrance family was aware of the secret passage, or what use — if any — they put it to.

While living with his parents again in this house, Torrance bought 1,200 acres of timberland. When a railroad construction boom doubled the price of railroad ties, he made a good profit. Torrance added that the work of supervising the cutting of the timber was good for him in other ways, too. "In the outdoor life I became strong."

Torrance then made secret cellars in the vicinity more or less obsolete by organizing the Bank of Gowanda — "the first corporation with which I was connected" — and later the Bank of Cattaraugus and the Bank of Springville.

He also built thirty or more houses in Gowanda. In 1882, he added an opera house and a brick block of stores to the village.

Additionally, he proposed a municipal water company, but "the question was put to a vote of the people and through the influence of the nonprogressive element and aided by a number of men who were more or less jealous of my activities, the project was defeated."

A Torrance proposal to install five hydrants in the village also was defeated at the polls. "I had anticipated these negative votes," Torrance said, "but the contest was more bitter than I had thought possible."

Undeterred, however, he then installed three demonstration hydrants in the village square and arranged a contest "between our gravity system for fire protection and the Silby fire apparatus which the enemies of the water scheme had meanwhile induced the village to purchase."

After a fire department parade gathered a crowd in the square one afternoon, a signal was given for crews to spring into action with both kinds of equipment.

"One hose company was flooding the public square with six streams over a hundred feet in the air from our gravity system several minutes before a steamer got into action with a single stream," Torrance recalled with some satisfaction years later. "The enemy was put completely to rout, and the village forthwith voted an appropriation for fire hydrants, and I and my associates were vindicated."

Soon after this contest, Torrance discovered the possibilities of Southern California during one of its biggest real estate booms and moved to Pasadena. His brother, Lewis, accompanied him and they formed a partnership to buy and sell real estate in the Golden State.

They arrived in 1887, the year in which Los Angeles — which still had no paved streets — opened its first public high school, the year the influential California Club was founded. It was the year before the Los Angeles Chamber of Commerce was chartered, the year before South Pasadena incorporated, the year before Charles Lummis formed the Association for the Preservation of the

In the family living room on the first floor of the South Pasadena Torrance house, Torrance's sister, Jennie Welch, and his mother, Mary Curtis Torrance, relaxed in 1912 amid mahoghany furniture, Persian rugs, paintings and *objet d'art*. Note the extensive built-in bookcases and the upright telephone on top of the bookcase immediately behind Mrs. Welch.

The close relationship between Jared Sidney Torrance and his cousin, Isabel Henderson, who founded the Torrance Public Library and was sent to the fledgling modern industrial city by Torrance to encourage the cultural and social life of the city, seems clear in this blowup of the guide to fuses. It is still on the door of the third-floor fuse box of Torrance's South Pasadena home. One is clearly designated as controlling "Mrs. H's room."

PHOTO BY WM. FRIDRICH

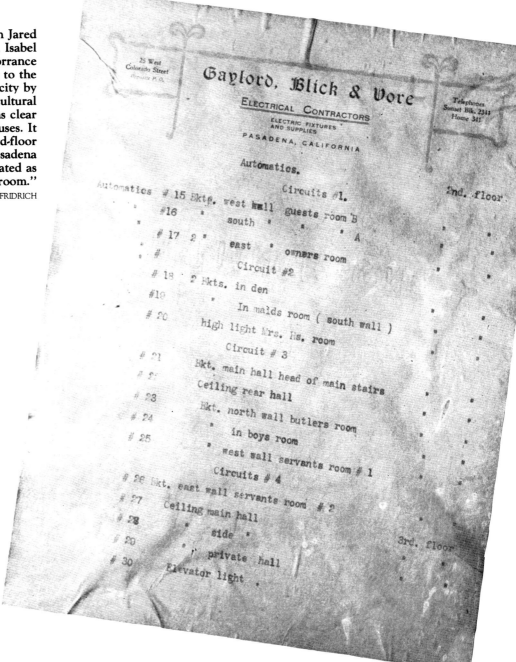

Missions which would later become the Landmarks Club. Torrance eventually would move to South Pasadena, and would be active in the California Club, the Chamber, and the Landmarks Club.

The first electric lights arrived in Los Angeles five years before Torrance did. By 1886 the system had more than one thousand subscribers. The City of Angels was in the midst of a decade during which it grew from 11,183 residents in 1880 to 50,395 in 1890.

Within a few years, Jared Sidney Torrance left his partnership with his brother and formed another with W.D. McGilvray. The firm of McGilvray & Torrance sold real estate and insurance and specialized in property in Altadena, then a wealthy and fashionable suburb north of Pasadena. An 1893 publication of the Pasadena Board of Trade said of McGilvray & Torrance: "The members

of the firm are young men of high social standing and are each imbued with thorough business principles and sterling probity of character."

Torrance and his brother bought controlling interest in the stock of the Pasadena Electric Light & Power Co. in 1888. Torrance served as vice president and secretary of Pasadena Electric and his brother managed that business and a related one, the Electric Supply & Fixture Co.

The latter firm, run in partnership with William Boorman, did electrical contracting and sold gas and electric fixtures. In 1898, the Torrances sold their interests in Pasadena Electric to what became the Southern California Edison Co., and the Pasadena operation was merged into the larger company the following year. Subsequently, Torrance served as a vice president of the Edison Co.

During the period from 1887 to 1910, Torrance was listed in Pasadena city directories as living at three different addresses on South Grand Avenue, including one house his brother had previously occupied. One house has been razed and replaced by a modern building. So has the place across the street, where Torrance's second wife, Helena Childs, lived with her husband Frank Childs, who managed the Arroyo Vista Hotel in Pasadena until his death about 1900. His widow, a leader of Pasadena society, became Torrance's wife in 1914.

But first, on February 13, 1889, Torrance married Annie Laurie Fowler in Pasadena. He was 37, she was 23 — the same age as Torrance's sister, Jennie. Annie Fowler was the daughter of John and Augusta (nee Childs) Fowler of Oakland, and bore Torrance his only children.

Jared Sidney Torrance, Jr. was born March 16, 1890 in Gowanda and died September 21 that same year in Gowanda. Their second son, John Fowler Torrance, was born in Gowanda on July 14, 1891 and died April 4, 1900 in an elevator accident in Pasadena at the age of eight.

After their wedding in 1889, Mr. and Mrs. Torrance left for San Francisco, the *Pasadena Union* reported, "where they will take a steamer for New York City via Cape Horn."

Mrs. Torrance died little more than four years later, on April 12, 1893. She was buried in the Torrance family plot in Pine Hill Cemetery in Gowanda. Her husband later also was laid to rest there, though his second wife was not.

In 1892, Torrance became a director of the Rubio Canyon Land & Water Association, which provided a water supply to Altadena, where Torrance actively sold real estate at that time. Torrance was president of that

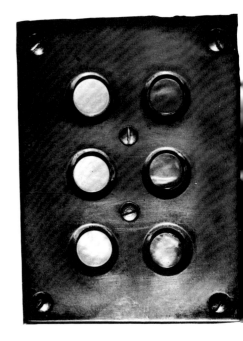

The grand staircase in the Torrance house rose from a large hallway near the front door of the house. It was illuminated by both electric light and a large stained-glass window depicting a classical water-bearing maid. This central figure seems particularly appropriate in view of Torrance's creation of a water company in Gowanda, New York and his efforts there to promote fire hydrants for the town. He also was a director of water companies which provided the liquid vital to the development of Altadena, Ventura, Chino and Fontana and was instrumental in the creation of the Dominguez Water Co. Torrance was a developer and financier who demonstrated a keen insight into the importance of reliable water supplies to develop Southern California real estate.
PHOTO BY WM. FRIDRICH

Torrance and his brother Lewis owned the Pasadena Electric Co. for more than a decade at the end of the nineteenth century. Torrance later became a director of the Southern California Edison Co. His enthusiasm for things electrical can be seen throughout his house, including a master switch panel in the living room from which he could control lights throughout the house, and switches like this one next to the stairwell. It allowed anyone walking up or down the stairs to turn the lights on or off as needed, so they need never be in the dark as they climbed the stairs.

PHOTO BY WM. FRIDRICH

The artist and the model who posed for this window in the stairwell of Torrance's South Pasadena home are no longer remembered, but the beautiful result of their collaboration lingers on. It is even more fully appreciated when seen in color. Torrance's home was an elegant one befitting his status as a wealthy member of the elite of Southern California, who traveled between their offices and exclusive clubs in Los Angeles and their homes in Pasadena and South Pasadena, and shaped Greater Los Angeles and all of Southern California in their most formative years.

PHOTO BY WM. FRIDRICH

association and throughout his life displayed acute awareness of the vital role water plays in the life of any community. Through Rubio Canyon, Torrance had dealings with Professor Thaddeus S.C. Lowe, who founded the Mount Lowe Electric Railway Co. to serve a resort Lowe built on the San Gabriel Mountains in the Angeles National Forest behind Pasadena.

The scenic railway began running up Rubio Canyon on June 29, 1893 to Rubio Pavilion at the 2,200-foot level. On July 4, 1893, stair-stepped cars running up a steeper incline began regular trips from Rubio to the top of Echo Mountain at 3,500 feet. There, the Chalet Hotel, Echo Mountain House, a giant searchlight that had been featured at two world's fairs and Professor Lowe's astronomical observatory comprised a complex of buildings painted white and thus called "the White City." Tourists could take meals and lodging there or traverse via another narrow gauge railway from the White City around 127 curves and over 18 trestles to the Alpine Tavern.

The year Mount Lowe opened was a year of financial collapse in Southern California. Four area banks closed in insolvency, and Professor Lowe soon ran into financial difficulties, too. Creditors, including Torrance, brought suit against him and in April, 1897, Torrance was listed as an officer and director of the Pasadena & Mount Lowe Railway, a corporation set up to take over Lowe's interests. On November 1, 1897, a judge appointed Torrance the sole receiver in the bankruptcy case.

Torrance promptly took charge, upgrading service to the public, improving the maintenance of facilities and equipment, and setting out to make the resort accessible to and inexpensive for family outings and picnics, abandoning Professor Lowe's original concept of Mount Lowe as a playground for the rich. Torrance cut fares in half, introduced excursion rates and refinanced the company's long-term debt. In 1899, he also successfully sought an Act of Congress to straighten out a legal tangle over property ownership at the resort. The legislation gave the company ownership of resort areas already developed, but provided only easements on federal land for the railway rights of way. Torrance's efforts during two years as receiver in charge of Mount Lowe, he recalled, involved "converting the enterprise into a paying proposition." He did that job so well

that on March 29, 1899, a month after Congress acted, the now-profitable resort was sold at auction.

"I resigned, reluctantly, of my own volition, but I was anxious to get into business for myself," Torrance said.

He summarized those two years on Echo Mountain as "exceedingly pleasant. The mountain air and scenery were a constant source of delight. The Echo Mountain House was an attractive hotel and I had the satisfaction of bringing the railroad out of bankruptcy into solvency, and it sold soon after to the Southern Pacific at a large figure."

Even more uplifting than the mountain-climbing railroad was one of Torrance's contributions to the development of Altadena. In 1902, he loaned a carriage house he owned for use as Altadena's first church, a nondenominational community church.

He also made what were described as "substantial" contributions in 1911 to help Dr. Henry B. Stehman, a former Chicago resident, move his La Vina Sanitarium from its original site to a 240-acre vineyard above Altadena. The sanitarium was founded with the help of Torrance's friend and Pasadena neighbor, Dr. Norman Bridge, another ex-Chicagoan. Torrance served on the board of La Vina and reportedly donated the second cottage erected on the vineyard property.

Torrance also was active in many civic-minded organizations in Pasadena, including the Valley Hunt Club. Founded in late 1888, for the first few years the activities of the club included riding to hounds across the nearby open countryside. The last hunt was in 1893 and thereafter, the members turned instead to picnics and cotillions.

On January 1, 1890, the club held its

Torrance's South Pasadena house also was equipped with an electric bell system to summon his live-in servants from their living and working quarters. His staff included a cook and a housemaid, who had bedrooms and sitting rooms in a separate section of the second floor, and their own separate dining room on the first floor. The 33-room house had five entrances and an electric elevator.

PHOTO BY WM. FRIDRICH

The entry hall of the elegant Torrance home in South Pasadena adjoined this parlor, where Torrance must have done much socializing. None of the furniture in the house today is from the Torrance family, but the extensive built-in bookshelves, gas fireplaces and other fixtures are mostly unchanged. The ceiling of the parlor above is hand-painted with pink roses, possibly a subtle floral reference to the fact that Torrance served as vice president of the Valley Hunt Club in 1894 and was president of that club in 1895 and 1896. The Valley Hunt Club originated the Tournament of Roses Parade in 1890 and conducted the parade itself for the last time in 1895. Thus it was during Torrance's tenure as Valley Hunt President that the club decided the parade promoting the wonders of Pasadena and the Southern California climate had grown so large that a new, specially created organization should run it.

PHOTO BY WM. FRIDRICH

first parade of flower-decorated carriages and sponsored an afternoon of public games to advertise the advantages of this city of 4,882 residents. Torrance was vice president of the club in 1894 and president for two terms, 1895 and 1896.

Eighteen hundred ninety-five was the last year the club conducted the Rose Parade. Members decided that the event had already grown so large and drew such large, enthusiastic crowds that it should be turned over to an agency specifically created to run it.

During Torrance's Valley Hunt Club presidency, he also laid out the first golf course in Pasadena, only a few years after the 1891 opening of the state's first golf course in Riverside.

The Los Angeles Stock Exchange was founded in 1899. Torrance was a member of the exchange and held securities in the Spring Street Market Co., a firm involved in the

establishment of that exchange.

In 1916, he listed 104 California corporations in which he recalled having been involved. He was president of 23. He was vice president of 16 companies, including the bond house of James H. Adams & Co., and firms involved in the development of Fontana.

While developing Torrance, Jared Sidney Torrance was president of Torrance, Marshall & Co., Dominguez Land Co., Torrance Land & Improvement Co., Torrance Water, Light & Power Co., and was the sole stockholder in Thomas D. Campbell & Co.

Torrance also was vice president of the Bolsa Chica Gun Club, and a director of the California Club of Los Angeles.

He was a major stockholder in the Union Savings Bank of Pasadena, founded on February 1, 1895 and opened March 1, 1895 in the Masonic Temple building on Raymond Avenue in Pasadena. Torrance's neighbor and friend, Dr. Bridge, was a director of the bank. Torrance, Col. L.P. Hause and M.E. Wood built the Masonic building in 1894-95 at a cost of $40,000.

Torrance also drew public notice in 1894 when the *Los Angeles Daily Journal* included his name on a list of 72 Pasadena-area residents whose real estate holdings in Los Angeles County were valued at more than $10,000.

When Southern Pacific Railroad wanted to establish a direct rail link to Pasadena in 1895, they turned to prominent real estate man Jared Sidney Torrance to purchase the Colorado Boulevard site of the Pasadena depot.

Despite his father's fling in Democratic Party politics, and Torrance's acquaintance with President Grover Cleveland and other influential politicians, Torrance developed a reputation for being politically independent.

On February 8, 1900, the California Legislature elected Republican Thomas R. Bard as a U.S. Senator from California. He served in that post until March 4, 1905. Jared Sidney Torrance, William R. Staats, Frederick H. Rindge, W.S. Botsford and John B. Miller

formed a group in 1900 to buy out Bard's ownership of one-third of the stock of Union Oil Co. of California. The stock was held by United Stockholders Associates, with Torrance as president and chief spokesman for the minority stockholders group. Union Oil had been founded in 1890 by Lyman Stewart, who still ran the firm.

"I regarded the service of Lyman Stewart as worth more to Union Oil than all the other directors put together," Torrance once said. "He possessed courage that was almost unlimited; he knew every feature of the oil business — the drilling end, the territorial end, the marketing end. But I did not have much respect for his ability as a financier."

Torrance served as a vice president of Union Oil and also was president of a Union subsidiary, Union Annex Oil Co. Stewart, who apparently shared Torrance's judgment of his own ability as a financier, placed Torrance in charge of Union's finances in Los Angeles from 1900 to 1910. Shortly after he was placed in that position, the company's stock was doubled to ten million dollars in capital.

In 1901, Torrance and Botsford swayed the board of directors against Stewart's recommendation that Union join a syndicate of California fuel oil producers. That action is viewed in an official history of the company as a key, far-

An indoor tile swimming pool vaguely reminiscent of the one at Hearst Castle was just below the rear of the Torrance house. It included changing rooms and showers. Details are in white marble or white tile, with stained-glass windows now in storage to prevent damage by vandals. Ms. Winter says the pool was so well constructed that it, too, is fully functional to this day.
PHOTO BY WM. FRIDRICH

reaching decision to keep the firm independent of any outside organization.

As vice president of another Union Oil-controlled company formed in 1905, the Union Provident Co., Torrance helped Union Oil founder Lyman Stewart control enough stock to retain working control of the company despite large offerings of Union Oil stock to the general public.

Also in 1905, Union formed the Union Steamship Co., with Torrance as a director, to buy four tankers. In 1906, when the great earthquake and fire in San Francisco burned Union Oil's storage tanks and records there and delayed expansion of Union's Northern California plant, and again when a storage tank in Oregon blew up while an employee negligently inspected it with a lighted lantern, and yet again when a Panama pipeline the company built proved to be a white elephant, Torrance's finesse in the area of finance was a godsend to Union.

Torrance also was on the board of other Union-related firms. These included Union Tool Co., a manufacturer of oil well drilling equipment which later was to play a major role in the founding of the city of Torrance; the Outer Harbor Wharf & Dock Co., which helped to promote and build a terminal at San Pedro Harbor adequate to accommodate ocean-going steamers; and Producers

Transportation Co., which built a pipeline to carry oil from the San Joaquin Valley to Port Harford in San Luis Obispo County, allowing Union to avoid the high rates charged by Southern Pacific to transport crude oil.

During a major Los Angeles building boom, 1902-1908, and particularly after the 1906 San Francisco earthquake led to stricter construction requirements, Torrance participated in development of a new central business district along Seventh Street, operating through his Seventh Street Development Co. and Seventh Street Fireproof Building Co.

At his death in 1921, he also still held major interests in the San Fernando Mission Land Co., a firm set up by wealthy businessmen in 1904 to buy 16,000 acres of land in the San Fernando Valley in anticipation of profits when Henry Huntington extended his trolley lines from downtown. Completion of the Owens Valley water project by the city of Los Angeles in 1913 and annexation of the valley into Los Angeles in 1915 opened the land to profitable development.

Some entirely different interests also claimed the attention of this indefatigable financier.

Charles F. Lummis, founder of the Southwest Museum for the Study of Indian Artifacts, and a colorful writer and public figure, opened a museum of sorts in the old Los Angeles Chamber of Commerce building on Broadway near Second Street in late 1903. In 1908, he asked Torrance to join his efforts to build a new museum facility.

"I am perfectly willing to be a voting member of the corporation," Torrance replied in an August 12, 1908 letter now in the museum's collection, "but I have so many demands upon my time that I am unwilling to be a candidate for any place upon any boards of directors, or of committees in the premises."

Before long, however, Torrance's resistance was worn down by Lummis' persistence. He became a member of the museum board, made donations totalling at least $22,000 toward the construction of the museum building and gave his name to the building's main tower, still known as the Torrance Tower. By 1917, Torrance was president of the museum's board of directors, a post he held until his death four years later. On March 3, 1920, a 240-foot tunnel and 108-foot elevator opened, providing easy pedestrian access to the museum from nearby streets, thanks to a $50,000 contribution made by Torrance and Dr. Bridge.

From 1911 until his death, Torrance also served on the board of the Barlow Sanitarium, a tuberculosis treatment facility that opened in September, 1903, next to Elysian Park in Chavez Ravine.

On June 6, 1914, Torrance married Helena Childs at his sister's home in San Francisco. Her parents were Daniel and Margaret (nee Reynolds) Heney of San Francisco. Torrance was 61, his bride 47. As he and his first wife had been, they were 14 years apart in age. Though Mrs. Childs had two children from her first marriage, she and Torrance had no children.

The newlyweds sailed from New York on June 20, 1914 for Southampton on the luxury liner *Olympic* of the White Star Line. The *Olympic* was a sister ship to the *Titanic*, and had some of the poshest first-class accommodations on the trans-Atlantic run at that time, including the first swimming pool ever on an oceanliner, a Turkish bath, an exercise room, large men-only smoking lounges, and dining and other public areas of utter opulence.

The Torrances planned a four-month honeymoon in Europe, which would have placed them there in early August, 1914, at the outbreak of the first world war, but his 1916 recollections do not include an account of that experience.

Torrance's mother, Mary, died on February 11, 1916 at the age of 84, in Pasadena. Among the things she bequeathed to him was a packet of family letters, which sparked his interest in tracing his family tree. At his wife's urging, he soon began writing his autobiography.

In March, 1921, he was still working with researcher Louise Gardner on the text for *The Descendents of Lewis Hart and Anne Elliott*, his book on his family history and genealogy which his wife published privately in 1923. Gardner was being paid ninety dollars per month for her help.

On March 7, 1921, Torrance revised his will, though the reason for the revisions and the nature of the changes are not known. Torrance had recently pledged $5,000 to the Pasadena Hospital's (later the Huntington Memorial Hospital) building fund, and his will included money that helped to establish the Torrance Memorial Medical Center in Torrance. But when Torrance suddenly felt unwell himself, he apparently was unwilling to enter a hospital.

On March 9, 1921, Torrance had teeth and knee x-rays taken. His condition deteriorated. Beginning on the night of March 25, 1921, this energetic city builder and vital financial wizard languished at his South Pasadena home under the nightly vigil of a nurse, Miss Ada Wilson, engaged for six dollars per night to attend him at his bedside. She sat with him for only four nights before he died on the twenty-ninth. After his death, his physician, Frederick A. Speik of Los Angeles, billed the estate for 29 visits, apparently daily housecalls during the month of March. Torrance's death was listed as due to pneumonia.

His death came just three weeks before the April 19, 1921 election in which Torrance residents were expected to vote to incorporate the city of Torrance, Torrance's crowning achievement. And indeed they did so, giving a dramatically lopsided 355-to-11 vote of confidence to his great dream.

The *Pasadena Star-News* described Jared Sidney Torrance as "one of the leading financiers of the West" and noted that he was a director of "more than a score

This modest stone marks the spot in the Pine Hill Cemetery near his hometown of Gowanda, New York where Jared Sidney Torrance's ashes were interred, though the year of his birth is incorrectly inscribed as 1853. Pine Hill also has the remains of his first wife, Annie Laurie Fowler, who died at 27; his son, Jared Sidney Torrance, Jr., who died at six months in 1890; and their second son, John Fowler Torrance, who died in 1900 at the age of eight. The cemetery was among the many recipients of bequests from Torrance's will. Torrance never lived in his namesake city in Southern California. Though he was an enthusiastic booster of Southern California, he turned to his family roots for a place to be buried. He could not have been buried in Torrance, California, either, since one restriction on deeds in the new town he founded barred cemeteries within the city limits and there are still none today.

COURTESY OF GOWANDA HISTORICAL SOCIETY

of big financial and commercial corporations of Southern California and a member of the Annandale Country Club."

Funerals at the home of the deceased were the custom of that time. Reynolds & Van Nuys in Pasadena was retained to conduct Torrance's funeral at his South Pasadena home. He was laid out in a $325 gray casket before cremation, which cost fifty dollars. Dr. Leslie E. Learned of All Saints Episcopal Church of Pasadena was retained to conduct a 3:30 p.m. Thursday service and received a $35 honorium. A hearse cost ten dollars in those days and one hundred chairs rented for the solemn occasion cost five dollars.

Though friends were asked to omit flowers, a truck was necessary to haul all the floral tributes that arrived anyway. The truck, and a detective hired to provide security for the private service, each cost five dollars. Torrance's ashes were carefully placed in a $45 bronze urn, inscribed for another five dollars, and carried to Gowanda for burial.

His widow, Helena Torrance, continued to take a lively interest in her husband's crowning accomplishment, especially in Torrance Memorial Hospital. She died in Pasadena on October 18, 1940 at 72.

For most Americans, the years 1921-22 were years of severe postwar recession, but at his death in 1921 Torrance left

behind a 2.9 million dollar estate which was reduced to just under 2.2 million dollars when all his debts were paid. His legacy included not only a new city, but charitable bequests helping to establish and maintain Torrance Memorial Hospital, which still was receiving monthly payments in 1984, according to a hospital spokesman, and money for the Torrance Public Library. Though Torrance never lived in his namesake city, he was intimately involved in its development throughout the last decade of his life. At his death, at least half of his personal fortune consisted of real estate, securities and other holdings in Torrance or firms doing business in Torrance.

His wife received $100,000, the family home in South Pasadena, most household goods and personal effects, and income from a trust fund for life. His brother and other relatives, his first wife's sister, his second wife's children and even his cousin, Isabel Henderson of Torrance, each received $5,000 or more — a large sum in 1921. Mrs. Henderson not only started the Torrance Public Library with Torrance's help, but served as a founding member of the board of Torrance Memorial Hospital Medical Center, as did Torrance's second wife, Helena Torrance.

The Pine Hill Cemetery, where Torrance's ashes were interred, received $10,000 for upkeep of the family plot from Jared Sidney Torrance's estate. Other grants were made to the

Southwest Museum, the Barlow Sanitarium, the La Vina Sanitarium and the McKinley Industrial Home Society for Boys in Los Angeles.

W. Jarvis Barlow, who founded the Barlow Sanitarium, was a long-time friend of Torrance's and recalled after Torrance's death that Torrance was known to his friends as "Sidney," and Sidney "always made close and intimate friendships." Sidney, Barlow said, was "a strong personality ... with a spirit of optimism and cheerfulness, great personal magnetism and charm."

Sidney also was a man "who could always grasp large affairs and showed unusual wisdom and optimism. A fair criticism of him might be that he burdened himself too heavily with great responsibilities, but this was due partly to the fact that he was happiest in producing, developing and working out new schemes for progress. Many examples of this may be seen through his career, noticeably his idealistic industrial plan consummated in the town which bears his name — Torrance."

Jared Sidney Torrance must have had a sense of humor, too. Dorothy Jamieson, whose mother was Isabel Henderson, recalled that when asked about the origin of the name of the town, Torrance invariably gave the same answer. "He always said," she recalled, "he didn't know why they named the town Torrance — but he liked it!"

Dust, recession and war: the town's troubled first decade

The "Modern Industrial City" begins instead as a small town beset by unsold vacant lots and the cataclysms of history.

In the beginning, Torrance was dust.

Those present on the day in 1912 when ground was broken for the new industrial town of Torrance, like Ida Schaffer, a Manhattan Beach resident who is a member of the pioneer Avila family of Inglewood, recall Torrance then as "a very dusty place." The prevailing winds were from the

local economy there, the family decided to sell out and move to Torrance.

He rented space in the ground floor of the Brighton Hotel at Cabrillo and Cravens avenues and opened the first drugstore, though he had to sublease to Hurum Reeve — a carpenter who was working in Torrance and wanted to open a hardware store — in order to

This 1914 photograph shows Jared Sidney Torrance, second from right wearing bow tie and carrying a cane, with early pioneer businessmen of the town. From left, they are Harry Paige, a grocer; George Neill of the First National Bank of Torrance; Fay L. Parks of Torrance Plumbing; George A. Proctor of the Union Tool Co. and later the town's first mayor; Charles Long; Hurum Reeve, a hardware store operator; Jacob Isenstein, a men's store owner; C.A. Paxman, who had an electric shop; Burr Peck, a painter; B.M. Knudson of the *Torrance Herald* newspaper; Vern Zuver, a plumber; A.H. Bartlett, secretary of the Torrance Chamber of Commerce and later the city clerk for many decades; Charles Walker, Torrance and Ben Hannebrink of Union Tool.

This is the official corporate seal of the Dominguez Land Corp., the successor firm to the Dominguez Land Co., both founded by Jared Sidney Torrance to facilitate the development of his namesake city. Torrance served as president of both firms, which were the major operating companies involved in creation of the town.

ocean then as now, and when the region was dry — as it generally is between May and October — the site of the future city often swirled with flying sand and dirt.

Harry H. Dolley, a pharmacist who opened a drugstore in Torrance with his father in the early days, recalled visiting on "Grand Opening Day" — a Sunday in the fall of 1912.

"It was a most discouraging day," Dolley wrote years later. "The wind blew hard and cold. The air was full of sand and dust from the plowed-up fields where houses and streets were being built."

But his family then had a drugstore in Azusa, and when a hard freeze that winter destroyed the Southern California citrus fruit crop which supported the

afford the steep one hundred dollars per month rent.

Little more than a year after the townsite was laid out, the first issue of the *Torrance Herald* said in January, 1914, "The Dominguez Land Corp. has had vacant lots and land about the city planted to barley." The planting of grain, along with many trees intended to provide shade and a windbreak, the paper said, would "obviate the possibilities of dust storms in the summer as well as obviate the unsightly and neglected vacant lots in the ordinary town or city."

And the only thing worse than the dust, the old-timers say, was the mud that came with the rains and made the mostly unpaved roads out of town impassable.

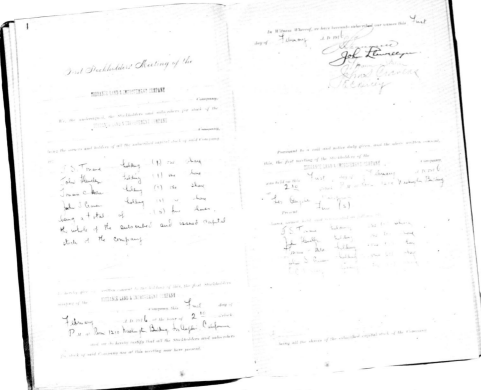

Torrance and his associates, in the venture to develop the West's first modern, model industrial city on former Rancho Dominguez property, used a variety of corporations to implement their plan. One such firm, organized in 1916, was the Torrance Land & Improvement Co. Torrance's partners in this firm were John Llewellyn of the Llewellyn Iron Works; a Torrance relative by his sister's marriage, Torrance C. Welch; First National Bank of Los Angeles executive John S. Cravens, who also was a former president of the Edison Electric Co. in Los Angeles; and E.C. Dicey. Other firms Torrance created included Thomas D. Campbell & Co., which promoted the town during its first year, and the Dominguez Land Corp., which managed land sales and other continuing interests locally.
PHOTO BY WM. FRIDRICH

Vacant lots, economic ills and unfulfilled promises of major industrial plants plagued the new town through its first decade.

The founding of Torrance to the east of Redondo Beach, in fact, was initially taken with so little seriousness by the *Redondo Breeze*, that the paper consistently misspelled the name of the new development as "Torrence" during the summer and fall of 1912.

An article in the *Redondo Breeze* of July 27, 1912 referred patronizingly to "Torrence (sic), a small place about three and one half miles southeast of Redondo" and focused on the August, 1912 opening of a Union Tool Co. plant there. It was an event of importance to Redondoans, the paper suggested, because 300 families would earn their livelihood there, "many of whom expect to reside in Redondo Beach" once a new road and a new Pacific Electric line made that possible.

It was not until late in 1912 that the small weekly newspaper, which would become the giant of South Bay journalism and move its plant to Torrance in the 1960s, correctly spelled the name of what would become the South Bay's most populous town.

The story of how the Torrance tract received its name also is an interesting one.

According to the minutes of the March 20, 1912 meeting of the board of directors of the Dominguez Land Co., the U.S. Post Office Department of that day would not allow the new development to be called "Dominguez" because there already was one Dominguez on the map in California and another in Colorado.

"Various variants of the name 'Dominguez' had been suggested, principally 'Dominguez City,' 'San Dominguez' and 'El Dominguez,' but the (Dominguez Land Co.) general manager (H.H. Sinclair) reported that none of these would be satisfactory to the Dominguez family and that they would prefer to retain the name 'Dominguez' for the present (railroad) station of that name (near the Dominguez adobe) and requested that the Dominguez Land Co. select some other name for the industrial city.

"Several directors suggested the name of 'Torrance,' but (Dominguez Land Co.) President (Jared Sidney) Torrance requested that the use of his name not be considered.

"A general discussion followed in which about thirty names were suggested, most of which had to be dropped on account of duplication in other parts of the United States. The names 'Southport,' 'Obrador,' 'Coronel,' 'Don Manuel' and 'Industrial' received the most favorable considerations, but not any of these was deemed to be satisfactory.

"An informal vote was then taken on the name 'Torrance' and it was unanimously decided that this name was

Nothing happens in the business world without an enthusiastic salesperson behind the concept. That was true in 1914 when this flyer "boomed" Torrance as "the modern industrial city," and promised 3,000 jobs and a population of 15,000 in the near future. While growth was to be delayed by bank panics, depressions and world wars, and while we have shifted dramatically away from "high temperature" to "high technology" industry, the optimism of the founders is amply vindicated 70 years later.
PHOTO BY WM. FRIDRICH

the logical and the most satisfactory name and should be used if President Torrance would withdraw his objections. President Torrance protested against the use of the name, but Vice President (H.H.) Sinclair assumed the chair" and a resolution, "proposed by Mr. (John S.) Cravens and seconded by Mr. (Maurice S.) Hellman was unanimously adopted," making Torrance the name of the new industrial community they planned to build.

Perhaps even more interestingly, Jared Sidney Torrance's decision to create a new industrial town on empty land between Los Angeles and San Pedro Harbor seems to have sprung out of rising real estate prices in the City of the Angels and a violent climate of labor-management struggle that came to a bloody crescendo in 1910.

General Harrison Gray Otis, owner of the *Los Angeles Times*, had crusaded for nearly 30 years against unions and made Los Angeles the strongest open shop town in the nation.

But the Central Labor Council, an umbrella group of 85 unions, put on a push in Los Angeles in 1910 which included a strike by metal trades workers. They made progress towards organizing and winning recognition for the union until October 1, 1910, when a dynamite explosion destroyed the *Los Angeles Times* newspaper plant at First Street and Broadway and killed 20 employees.

Otis found a time bomb at his home that afternoon, which police removed from the house before it exploded. And a dud was planted at the home of the secretary of the powerful anti-union Merchants and Manufacturers Association.

On November 8, 1910, perhaps not coincidentally, Los Angeles also turned out the largest bloc of Socialist voters for a state-wide election.

On Christmas Day, December 25, 1910, another blast — this one at the Llewellyn Iron Works in Los Angeles — further escalated the climate of unrest and labor violence.

Nationally famed detective William J. Burns was brought into the case and persuaded Ortie McManigal, a member of the International Association of Bridge and Structural Iron Workers headquartered in Indianapolis, to sign a sworn statement implicating John J. McNamara, secretary-treasurer of the union, and his brother, James McNamara.

Attorney Clarence Darrow undertook their defense, but after Darrow's chief investigator was arrested for attempting to bribe a juror, James confessed to placing 16 sticks of dynamite in the *Times* building. He was sentenced to life imprisonment; his brother to 15 years.

In this atmosphere, the new city of

Joseph F. Sartori, founder and president of the Security Trust & Savings Bank in Los Angeles, was one of Torrance's partners in creation of what became the city of Torrance. In 1907, Torrance and Sartori also had been colleagues in the Normal School Co., a firm created to buy the already-outgrown downtown Los Angeles site of the State Normal School. The property was sold to the city of Los Angeles in 1913 so Fifth Street could be opened and the Los Angeles Public Library could be built on the site. Sartori was a founder of the Los Angeles Country Club and for 49 years reigned as its organizational and financial genius.

Torrance was conceived as a kind of capitalist's concept of a worker's paradise — in which living conditions would be so wonderful that labor unrest would vanish.

Plans for the new industrial city were announced in March, 1912. That same year, the Los Angeles Police Department created its infamous Red Squad to battle against union organizers and others who sought to stir economic and social unrest.

Despite the climate of labor-management antagonism and violence, the Union Tool Co., a subsidiary of the Union Oil Co., and the Llewellyn Iron Works of Los Angeles wanted to expand, Torrance recalled in 1916. The cost of land near Llewellyn's existing Los Angeles plant — then $2.50 per square foot or more than $100,000 per acre — was considered to be "prohibitive." So cheaper land in Torrance seemed highly attractive for new facilities.

In 1911, Los Angeles had a population of 319,198 and was second only to San Francisco in California. Pasadena had grown to 30,291 and South Pasadena — where Torrance lived — claimed a mere 4,649 residents.

The region in which Torrance chose to build his new industrial town was rural land less than five miles east of the summer resort city of Redondo Beach, which had 2,935 year-round residents in an era when 60 of California's 125 cities had fewer than 2,500.

The Torrance project, as presented in 1912, included a plan to dredge the marshy lowlands between Torrance and San Pedro to create a ship channel that would allow the great new industrial plants of Torrance to load and unload raw materials and finished goods directly to and from ocean-going vessels.

Though some have doubted the seriousness of this part of the plan, the earnest intent is shown by the fact that during the Dominguez Land Co. meetings, directors considered naming the town "Southport." We know also that Torrance's holdings at the time of his death in 1921 included an ownership position in securities of the Standard American Dredging Co., where he also served as a director.

Torrance means "man of the hills" in Scottish, and Torrance seemed particularly fond of his father's house in Gowanda overlooking the village in a valley below. His hillside home in South Pasadena also had broad vistas. His namesake city, however, was built on mostly flat land.

To found the town, Torrance negotiated with the attorney for the Dominguez family to buy about 2,800 acres from the Dominguez Estate Co. for $980,000 and added 730 acres to that from a Dominguez heir for another $550,000.

Then the Dominguez Land Co. was formed under Torrance's guidance, with $500,000 in capital stock outstanding. A successor corporation, the Dominguez Land Corp., was later formed with Torrance as president and capitalized for two million dollars. A 1.5 million dollar bond issue by the latter company "practically paid for the land," Torrance said, and "became the operating company."

Other officers of the corporation included John S. Cravens, a Pasadena resident and a vice president of Los Angeles First National Bank who served with Torrance on the boards of the Barlow Sanitarium and the Southwest Museum. Cravens also had membership in the California Club in common with Torrance.

Cravens was an Episcopalian and a Republican. He served as a one-dollar-a-year member of the Council of National Defense in Washington, D.C. during World War One.

Joseph F. Sartori of Los Angeles, another director of the Dominguez Land Co., was a banker who organized the Security Trust and Savings Bank in Los Angeles, and in 1929 became president and director of the Security First National Bank of Los Angeles. He was active in securities and investment firms.

Before his death in 1946 at the age of 87, Sartori had served as a Los Angeles director of the Federal Reserve Bank of San Francisco, president of the California Club, and a director of the Automobile Club of Southern California. He was a staunch Republican.

Both Cravens and Sartori had streets in the new town named for them.

If there was to be a vista from downtown Torrance, it would be a view of Mount San Antonio — popularly called Mount Baldy — beyond the depot, which was built at the northeast end of El Prado, a broad street designed to stretch from the station to a town square at what is now Carson Street. A city hall was planned for the site now occupied by Torrance High School

and the street name "El Prado" meant "parade."

Torrance arranged for four industries to lend their support to the new industrial city.

He had been a vice president and finance director for the Union Oil Co. and a member of the board of directors of the Union Tool Co. In June, 1911, he offered Union Tool the privilege of buying 25 percent of the stock in the Dominguez Land Co. if they would move to Torrance. In September, 1911, he succeeded in persuading Union Tool officials to buy a 25-acre tract in the new town and build a $500,000 plant there. Union Tool, with 500 employees in Torrance in 1912-13, was one of the largest manufacturers of oil well machinery and tools in the world. By 1921, its Torrance plant claimed 1,100 employees with a monthly payroll of $200,000.

D.S. Faulkner, a Union Tool vice president, recalled in 1947 that he came to Torrance in January, 1914. He says the company encountered "many difficulties ... of building complete manufacturing facilities in the middle of a large ranch" but "the plant was eventually completed and manufacturing operations started in December, 1912.

"When manufacturing did get under way, only three or four houses had been completed, and all of them (were) occupied by the following employees of the Union Tool Co., in the order of their moving in: Messrs. L. Garretson, John B. Smith, Dick Smith and Clinton Northrup.

"The westerly winds, which in summertime generally keep the temperature of Torrance five to ten degrees below the neighboring city of Los Angeles, were a great nuisance in those early days. They carried large quantities of sand from unoccupied plots of land directly into our machine tools, necessitating an unusual amount of maintenance work.

"But on the other hand, those vacant fields provided some of the best crops of mushrooms anywhere and harvesting this crop provided some of the principal noon-hour diversion."

The Dominguez Water Co. also was created to build a $750,000 system to supply water to nearly 20,000 acres of land in the Torrance vicinity, including water for residential, commerical and industrial use in the new town, and for agriculture on the adjoining lands still held by the Dominguez heirs.

The Torrance Power and Light Co. was created to provide electricity to factories and homes. Plans were announced for crude oil and natural gas pipelines to serve the town with energy sources.

"After protracted negotiations," Torrance recalled in 1916, Pacific Electric Railway agreed on December 26, 1911, to build a line to the town and by July 1, 1916, move their railcar construction and repair shops from Los Angeles to a 125-acre site in Torrance, a site turned over to them free of charge. Construction of the facilities, which would serve the line that then operated more trolley cars than any other electric street railway in the world, was expected to cost $750,000, but was not begun until 1916 and completed in 1917. In 1921, Pacific Electric employed 530 men

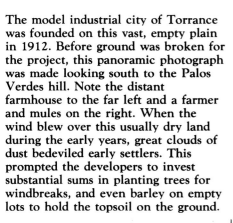

The model industrial city of Torrance was founded on this vast, empty plain in 1912. Before ground was broken for the project, this panoramic photograph was made looking south to the Palos Verdes hill. Note the distant farmhouse to the far left and a farmer and mules on the right. When the wind blew over this usually dry land during the early years, great clouds of dust bedeviled early settlers. This prompted the developers to invest substantial sums in planting trees for windbreaks, and even barley on empty lots to hold the topsoil on the ground.

One of the earliest industries in Torrance was glassmaking. In fact, in those days, going down to the glassworks to watch the skilled artisans shape and form silica and sand at white hot temperatures was a favorite pastime. Frank Paour contributed this exquisite ladle to the Torrance Museum. It was blown about 1918 by an artisan in his off-duty hours. The Torrance Window Glass Co., managed by Charles Lyman Bisbee, came to Torrance from Ohio in 1914 and boasted that "we make the finest glass in the United States." The company, later known variously as the Western Sheet Glass Co. and the Torrance Flat Glass Co., operated on an eight-acre site and employed as many as 250 men. But the painstaking process of blowing window glass by hand was made obsolete by less costly and less time-consuming machinery to produce flat glass, and despite efforts to keep up with new technology, the glass company passed from the scene in the early 1930s.

PHOTO BY WM. FRIDRICH

The Union Tool Co. was the first manufacturing plant established in Torrance and is shown here under construction in the fall of 1912. The firm remained the town's largest employer well into the 1920s. A view of the completed facility is shown from a picture postcard issued shortly after the plant opened in late 1912.

in Torrance and had a monthly payroll of $77,000.

A Southern Pacific spur line from the main line from San Pedro to Los Angeles also was established at the request of Union Tool officials. They wanted a full-service, standard gauge train service to ship their goods to points throughout the United States.

Torrance described himself as "one of the largest stockholders" in the Llewellyn Iron Works — then on North Main Street in Los Angeles. The firm, one of the largest industries in the Southwest at that time, fabricated and erected structural iron and steel, made iron and steel water pipe, and built elevators and large storage tanks for oil.

Torrance contracted with the proprietors, Reese, John and David Llewellyn, to sell them 15 percent of the Dominguez Land Corp.'s stock and 24 acres of land for a new plant, which they pledged to construct by late 1914, with the help of financing also arranged by Torrance.

The plant was not actually started until 1915 and completed in 1916, however, due to intervening hard times. By 1921, Llewellyn employed 500 in Torrance and paid $75,000 monthly to its workers.

The fourth firm in the original Torrance project was the Pacific Metal Products Co., which built a plant on a five-acre site and opened during the winter of 1912-13.

Other plants built during the town's pre-incorporation decade included the Hendrie Rubber Co., the Torrance Pearl Manufacturing Co. — later known as Salm Manufacturing — the California Shoe Manufacturing Co. and the Hurrle Window Glass Co.

The internationally noted landscape architects, the brothers John C. and Frederick Law Olmstead, Jr. of Boston, were employed to lay out the townsite. They were the sons of America's foremost landscape authority and architect, Frederick Law Olmstead, who died in 1903 at the age of 91.

Torrance was also an Edison Co. director, and H.H. Sinclair, a former Edison Co. engineer, was hired as the general manager of the Dominguez Land Corp.

The Olmstead firm was paid $5,000 to design the new city as a model that would be admired and copied elsewhere, the first industrial city built from the ground up in the West. Their contract with Dominguez Land also called for a $3,000 per year consulting rate after the initial fee, and expenses.

The Olmstead plan called for all telegraph, telephone and electric wires in Torrance to be placed in underground conduits, and water, sewer and gas lines to be laid in alleys to avoid tearing up the streets later to repair those lines.

The new town was to have paved streets, a water distribution plant, a sewer system, street lighting, the construction of one hundred or more houses, six brick commercial blocks, a railway passenger depot and other features, "all first class," Torrance said.

In April, 1912, it was announced that the Dominguez Land Co., with offices in the Title Insurance Building in Los Angeles, had hired architect Irving Gill of San Diego to run Dominguez Land Co.'s in-house architectural department. Gill later became one of California's most celebrated architects — he also laid out Palos Verdes Estates — and his work in Torrance is regarded as formative to his style. During his tenure in Torrance, he worked in a variety of types and methods of constructions,

particularly in concrete.

During 1912, Gill was preparing plans for the Pacific Electric depot, a city building, an administration building, stores, a hotel, rooming houses and about one hundred cottages. Some were so simple in design and of such austerely cold concrete construction that the model homes for model workers proved difficult to sell to working men more at home with the wooden columns, carved moldings and broad porches of that day.

In July, 1912, a $20,000 contract was awarded to the California Real Estate & Building Co. in Los Angeles to build the depot, the Dominguez Land Co. administration building and an office building.

Investors in the project — "men of means," Torrance said — decided "that the first consideration should be to do things right. Plans were carefully considered and all construction work was of the most thorough character. Sewers, paved streets, and all public utilities were constructed in advance; alleys which contained all pole lines and water and gas mains were provided throughout the townsite; ample reservations were made for public parks, an athletic park and for playgrounds; a civic center was designed, and upwards of 300,000 trees were planted in streets and windbreaks; and several acres were reserved for public schools to be donated to the public."

An expert horticulturist, J.F. Rupprecht, was brought in to run the Torrance nursery that nurtured the many trees, including 20,000 eucalyptus, 15,000

arborvitae, 20,000 Japanese pines, and assorted magnolias, Himalayan cedars, palms from South Africa and the west coast of Mexico, Catalina cherry trees, dragon lilies from Australia, and 150,000 flowering shrubs.

The layout of the town, with its view of Mount Baldy and factories to the east of houses and stores, so prevailing winds would carry factory smoke away from them, also called for a graceful concrete bridge over Torrance Boulevard, a bridge designed by Gill. The bridge kept trains from blocking major streets as they traveled to and from the depot and kept their noise and vibrations away from the new residential areas.

Architect Irving Gill drew the assignment of designing the railroad depot, the bank building and other buildings in the new downtown.

The commercial district was limited to buildings of brick construction at least two stories high, while a core of expensive homes in the heart of the city's residential district was assured by the requirement that the homes of the most influential citizens who resided on Post Avenue must cost "at least $5,000."

But most houses for the average working men were more reasonably priced and were sold on plans that made them attractive to working family men fleeing the radical labor-management turmoil of the urban Los Angeles of that era.

"Very particular attention was given to the proper housing of the future employees of the factories locating

This shot, inside the tire plant, shows tires in various stages of assembly and the equipment used to produce them. Bear in mind that what looks like a bicycle tire to us today was, in fact in the 1910s and 1920s, a servicable tire for an up-to-date family's flivver.

Another of Torrance's early industrial manufacturing plants was the W.C. Hendrie Rubber Co. factory which manufactured tires. Note that the tires could be shipped by rail directly from the Hendrie plant throughout the United States, and note the undeveloped vistas to the south of the plant, looking toward Palos Verdes and San Pedro.

there," Torrance said of the planning for his new town. The idea was to create "a model industrial city," he said.

George W. Neill, president of the Torrance Development Co., wrote in the *Torrance Enterprise* of November 5, 1920, that the aim was to "establish an environment that would produce maximum efficiency in the men as well as the factories.

"Several elements enter into making efficient workmen," said Neill. "The first is a living wage and that means more than bread and clothing and a roof over the head; that implies opportunities for recreation and culture, education for the children, money saved for sickness and old age.

"It means sufficient pay for the workman to own his own home, thereby becoming a better American citizen and one having an active interest in the development of the community in which he lives.

"In Torrance, the great majority of the people own their own homes, which speaks well not only for the workmen, but the industries. These homes are sold on easy payments, ten percent cash, the

balance in 60 equal installments."

An article titled "Moving the Factory Back to the Land," published in *Sunset Magazine* in 1913, said the Torrance project was good not only for workers, but for employers, too. The new, modern Union Tool Co. plant in Torrance was expected to cut production costs for the firm by 18 percent and increase output 20 percent with the same payroll.

In the meticulously planned new model industrial city, the article said, "The well-being of the worker has at last been clearly recognized as the source of the largest, most permanent profit, and to the enhancement of this well-being has been given the best thought of J.S. Torrance, father of the project.

"This industrial city was to be the crowning achievement of a long career filled with constructive effort. It was to prove that a worker decently, pleasantly housed upon an ample plot of ground of his own, increases in efficiency and contentment, that these qualities are most important industrial assets and that their growth could be stimulated by laying the groundwork of a model city."

Despite these lofty ideals, land in the new town of Torrance was designated for use in five ways: "business, residential, industrial, unclassified and special quarters for non-Caucasians."

The restrictions placed upon deeds of all property sold in Torrance forbade the manufacture or sale of alcoholic beverages a full eight years before national Prohibition was adopted. If the Torrance provision were violated, the deed restrictions provided that title of the land held by the violator would revert to the Dominguez Land Co.

The developers also banned slaughter houses, tallow chandleries, factories making soap, candles, fertilizer or glue, tanning plants, explosives manufacturing, and cemeteries. George Cate, a Redondo Beach undertaker, noted the ban on cemeteries in Torrance and advertised his services heavily here in the early days.

The restrictions also said: "Excepting in the Foreign Quarters, no portion of any of the property herein referred to shall be sold or conveyed to any person other than of the white or Caucasian race," which was "deemed to exclude Hindoos or other Asiatics." Also

forbidden were leasing or renting to non-whites and "no portion of any of the property herein referred to shall be leased or rented to any person other than of the white or Caucasian race, excepting that persons of any nationality may act or serve as employees during the actual possession and occupancy of the owners."

"Rigorous restrictions were adopted," Torrance admitted in his autobiography in an apparent reference to deed restrictions. "And indeed, some of them, in reference to racial matters, tread pretty hard on the toes of the Constitution of the United States."

An additional restriction was added by state-wide approval in November, 1920, of the Alien Land Law initiative, which barred Japanese from owning or even renting land in the state of California.

Like railroads and factory smoke, Latinos, Japanese and other minorities were to be segregated from the mainstream of Torrance life for many decades. The deed restrictions and other racial measures led to the development of an area in Torrance which in 1921 was called the "Mexican Village" of the Pueblo Lands.

A new town can make do for a spell without some businesses, but grocery stores are immediately necessary. Harry E. Paige had his store in the El Prado Apartments in 1917. No long checkout lines in those faraway times; no unit pricing, either! Soon thereafter, he moved his store across the street, where daughter Rose helped "when I could reach up far enough on a shelf." His baking and coffee grinding used to fill the air with wonderful aromas.
COURTESY OF ROSE PAIGE KING

Hurum Reeve opened a hardware store on Guadaloupe Avenue eight years before the city was incorporated. The street name was changed in 1923 to Post Avenue to honor Judge George W. Post, banker and Dominguez Land Co. manager who was considered the second most important man in the founding and nurturing of Torrance through its difficult early days. If you were a good customer of Reeve's in 1913, you probably would have received this elegant 1914 calendar as a Christmas gift.
PHOTO BY WM. FRIDRICH

Jacob Isenstein, a Torrance merchant whose son was Albert Isen, mayor of Torrance during the 1950s and in the early 1960s, was the proprietor of the Mexican Village.

A 1922 city directory listed the occupants of the Mexican Village as Pablo Terazas, Selvera Rios, Julio Lopez, Angel Navaro, Encarrnason Gonzales, Jose Reyes, Modesto Ruiz and Gabriel Garcia. Lopez was a Llewellyn employee, while Navaro, Gonzales, Reyes and Ruiz worked for Union Tool; Garcia was a farmer.

More numerous in that early directory were persons with Japanese surnames, who lived on farmland surrounding the town, and whose names were included without full first names. These included K. Furuchi, J. Furushiro, D. Heramoto, T. Horita, M. Iida, J. Ikemoto, M. Ishii, S. Kaino, M. Kajikawa, T. Kato, K. Kawanishi, S. Kaywamoto, C. Kobayashi, Y. Kubo, I. Kuda, S. Miyamoto, T. Morishita, S. Nakayama, K. Sakamoto, S. Soto, H. Takazumi, T. Takutagawa, S. Tuzaki, E. Ueda, S. Uyesaka and D. Yabuka.

In spite of such segregation, George Neill called Torrance "the Garden City," suggesting that industrial employees there could also live off the fruits, vegetables and livestock they could raise on small ranches near their industrial

jobs in Torrance and put most of their wages in the bank.

"Where in the world could a better location have been found for America's first industrial Garden City?" said Neill.

"Within a few minutes' ride from the beach where the broad Pacific unceasingly rolls, within an hour's ride over splendid boulevards from the beautiful mountains adjacent to Los Angeles, amid flowers and sunshine, surely posterity will bless J.S. Torrance for his vision and wisdom in giving the industrial worker an opportunity to live under such an environment."

Some, at least, were persuaded. On August 12, 1912, the company contracted with the Western Building & Investment Co. — Frank R. Strong, president — for the construction in Torrance of 25 cottages designed by Gill. Western was to receive cost plus seven percent for the houses.

A few months before that, the open fields where Torrance was to rise became occupied by a variety of construction camps, Phoebe Sykes recalled in a *Torrance Herald* interview a decade later.

Her husband, A.E. Sykes, put up a tent store near what is the intersection of Carson Street and Cravens Avenue to serve the workmen preparing the site of

the new town. Nearby was a carpenter's camp and a small cook house where a Chinese cook served hot meals to the engineers and survey crews working on the property.

Their camp, Mrs. Sykes recalled, was "situated where the only trees in Torrance grew at that time, near the north end of Gramercy, where was also the only building in Torrance — a four-room ranch house and barn."

Also living in tents while they did their work were the graders, the street and sidewalk contractors, the construction crew erecting the Union Tool plant and pipefitters, who chose a site west of Madrid Avenue.

Sykes sold tobacco, newspapers, candy, suspenders and overalls, and even collected laundry at his tent store. Candles were also a particularly hot item there.

"So great was the demand for candles," the newspaper said, "that Mr. Sykes had to scour the city of Los Angeles and practically bought up the whole supply."

After the Pacific Electric depot opened in Torrance, the Sykes family ran the newsstand there from 1915 to 1923.

The cook house near Carson and

Cravens later became the Torrance Volunteer Fire Co.'s shed, in which the first hose cart was stored between fires. The structure was torn down in 1923.

Henry Burmaster was the first postmaster appointed in Torrance and opened the first Torrance Post Office on September 14, 1912. "The mail came down from Los Angeles once a day by one of the regular passenger cars of the Pacific Electric," Harry Dolley recalled.

Mail was distributed at the post office only until home delivery by carriers in Torrance was instituted on January 1, 1924. Long-time resident William Deane's father was the first uniformed postman in town.

In those days, though some wells in the Los Angeles basin were already showing the strain of the burgeoning population drawing from them and Los Angeles was constructing its first aqueduct, it was estimated that the supply available from the Dominguez wells was enough to support a population of 50,000 in Torrance.

"Before the public was even invited to visit Torrance," Neill said, "a million dollars had been spent for improvements and establishment of those utilities which make for sanitation, service, value and beauty. Twenty miles of paved streets were laid; a complete sewer system was installed. A reservoir of seventeen million gallons capacity was filled with artesian water, pumped from wells 1,400 feet deep."

The new town also had 84,000 feet of water mains and twenty miles of paved sidewalks and curbs.

As soon as public facilities in the town were that far along, the Dominguez Land Corp. began a campaign to sell business and residential lots and acreage.

A brochure issued in February, 1913, by

These photos show the town's earliest homes on Torrance's first two residential streets, Gramercy and Andreo avenues, in February, 1913, before a nation-wide financial panic and the start of World War One plunged the fate of the new industrial city into uncertainty.

COURTESY OF JEAN (SMITH) BROOKS

Harry McManus, who also served as chief of the Torrance Volunteer Fire Co., was assistant chief in 1913 when Walter Loucks was chief. Others on the force then were William Poulton, Ben Hannebrink, George Proctor, George Probert, Carroll Ashley, John Mitchell, Billie Louvenson and George Watson. Their only piece of equipment was the hand-drawn hose reel, on display in the Torrance Museum today. Hannebrink was chief in 1918 when the first chemical fire truck was acquired. A combination fire station, police department and jail was built on Cravens in 1923. The legendary old railroad rail, hung from a tripod and walloped with a sledge hammer, was used to call forth the volunteers. It is imbedded in the rock wall of the fire station built in 1956 at Crenshaw Blvd. and Carson Street.

Thomas D. Campbell & Co., sales agents for land in the new town, bore the slogan: "Torrance, the Modern Industrial City."

The brochure quoted a magazine article by the Rev. Dana Barlett describing Torrance as "America's first great industrial Garden City."

"The living conditions at Torrance are conducive to health and happiness for the workingman and his entire family," the brochure says.

In addition to Union Tool, by early 1913 a Pacific Metal Products Co. plant was manufacturing barrels and chains in Torrance and the Moore Truck Co. was building a truck plant in the new town, according to the brochure. Other firms committed to locate there included the Fuller Shoe Co., W.C. Hendrie Rubber

Co., Acme Brass Foundry, Out West Gem & Button Co., Holder Lumber Co. and the Southern California Lime & Cement Co.

Photographs in the brochure show a worker's house, an oil storage tank facility, the depot, an office building and the First National Bank of Torrance already built.

Also planned in the immediate future were a hospital building and a public library, but those plans would be shelved for more than a dozen years by the rocky fortunes of the new town.

Torrance, looking back in 1916 on the founding of the city that bears his name, recalled that he and his associates "started with the most brilliant prospects and future hopes, but we started one year too late; 1913 was a panic year and there was nothing doing in real estate."

"Sales," Torrance said, "were progressing very satisfactorily and closely approached the million dollar mark when the (nation-wide financial) panic of 1913 intervened, and the campaign ended."

W.H. Daum, a specialist in industrial real estate, testified in a case brought by the Dominguez Land Co. in 1927 against the federal agency that preceded the Internal Revenue Service that Torrance was built near land he had visited regularly beginning in 1886.

"I commenced shooting ducks on it about forty years ago," Daum said, "and had been over the tract repeatedly, how

This graceful bridge, designed by the Dominguez Land Corp.'s in-house architect, Irving Gill, allowed Los Angeles-bound motor traffic to pass without interruption from Torrance and carried the noise and vibration of the rail cars away from the city's residential area. The bridge served the downtown Torrance depot and made it possible for goods manufactured here to be shipped via Los Angeles or San Pedro. The Pacific Electric line also slowed the residential development of the town somewhat, since it made it possible for workmen in Torrance's factories who lived in Gardena, Redondo Beach and even Los Angeles, to commute daily to work. Note the heavy traffic of 1921 on what is known today as Torrance Boulevard.

Abalone shell knives, crafted by artisans at Salm Manufacturing which was located here from about 1918 into the 1930s. They're on display in the Torrance Museum, along with some lovely examples of artistic, multi-hued glass utensils blown here.

PHOTO BY WM. FRIDRICH

These unidentified men were among the craftsmen who worked at the Salm Manufacturing Co., creating *bric-a-brac* and *objet d'art* from abalone shells. The quality and beauty of American craftsmanship in those days is not a nostalgic legend. It is a fact, perhaps inevitable on a planet approaching five billion inhabitants, that "they don't make things like they used to." The former natives of the South Bay, the Chowigna Indians, would have appreciated these men's work. Chowigna work with abalone shell was so highly regarded that Shoshonean brothers from beyond Cajon Pass would come to Suegna near Wilmington or to the salt lake in Redondo to trade for it.

often I could not say, on the same mission."

Daum said public reception in 1912 "was one of very great favorableness to the Torrance project. It was, you might say, a new experience in city building and in development of the West.

"In the fall of 1912 and in the early part of 1913, Torrance represented about as active a market as we had any place around Southern California."

Even so, testimony in that tax case showed, from October, 1912 through February, 1913, the business lots outsold the residential lots in Torrance by a considerable margin. Most of the residential sales were made to contractors and builders, who bought to build upon and sell the houses they built.

As a result of a national recession in 1913 and a return of poor business conditions in late 1914 as World War One began in Europe, the new Llewellyn Iron Works plant was not built in Torrance within the first 18 months as originally planned. It finally was built in 1916. Initially, it was equipped as a large open-hearth steel mill capable of producing two hundred tons per day and in 1917, a rolling mill was added.

During the era 1914-20, other locations

closer to Los Angeles also were subdivided with an eye to industrial development and worker housing, including sections of the City of Vernon, Huntington Park and Burbank. Since labor was more readily available to industrial concerns in areas closer to Los Angeles, the prosperity of those projects detracted from the potential viability of the Torrance area.

Harry Dolley, the druggist, recalled that "in 1913, times were very bad. It was nip and tuck if the drugstore, the hardware store or the grocery store (begun by Jacob Isenstein at the same site) would stay in business."

"One day, Hurum Reeve took in only 35 cents," Dolley says. "Finally, realizing the difficulties the merchants were having, the land company eliminated rents for one year, in order to retain the merchants to supply the needs of the people."

At the time, he recalled, the only streets really built were Carson, 222nd, Cabrillo, Arlington, Gramercy and Andreo. "The rest of the town had been laid out, but was just sand and weeds."

All but one of the buildings in the town when Dolley arrived were commercial buildings designed by Gill and put up by the developer, Dolley says. The exception was a small, two-story building on Cabrillo owned and built by a butcher named Jones.

"He was a character if there ever was one," Dolley said. "He used to come out early in the morning, look up and down Cabrillo with not a soul in sight and remark: 'Looks more like Chicago every day!' "

Union Tool was built as scheduled, employed about 500 men in July, 1914, and also suffered under the adverse economic conditions of those early years. It shut down after the outbreak of World War One, then restored about four hundred jobs by August, 1916.

In 1916, Pacific Electric was reported about ready to begin constructing their massive car shops in town, Torrance said. But at the time he also said, "There is absolute stagnation, however, in the real estate business and sales are nil."

"We are erecting an additional hundred bungalows to meet a prospective early demand — but they will, for the greater part, have to be rented, as no one seems to be in a mood to purchase real estate in any form."

Writing in 1916 before the United States entered the first world war, Torrance admitted that the California Shoe Manufacturing Co. had already gone out of business and the investors in the Dominguez Land Co. had been disappointed up to that time. But he still hoped his industrial town venture would "eventually prove a material success."

In the meantime, he said, "the residents of Torrance will enjoy an environment which will make for good health, good morals and industrial welfare and prosperity, and if conditions return to normal within a reasonable time and the wheels of Western progress are again put in motion, the public-spirited men behind the enterprise should reap a substantial reward."

Torrance made some visits to his new city in his 1912 Packard — the only car he still owned at his death in 1921, though he'd also owned a Detroit Electric in 1917. Street cars and local passenger trains then provided excellent service throughout Southern California. Automobiles were luxury novelties more than necessities in those days, though the adventurous folk who pioneered Los Angeles already had the highest per capita number of automobiles in the nation.

For the privileged circles in which Torrance moved, however, there was little reason to risk the uncertain conditions of often-unpaved roads from Los Angeles to Torrance, when you could as easily make the important trips by private railroad car.

On one such visit to the fledgling city, the South Pasadena millionaire brought along his friends — bankers, investors, prominent businessmen from Pasadena and Los Angeles, and even Walter Raymond, the proprietor of the prestigious Hotel Raymond of Pasadena, which was a fashionable wintering spot for the wealthy and socially prominent from all over the United States.

"The party left Los Angeles in a special

The first Torrance float to appear in the Tournament of Roses Parade was this one depicting the industrial might and beauty of the modern industrial city in 1914. Note workmen at the anvil, center. It is interesting to note that the float was entered by Thomas D. Campbell & Co., which was a firm whose stock was solely owned by Jared Sidney Torrance, who had been president of the Valley Hunt Club two decades before, when it ran the parade. The tradition was revived during the 1960s and is carried on today by the Torrance Rose Float Association.

The young woman with a parasol at the rear of Torrance's first Tournament of Roses Parade float was Wanda Stacowitz, a Torrance beauty who became a talented professional opera singer after traveling to Italy to study opera in Milan. Madame Butterfly was her favorite role, according to Karmee Dolley. Returning to Torrance during the Great Depression in an age when opera was an oddity in Los Angeles, she soon left for New York City, where she sang and taught. Her father was a Torrance blacksmith.

COURTESY OF KARMEE DOLLEY

Though Torrance was still a small town when World War One began, its young men rallied to the flag. In 1920, these veterans gathered to break ground for the Bert S. Crossland Post No. 170 of the American Legion at the eastern edge of town. Standing on the ground are, from left to right, Tommy Lewis, Horse Aiken, Bill Stanger, four unidentified men, Ralph Satchell, Wallace Post, Lloyd Wartham, Tom Moran, Verne Babcock, Joe Malin, someone identified only as Martoise, an unidentified man, Jimmy Jones, Al Griner, James "Scotty" Scott, Betty Frenger, Nelson Reeves, Ted Frenger, Bob Deinger, an unidentified man and Fred Reese. Standing behind them on the platform to the right are, from left, Jim Day, Tom Atkins, an unidentified man, Dick Jenkins, Jack Williams and three more men whose names are not known. Bert Crossland was the only Torrance soldier to make the supreme sacrifice in World War One.

car of the Pacific Electric," reported a contemporary newspaper, "visited the industrial city and later returned to the car, where luncheon was served."

The visitors "made an inspection of the plants established in the town and of the model bungalows erected for the workmen."

The town itself did not grow as rapidly as some might have expected, at least partly because rail transportation made it possible to commute from more established areas.

In the early years, some workers were reluctant to move to Torrance because of a lack of schools. The first school opened in the fall of 1913 and by 1920, school buildings were in place on what is now the Torrance High School campus.

Harry Dolley remembered the first school as "a little cement building on the east side of Cabrillo between Carson and 220th Street. It had one teacher and the number of students you could count on the fingers of your two hands."

Dolley's sister stayed with friends in Los Angeles to attend high school.

Already some locals were beginning to feel that the town of Torrance was simply too small for another reason, too.

The *Torrance Herald* of September 3, 1920 urged the establishment of "a motion picture show" in the town, suggesting, "the jeer of the young men that 'this town doesn't even have a picture show' ought never to have been permitted, and should no longer be allowed to be true. Some way should be found to give Torrance a motion picture show at once if it has to be housed in a big tent."

Harry Dolley remembered two one-story buildings across the street from the depot in the early days, of similar design with heavy columns. One housed Thomas D. Campbell & Co. and the town post office. On the other side, the First National Bank of Torrance eventually was established.

But in the early days the nearest bank was in Gardena, which created a

71

problem every two weeks when Union Tool paid their employees by check.

"On paydays, my father would take the streetcar to Gardena and come back with $1,000 in gold and silver," Dolley said. "There was no paper money in those days. Most of the paychecks were cashed in the noon lunch period. Then my father would take the checks back to the bank in Gardena and pay back the loan of $1,000, for which the bank charged us one dollar."

Harvel Guttenfelder, another pioneering resident of Torrance, recalls another story about finances and a town marshal named B.M. Anderson.

"He had a motorcycle and acted in all the capacities of a police officer," Guttenfelder says.

"On payday at the Torrance Glass Factory, he would be down there, and one of the local merchants by the name of Ben Rappaport would go down with a pocketful of money to cash the men's checks.

"But the policeman would make the men go over to the other side of the street to the wives and children and give them the money for next week for rent money and groceries and necessities, and whatever was left, he was privileged to go out into the center of the street, where a poker game was in progress and sometimes lasted all day.

"Usually one fellow would end up with all the money on one payday and all the rest of them would all be broke! But the rent was paid and there would be groceries on their tables for another week!"

Though the Gill-designed buildings in Torrance were mostly fireproof — concrete and steel, with wood generally only used for doors — the Torrance Volunteer Fire Department was one of the first groups formed in the town. It was founded on November 12, 1912, in a tent at a meeting called by D.W. Gregory of the Dominguez Land Co. The seven men present named Harry S. McManus as their first chief.

McManus, Dolley said, was "a good Irishman," and "just about all the men in town" later joined the fire volunteers.

"All the equipment we had was a two-wheeled hose reel with a couple hundred feet of hose, which was kept in a little open shack on Carson Street at the head of Andreo.

"Instead of having a bell to ring when there was a fire, the boys at Union Tool took a piece of railroad track, bent it into a circle about four feet in diameter and hung it on a tripod with a sledge hammer, next to the firehouse. The first volunteer who got there sounded the alarm."

Dolley also recalled the May 1, 1913 formation of the Torrance Athletic Club, which had seventy charter members and "two pool tables in the Murray Hotel."

George Proctor, later the first mayor of Torrance, was president of that club and promoted amateur boxing matches in the clubroom, Dolley says. Later the matches moved to an outdoor ring the club helped build west of Western Avenue — possibly on fifteen acres Sidney Torrance reportedly gave them for an athletic field.

Athletic club members also formed a Gun Club, Dolley says, to hunt ducks in what was then called "Nigger Slough" — low land on which water sat without running off, from as far back as Gardena to the area near Los Angeles Harbor. The slough got its name, Dolley said, because of "the black adobe mud which was on the bottom."

Fay L. Parks founded Torrance's oldest plumbing firm, the Torrance Plumbing Co. He is shown with his truck, complete with two three-digit telephone numbers — two numbers, one letter each — and looking somewhat overdressed for his work.

The first and only bank in Torrance during the initial decade of the town's growth was the First National Bank of Torrance, founded by Judge George W. Post in 1913. The bank building, another of the Irving Gill designs, stood at the center of El Prado and Border Street, opposite the Pacific Electric depot. The one-story bank portion of the building later was razed for a parking lot and the three-story office portion of the building, which in the early days housed the offices of the town's first doctors and attorneys, became a hotel.

It's useful, even perhaps humbling to remind ourselves in these electronically pell-mell times, that our forebears were able to create a prosperous nation with nary a single microchip to help them. One way they did so, and got some exercise in the process, was with this adding machine, circa 1903, which is now in the Torrance Museum, the gift of Mrs. L.F. Stevenson. It was used at the Moneta Water Co., 2214 W. 182nd Street, then called Electric Avenue because the Pacific Electric's big red cars ran down it. Mr. Stevenson was general manager then.

PHOTO BY WM. FRIDRICH

73

He would row into the slough in a small, hand-made boat and hide in the tules, Dolley said.

"I used to get up at 4:30 a.m. every Wednesday and Sunday morning and hunt until after the sun came up. The best day I had was the time I got 13 ducks in one morning. They were teals, springs and pintails. We saw no mallards."

Shortly after formation of the volunteer fire department and the athletic club came the creation of a police department, Masonic lodge, chamber of commerce and several churches.

The Torrance Relief Society, founded in 1917 to aid families of men who enlisted or were drafted during World War One, continued into the Depression of the 1930s in its role of providing local aid to needy families.

Leonard Babcock, a former buyer for the Torrance Unified School District, recalled coming to Torrance with his parents in 1919, when it was a small, rural town and a blue-collar kind of place.

"There really wasn't much here when we came," he said, "and if you went very far any way, you were in sand and dirt."

His uncle, Edgar Morford, worked at the glass-blowing factory.

Babcock recalled playing marbles, mumbletypeg, spinning tops and rolling a hoop down the road for diversion as a child and attending an eight-room schoolhouse on the Torrance High site when there were not more than 125 pupils in all grades combined.

Babcock also recalled Phoebe Sykes had a newsstand at the Pacific Electric depot and as a boy he would get the *Los Angeles Record* and the *Los Angeles Herald* from her to sell for two cents each at the Pacific Electric car shops as the men got off work.

"We used to spread out the papers, and as the men left work, they would toss the money, pick up the paper, and run to get on one of the big red cars to take them home. Most of the men who worked in the P.E. shops at that time lived in Gardena and Los Angeles.

"We had two grocery stores in town, where you phoned in and placed your order and they delivered. We had a vendor for fresh fruit and vegetables who came down the streets and sold direct from his wagon. The Union Ice Co. delivered ice for ice boxes and this is another joy that is gone. On hot summer days, when the ice truck was on your street, the ice man would chip ice the size wanted for the ice box. There were always chips just the right size for eating that he allowed you to have, and nothing ever tasted better!

"The idea of selling direct to the home was carried on by those who sold bread and cakes, also, and the smell was *so* good from those trucks.

"One of the very nicest things about the new city of Torrance was that it was a close-knit family community," recalls Babcock of the town's early days, when no one locked their doors and everyone knew their neighbors.

"Everybody knew everybody else," agrees Dolley. "It was a wonderful time."

The Pacific Electric depot in Torrance was one of the first and most important buildings. The cigar stand at the left front of the building was operated by A.E. Sykes, who earlier had run a tent store selling goods to the survey, grading and construction crews that laid the groundwork for Torrance. The view appears to be from a hotel window across the street from the depot, with the red tile roof of the First National Bank of Torrance in the foreground. The picture was probably made before 1916, because the California Shoe Manufacturing Co., seen between the depot and the railroad bridge to the far left, had gone out of business by that date. The depot, like many other major buildings erected in Torrance before 1920, was designed by Irving Gill.

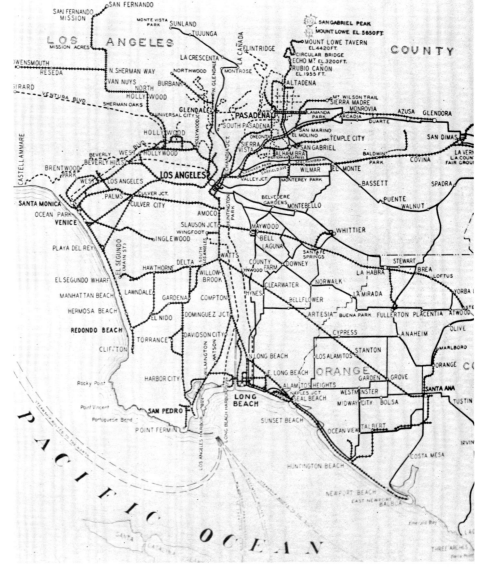

The Pacific Electric line was the most extensive electric interurban railway system in the world, with more than 1,000 miles of track spanning the reaches of Southern California during the early years of Torrance. As this map clearly shows, Torrance was on a spur line off the main line between Gardena and San Pedro, and to visit the bathhouse, salt water plunge, dancing pavilion and other seaside amusements at Redondo Beach from Torrance, it was necessary to travel via Gardena and El Nido.

The city incorporates and oil makes the 1920s roar

Torrance becomes a city of its own and Prohibition keeps the town dry except for its new major oil field.

The Torrance oil boom of the early 1920s spurred local prosperity and brought new people and business to a town already manufacturing oil drilling equipment at the Union Tool Company long before oil was discovered locally. And it even inspired this postcard, which purports to show the oil field "looking north on Carson Street." Carson, of course, runs east and west.

COURTESY OF KARMEE DOLLEY

We've all heard the jocular phrase — "for medicinal purposes" — about whiskey, but during Prohibition, those who had been advised by their doctor to have a little nip everyday, or those who just plain wanted to have a drink without patronizing a bootlegger or a speakeasy, had to ask their physician for a prescription like these. A druggist like Harry Dolley would then fill it. The sufferer, whether suffering from a medical condition or merely from a thirst, could then proceed home confident that he need not fear the dreaded federal alcohol agents. "The Noble Experiment" failed, of course, though it did wipe out the vicious saloons which had preyed on the poor and the workingman. (Or, as one cynic put it, working people saved millions that would otherwise have gone for booze — then they were able to lose it all at once in the stock market crash.)

PHOTO BY WM. FRIDRICH; PRESCRIPTIONS FROM KARMEE DOLLEY

For the small, unincorporated town of Torrance, there were big things ahead during the 1920s. Within the decade, a movement to incorporate the town — which the Torrance Chamber of Commerce initiated in 1919 — would come to fruition, a major oil field would be discovered near the new city, and the prosperity of the 1920s would be even more assured for many

new city, arguing that farms do not require city services and should not be compelled to pay city taxes for services they don't use.

Lomita farmers soon joined the protest, and in November, 1920, the Dominguez Estate Co. and the Del Amo family added their voices to the protest against the far-flung proposed boundaries for

in Torrance.

In July, 1920, in fear that Los Angeles would try to annex the new industrial and residential community created by Jared Sidney Torrance and his Dominguez Land Corp. halfway between the City of the Angels and its harbor at what would become known as Angels Gate, Torrance residents petitioned the Los Angeles County Board of Supervisors for an incorporation election.

Most of the leading citizens of the town supported the plan, but in September, 1920, owners of farms west of Torrance gathered at the L. Edwin farm. Edwin was named president of a farmer's group called the Tract Owners Association. The group directed their secretary, Charles N. Smith, to protest the attempt to include their farms in the proposed

Torrance. The Del Amo land, near what is now Hawthorne Boulevard, was also farmland and arguably more oriented at that time toward Redondo Beach, where Dr. Del Amo had a fine home on the Esplanade. As a result of the protests, the supervisors decided that the incorporation election originally set for February, 1921 would have to be readvertised due to an "error." The election set for April 22, 1921 included narrower boundaries. As a result, the Del Amo property did not become part of the city of Torrance until it was annexed by another election on February 23, 1926. It is, of course, now the modern commercial and financial center of the city.

Until incorporation, the Dominguez Land Corp. continued to play a major role in the development of Torrance.

LEGEND:–

Single Family Dwelling,
See Ord.75 for Dist. I-A   **I**

All Kinds of Dwellings,   **II**

BUSINESS & PUBLIC USE:
Retail Business, Offices
and Dwellings,   **III**

Public and Semi-public
use,   **IV**

Wholesale and Retail
Business and Dwellings,   **V**

Hospitals and Institutions,   **VI**

INDUSTRIAL:
Factories and Warehouses,   **VII**

Heavy Industries,   **VIII**

ADOPTED BY ORDINANCE No 51. April 17, 1923.

Two Family Resid.   **I-A**
ORD No 75

DIAGRAM
OF USE DISTRICTS
BUILDING ZONE MAP
OF THE
CITY OF TORRANC

After Jared Sidney Torrance's death in 1921, M.R. Osburn succeeded him as president of the Dominguez Land Corp. His presidency came at a time of transition to Torrance's new status as an incorporated city. Disputes between the new city government and the company in those first years centered on ownership of a sewage plant and streets and alleys in Torrance.

When this zoning map of Torrance was adopted by city government two years after the town's incorporation, Torrance already had designated land use for eleven years. From the very beginning in 1912, specific areas had been set aside for industry, commerce, residences and "foreign quarters."
COURTESY OF DAVE GEIER

Now picture saying this with a straight face in 1920: "Torrance, The Beauty Spot of Southern California." Good, you may have a career in real estate sales! Three times weekly these tours left downtown Los Angeles for "the famous industrial city," with "a dainty lunch" thrown in, here amidst our new city's splendors. Judge Post and George Neill were busy trying to save Torrance's first businessmen, while T.M. Miller Co. was busy coaxing others here to join them.
PHOTO BY WM. FRIDRICH

But apparently seeing the shape of things to come, Judge George W. Post, vice president and general manager of the company, resigned from those posts in January, 1921. He had held them for six rather difficult years in the history of the town.

A month before, on December 14, 1920, Sidney Torrance himself testified at a supervisor's meeting in favor of incorporation. Though transcripts of that meeting were not kept, unfortunately, a contemporary newspaper account says Torrance urged incorporation and announced that some of the biggest factories in the West were planning to locate in Torrance. He suggested that a population of 20,000 people would soon be living here.

Actually, though, that prediction was overly optimistic. As things unfolded, that mark was not in fact exceeded for another thirty years, until the 1950 Census found a great influx of workers

in World War Two aircraft and shipbuilding industries had suddenly made Torrance a very popular place to live.

The "error" the supervisors used to postpone the incorporation election cheated Sidney Torrance, the man who uniquely and personally created the city, out of the pleasure of seeing his civic brain child pass from a difficult adolescence into the full responsibilities of cityhood. Torrance died just 23 days before the April 22, 1921 vote that incorporated the city — by a 355-to-11 margin.

On April 25, 1921, the supervisors certified the results of that election, though the incorporation technically did not become official until December 12, 1921, when Frank Jordan, California's Secretary of State, formally recorded it in Sacramento.

The city of Torrance had sprung from sparsely populated open fields and dry farmland in 1912, to an estimated population of 350 in 1915 and a newly incorporated city of 1,800 in 1921.

A telephone directory published in the *Torrance Herald* in October, 1920, showed only 94 Torrance residents and businesses with phones.

By mid-1921, Torrance claimed 15 miles of paved streets, 20 miles of electric lines, 25 miles of sewer lines, 30 miles of water lines, and included just under four square miles of territory.

A 1921 Torrance Chamber of Commerce brochure quoting one of the leading economic indicators of that day said post office receipts in Torrance for the first quarter of that year were $2,465.20, up 68 percent from $1,465.26 for the same period in 1920.

The first meeting of the Torrance Board of Trustees — a body akin to the city

79

Plowed fields and a hen house are overshadowed by oil wells in 1920s Torrance area.

council of today — convened on Monday, May 16, 1921 at the Dominguez Land Corp. offices in Torrance. George A. Proctor was elected president of the board, a position equivalent to mayor today. Proctor had been president of the chamber and before the incorporation election had declared: "Torrance must incorporate as a safeguard against the ambitions of Los Angeles to annex all desirable communities. Once, Los Angeles forced large industrial plants from its city limits because of their 'dirty smokestacks.' Now we should keep our industry and community to ourselves."

Other members of that first board of trustees included Wallace H. Gilbert, Richard R. Smith, Joseph Stone and James M. Fitzhugh. It is perhaps interesting to note that these five men came to their city offices from the city's leading industrial firms — Proctor,

A welder takes a cigarette break at the Columbia Steel plant in Torrance. The Llewellyn Iron Works became part of the Columbia firm in the mid-1920s. Columbia was later a wholly owned subsidiary of U.S. Steel.

Once the news of the first gusher in Torrance hit, there was a scramble to drill new wells, and wooden oil derricks like these sprouted where only cattle grazed before. This scene reportedly is Sepulveda Boulevard, then known as Long Beach and Redondo Road, at Arlington Avenue. At least four cafes are visible and all may have catered to the oil field crews. Lacey & Son Contractors are about halfway up the road on the left side of the street. Most indicative of the easier pace of that earlier time, however, may be Frank's Auto Supply Station in the middle foreground, where an attendant seems to be dozing at the pump between customers. Though the picture captures the spirit of Torrance's oil boom, the location has not been confirmed as actually in Torrance.

COURTESY OF PAUL COMON

Smith and Stone were Union Tool Co. employees, Fitzhugh worked for the Llewellyn Iron Works, and Gilbert was a Pacific Electric Co. car shops man.

The issues with which that first board dealt during its first year were similar to those that city councils now grapple with. They served until an April 10, 1922 election, and all but Smith were re-elected. He was replaced by Edwin H. Nash, a Llewellyn employee.

During that first year, Robert J. Deininger of Dominguez Land was the city clerk; Harry Dolley, the druggist, was city treasurer; Perry G. Briney was city attorney; and Herman R. Postle was city engineer. Other officials that first year included William Gascoigne, street superintendent; city marshal, or police chief, Ben Olsen; city recorder, A.G. Pruitt, who was also in the real estate business; Ben F. Hannebrink, the fire chief and a Union Tool Co. employee; Isabel Henderson, city librarian; and Dr. Jesse S. Lancaster, city health officer.

During the first year of city government, the board adopted an official city seal,

approved the purchase of six cuspidors for city hall, considered matters relating to street conditions and street lights, rented a concrete garage near the Carson Street fire station for $2.50 per month to use as the first city jail, and voted to pay the city marshal $150 per month.

The first city building code was adopted at the board's sixteenth meeting on September 20, 1921.

On October 18, 1921, the board adopted the first dog license law, with a two dollar fee for males and spayed females, and a four dollar fee for unspayed females. At that same meeting, the city marshal reported "quite a bit of speeding in the evening" and asked the city to buy a motorcycle to pursue breakers of local speed limits. That purchase was approved at the next meeting, and at the following meeting, it was reported that Torrance's first traffic motorcycle had been purchased, used, for $225 from a Mr. Peterson of Redondo Beach.

On December 6, 1921, a city

Street Scene, Torrance, California.

Torrance Business District, Torrance, Calif.

Two views of the downtown Torrance business district of the 1920s show El Prado between Sartori Avenue and the Pacific Electric depot on Border Avenue.
COURTESY OF KARMEE DOLLEY

administration pinched for revenue to continue its operations, turned off 80 street lamps "in locations where they would not be missed" to save $90 per month on the city electric bill. Also at that meeting, Helen O'Leary of the Torrance Woman's Club asked for an ordinance to be enacted "making it a criminal offense for a boy to carry a slingshot or BB gun" in Torrance due to "the indiscriminate use of slingshots and BB guns by the boys of Torrance in shooting birds."

In February, 1922, the board authorized taking a $150 trade-in allowance for the used motorcycle they had bought for city peace officers only four months before, because it needed too many repairs. They also heard a plea for money from the city librarian, who was paid only for half a month in January, 1922 because the Torrance library joined the county library system in mid-month.

Also that first year, Dr. Lancaster told the board that the Mexican Village was operating with open cesspools and health conditions there were "very bad" but would soon be remedied.

Though the board met at the Dominguez Land Co. office initially, the honeymoon between the company that founded and guided the town through its early years and the new city government soon was over. Throughout that first year, the two repeatedly tangled over ownership of streets and alleys in Torrance — the Dominguez Land Co. wanted to retain title to them while the city suggested they be deeded over to the city for public use and

maintenance. They also clashed over the city's efforts to acquire a sewage treatment facility, begun but not completed under Dominguez Land's administration.

Though deed restrictions in Torrance had banned alcoholic beverages from the founding of the town, Federal Prohibition — under the 18th Amendment to the U.S. Constitution — added further strictures from 1920 to 1933. To further reinforce Torrance's position as a "dry" community, City Ordinance No. 18, introduced in January, 1922, also prohibited all alcoholic beverages within city limits.

According to Karmee Dolley, prescriptions for alcohol for "medicinal purposes" were in considerable demand in Torrance during Prohibition and were filled by her husband, Harry, at the family drugstore.

According to a story in the *Torrance Herald*, Torrance's first mayor even found a chuckle in the early days of Prohibition. The September, 1920 issue

Fred Palmer's Service Station on Carson Street at Arlington Avenue pumped gas and sold General and Brunswick tires during the 1920s.

Harry Dolley was a pioneering Torrance drugstore operator, as the telephone number of his store — 10 — shows. This was one of the containers he dispensed with medicine and good advice to his customers.

PHOTO BY WM. FRIDRICH

The 1920s' oil boom in Torrance brought increased economic activity to the community in two ways. Not only did local landowners who hit oil prosper, but local firms like Union Tool that manufactured oil drilling and related equipment also did increased business. The Bank of Italy — now the Bank of America — was actively expanding into state-wide branch banking at the time, and Torrance was a logical place to locate since the only competition was the bank that had served alone through the town's first decade — the First National Bank of Torrance. The Bank of Italy was at the corner of Sartori and Marcelina avenues in 1928 when this photo was made, as it is today.

of the paper reported another local had advised Proctor that wood alcohol was dangerous to drink. "I should think it would be," Proctor replied. "Think of the danger from splinters!"

Even a very new city needs law and order; Torrance was no exception. Five months after the board's first meeting, Ben Olsen, the marshal, was given the additional title of dogcatcher. He resigned December 13, perhaps convinced that a Christmas bonus wasn't in the cards. He signed on again soon after.

A year later, there were rumors of bootlegging in the Pueblo and stories of loafers hanging around the schoolgrounds. And the chief of police allowed that he was tired of using his own car to transport prisoners. It took him until mid-1923 to pry the money out of the city's board of trustees for a city Essex.

In 1924, the police chief had to get after the Edison Company. Four different times they forgot to turn on the lights in the evening.

Exasperation with crime and criminals is not as recent a phenomenon as we think. Witness this paid notice in the *Torrance Herald* on July 29, 1921:

"The four boys who visited my melon patch on Redondo Blvd. last Saturday night and maliciously destroyed green melons and vines are known. Anyone entering my premises for the purpose of destroying my fruit and vegetables or stealing same will meet with a pitiful fate from now on. J.E. Chandler"

Things seemed better a few months later. At the end of the first Fiesta that year, Judge George W. Post said he had found just one crooked concession!

The first movies in town had been shown in 1912 on the ground floor of the Myrtle Apartments on El Prado. John C. McVey opened his theatre in 1921 in what was originally a privately owned city auditorium. Citizen pressure groups made themselves felt then. In late 1923, Mr. and Mrs. McVey, managers of the Torrance Theatre, agreed not to exhibit Charlie Chaplin's *The Pilgrim* because "it burlesques the ministerial profession."

When the increased number of officers on the Torrance force held their first Policeman's Ball sixty years ago, they had the jazz orchestra from the *S.S. Avalon* playing in Legion Hall. Soon after an otherwise successful evening, the papers reported that an oil field worker was fined $100 for creating a disturbance at the ball. "That," noted one witness, "is like spitting in a bulldog's face."

Our favorite typographical error from the 1920s is the newspaper story about the young waitress who attempted suicide by taking poison. "Officer Clark responded ... she fought, but was finally given a strong anecdote and recovered." What a storyteller Officer Clark must have been!

On a more serious note, the handcuffing by police of a nine-year-old boy "for fun" and other complaints led to a shake-up on the force. It did not prevent the new city from being shaken in July, 1924, by its first major scandal.

In brief, five men from Compton had been stopped for reckless driving. When they and Officer Stanley Abbott arrived at the station, a fight apparently ensued. Chief Byron Anderson came down to the jail, and spent some time alone with the five arrested men. Dr. Shidler was called down to the jail, examined the men and made this informal but comprehensive affadavit: "I have this

Two more views of the downtown Torrance business district of the 1920s. Cabrillo Avenue included an electric railroad line down the middle, and next to the furniture store on Sartori Avenue — erroneously called "Sartori Street" on this postcard — was the Torrance Hardware Co., which offered hardware and furniture, and was run by Hurum Reeve who lived in one of the town's most elegant homes at 1504 Post Avenue with his wife, Jessie.

COURTESY OF KARMEE DOLLEY

Though no record of Bailey's Market can be found in city directories of the period, this photo shows a typical setup and prices from the 1920s. Can you believe Camels, Luckies, Old Gold or Chesterfields were two packs for 25 cents? Chuck roasts for 14 cents per pound? Or fresh ground round for only 19 cents per pound? And how about today's special — salami, weiners, minced ham, liverwurst or bologna — only 17 cents per pound? Even the cat on the sidewalk in front of the market seems to be contemplating *that* special!

—Sartori Street, Torrance, Calif.

Looking North on Cabrillo Ave., Torrance, Calif.

day examined these five men and find that each and every one has been drinking and is in no condition to be driving on the highway."

Yet a few days later, when they came to trial, all charges were dropped for insufficient evidence except one count of reckless driving.

Within a month, persistent rumors of extortion and the zeal of the *Torrance Herald* resulted in the arrest of Police Chief Anderson, City Recorder James L. King and attorney A.P. Morewood. The charges were extortion of $950 from the five accused. Recorder King was soon dropped from the indictment. Officer Stanley Abbott disappeared for two months, stalling progress.

When Abbott returned voluntarily, the case went forward. A jury, with ten women serving, began hearing evidence in December against the former chief and the attorney.

Across the gulf of sixty years, it seems clear that extortion involving Chief Anderson and attorney Morewood, with Officer Abbott expecting a substantial share for his role, did take place. One thing that added considerable titillation to the testimony was the frequent reference to the need by those receiving the money to see that some of it got to a man consistently referred to only as "the political boss of Torrance."

This was the kind of stove raffled off on opening day at the Torrance office of the Southern California Gas Company in 1924. Visitors to the office that first day included A.B. Macbeth, F.J. Schafer, H.L. Ziegelmeyer, F.T. Nagle, M.A. Bentley, Mr. and Mrs. T.J. Protheroe, Mr. and Mrs. R.W. Campbell, Mr. and Mrs. F.C. Ingram and their grandson, Master Cavanaugh, and C.B. Sadler and family. The Clark Jewel gas range was won at an 8:30 p.m. drawing that Thursday evening by Mary A. Henderson of 1616 Cypress Street, Lomita. The publication *Gas News*, of August 1, 1924, reported that "the prize was promptly delivered and connected, and Mrs. Henderson cooked the Saturday evening meal, from Scotch broth to scones."

COURTESY OF THE SOUTHERN CALIFORNIA GAS CO.

This was the Redondo District distributing station of Southern California Edison on Torrance Boulevard in the 1920s. In this picture, construction crews, local crews and the garage force assembled. They handled everything in the area below 33,000 volts. C.W. Koiner was the distribution manager then.

COURTESY OF CANDY PALMER

The Torrance office of the Southern California Gas Company opened on July 10, 1924 and also served Lomita, Gardena and Moneta, with 5,000 residential meters and 100 industrial gas connections. Today, the Torrance office serves 98,576 residential customers, 4,617 commercial connections and 888 industrial plants — a total of 104,081 customers. The first office, pictured here, displayed a stove which was raffled off as the grand opening prize.

COURTESY OF SOUTHERN CALIFORNIA GAS CO.

Town Trustee J.S. Torrence — no relation to Jared Sidney Torrance who had died three years earlier — testified that he was not "the political boss," and that he had received none of the money.

Complicating matters, Officers Dillon and McMillan were dismissed from the force during the trial. Torrance City Attorney Perry G. Briney testified that it wasn't because they were going to testify for the former chief. It was because they kept going out drinking with the accused, and because one was alleged to have said that, with all that money changing hands, he was upset because he had not received any.

Two days after Christmas, after only an hour of deliberation, the jury found Anderson and Morewood guilty of extortion. A week later, Judge Collier gave them two to ten years in San Quentin and recommended action against City Recorder King, who quickly resigned.

The final bizarre twist in the case of Chief Anderson began a few years later. Anderson had served minimal time for the extortion. A Lomita bank was held up by a white man, face blackened for disguise, driving a blue Buick with one flat tire. In spite of that handicap, the man got away.

A few weeks later at Citizen's State Bank in Long Beach, his luck ran out. Byron Anderson, former police chief of Torrance, was arrested, and later convicted of robbery and returned to San Quentin.

John Stroh, later the chief here, said in an interview with Captain Jim Weyant in 1970 that his first assignment in Torrance, before he was even officially an officer, was to pick up Anderson and Morewood and transport them to Los Angeles County Jail on a very foggy night. He also noted that the first city marshal, Ben Olsen, was a better judge of character than most. He resigned rather than work for Anderson.

The Stroh family had a remarkable career in law enforcement. Chief John Stroh served 30 years; his daughter, Lucy, served 19 — much of it in Compton where she felt she could succeed on her own and not be seen as benefiting from being John Stroh's

Shortly after World War One, this ceremony was held in front of the Union Tool Company facility in Torrance to dedicate a memorial to those who served and died in that struggle to "make the world safe for democracy." In that era, nearly every town had its own band and Torrance was no exception. A dozen or so musicians are seen on the low platform to the left of the main stage, which is decked with bunting. It is interesting to see, too, that at this early date there were more than three dozen automobiles and trucks captured by the photographer in this one scene. Note, also, that the majority of those attending this gathering — both men and women — are wearing hats.

Along with a library, a hospital for his new city was a passionate priority of Jared Sidney Torrance. Though he did not live to see Torrance Memorial Hospital open on the knoll on Engracia Avenue, his will made generous provisions for it. In fact, more than sixty years after his death, Torrance Memorial still receives a monthly income from one of his bequests. Mrs. Helena Torrance, his widow, took an active part in hospital affairs until her death in 1940. She is seen here in the hospital lobby in 1925. The nonprofit hospital moved to Lomita Boulevard near the airport in the 1960s. Physicians like Dr. George P. Shidler and Dr. Jesse S. Lancaster played important roles in the early life of the city. They had offices in the First National Bank building with their old friend from York, Nebrasksa, Judge George W. Post. The first dentist in town, incidentally, was W.J. Neelands.

daughter — and his son, Jerry, also served 19 years.

A policeman's joke from the period claimed that there was an officer then who saw to it that there was never an accident reported on Figueroa. He would have the cars pushed over to Main before he wrote his report. He never was able to spell "Figueroa."

In late 1924, the Ku Klux Klan was active in Torrance, as it was throughout Southern California. There is some evidence that Klansmen in Pasadena who wanted to be police officers, and who were rebuffed by a "no-nonsense" police chief there, came here to join the force.

Most Klan activity in the 1920s was limited to anonymous threats, but sometimes this extended to dozens of placards tacked up on telegraph poles overnight with the same threats on each card. Judge John Shidler recalls "KIGY" for "Klansmen, I Greet You," chalked on every street corner during the mid-1920s, too.

And in September, 1924, Torrance had its first Klan wedding at, of all places, Legion Hall. Reverend Wm. Sullivan officiated under the auspices of "Crusaders for America," an organization like the Klan for Canadian-born Americans. About 500 attended.

There was a wonderfully minor-league

air about some crime here in those days. In November, 1924, a one-man crime wave — a prowler — ravaged and looted his way through the heart of town. Here was his mind-boggling haul, as recorded in the *Torrance Herald*:

"Hurum Reeve (1504 Post) — Mr. Reeve's pants and 21 cents; Clayton Severns (1307 Amapola) — $13 and a watch; Edwin A. Myers (1222 Amapola) — $35; Robert Parke (1318 Amapola) — $2 and a pocketbook; Oscar Carlson (1313 Cota) — Ransacked only; Arthur Mullin (1323 Cota) — Prowler heard; most of other loot found on porch including Hurum Reeve's pants."

In June, 1923, a combination police headquarters, fire department and city hall was constructed in the 1500 block of Cravens Avenue by the Brewer Construction Co. under a $6,915 contract. The new civic building included a one-room jail with four wire-glass windows.

But the construction of the first city hall complex specifically designed for that purpose was not the only sign of the passing of an era in Torrance. Sidney Torrance had died in 1921 just before incorporation became a reality, but in 1923, the man many people credited with being the second most important figure in the development of Torrance also died.

Harry Dolley recalled the story of Judge

FREDELLE A. YOUNG

EDNA STAIR

WM. 7. WALKER

EDWARD AIKEN

JOSEPH BISHOP

MARION BISHOP

WAYNE MALONE

JOSEPH GILL

JAMES GILL

POLLY POST

PATRICIA POST

POLLY J. BARTLETT

WM. J. ROSS, Jr.

CARL LAKE

GEORGE W. NEILL

Beginning in 1921, the First Evangelical Church at Marcelina and Arlington avenues took hundreds of pictures of all the babies and young children of the congregation. A lot of well-known Torrance family names are included in these representative shots. Clearly the church photographer had a wonderful way with young people! Incidentally, they called these pictures "The Cradle Roll." They are on display at the Torrance Historical Museum, with information slips beside them so that browsers can provide data about what happened to these young people as they grew up and went out into the world.

PRESENT-DAY PHOTO BY WM. FRIDRICH

Eighteen members of the winter Class of 1924 at Torrance High School posed for this photograph before graduation. It was then not uncommon for young men to drop out of high school to work on the family farm or seek blue-collar factory jobs in Torrance plants to help support their younger brothers and sisters. That fact may help to account for the presence of twice as many young women as young men in this class. Individuals in this photo have not been identified, but the Class of 1924 included Ione Barnett, later a USC grad, teacher and movie studio secretary; Chris Bartsch, later a National Supply employee; Ethel Bodley, who died within 20 years; Loretta Condley, an insurance company secretary in later years; Blanche Fix and Lillian Elman, both later housewives, each with two children; Albert Isen, later a USC and law school graduate, attorney and mayor of Torrance; George Hannan, later a senior clerk of the U.S. Post Office in Torrance; Ruth McKenzie, later the wife of C.L. Ingold, an optometrist; Gwendolyn Miller, later a housewife with three children; Helen Morse, a future UC Berkeley grad; Frank Perkins, a veteran of the U.S. Army and a phone company employee; Vivian Pratt, a nurse at Bullock's in Los Angeles; Wilson Woodburn, a state employee; and Clifford Simpson, Clara Totten and Harriet Vieths.

George W. Post from the early days of 1913.

After Thomas D. Campbell & Co. completed its job of initially promoting the town, according to Dolley, the Dominguez Land Co. moved its offices to Torrance and Mr. and Mrs. H.H. Hedges came to town; he to manage the Dominguez Land Corp.

"In a short time they had both antagonized the home guard," Dolley said, "because they didn't know how to handle people."

Judge George W. Post and George Neill, natives of York, Nebraska, had moved to Torrance in 1913 and opened the First National Bank of Torrance. That little town in the Midwest was also the starting point for two other Torrance pioneers — Dr. Lancaster and Dr. Shidler.

"In a short time, Mr. Hedges was out as manager (of the Dominguez Land Corp.) and Judge Post and George Neill took over and did a very good job of it. George Neill was a real diplomat. He could say no and make you think he was doing you a favor."

Judge Post arrived in Torrance at the age of 65, and founded the First National Bank of Torrance, Torrance's only bank for its first decade. Post, through the bank and Dominguez Land,

Church activities have played a major role in the life of our city since its founding. This was the choir of the Methodist Church in 1928. Left to right, back row: Tom Ulrich, David Turner, Bill Creighton, Oliver Hamilton, Bill Mechian and Guy L. Mowry. Middle row: Maria Wright Madden, an unidentified lady, Mabel Ella Sweet, Sara Hogue, Lola Mae Tomkins and Nellie Sinclair. Front: Dick Hogue, director; Juliet Johnson, accompanist Laraine Ulrich, Mabel Hall Borgener, Gertrude Mowry, Rose Paige King, Phyllis Hamilton and Mary Brown. The congregation was founded in 1921 in the old Dominguez Land office tent on El Prado under pastor Rev. Gordon A. Riegles. In 1923, ground was broken for their permanent church at El Prado and Manuel.

COURTESY OF ROSE PAIGE KING

helped see the fledgling town through the difficult years of recession and world war.

Post was born the son of a Presbyterian minister in Ohio, and lived in Missouri until the outbreak of the Civil War, when his family's pro-Union sentiments made life there too difficult and the family moved to Iowa. At 16, Post enlisted in an Iowa unit of the Union infantry.

Admitted to the Iowa Bar in 1871, he moved to York, Nebraska where he practiced law until 1875, when he became a district judge in Nebraska and later the first collector of internal revenue for Nebraska and the Dakotas.

Post convened the first Republican State Convention in Nebraska and was a member of the York County Republican Committee for many years.

He later turned from public affairs to banking and finance and organized,

consolidated and served as president of several banks. He also was park commissioner, councilman and mayor of York.

When he died of pneumonia ten years later in 1923, he was eulogized as second in importance only to Jared Sidney Torrance in the founding and fostering of the "modern industrial city."

In fact, the *Torrance Herald* reported, "Every business firm in Torrance closed its doors in honor of Judge Post, the man whose activities have meant so much to the progress of the city."

Said the *Torrance Herald* obituary: "When he lent his aid to the man whose name the city now bears, many distressing problems confronted them. Judge Post gave to the task his wide legal, financial experience and his stalwart character.

"In 1914, when the European war started, many men with investments in

The paymasters of the wages of sin, several hundred bottles of contraband hootch — mostly Scotch — on proud display in front of the Torrance Police "posse" that rounded it all up about 1926. Two men are holding some of the evidence. But Lester E. Stanley, second from right, who was the city's first motorcycle officer, always told his daughter, Mrs. Audrey Welles, that all the hootch was destroyed. Fifth from left is John Stroh, later the chief, whose daughter, Lucy, became the first woman desk sergeant here during World War Two. Officer Stanley once gave Wallace Beery a ticket for speeding and was surprised and displeased later to find that it had been "taken care of." He used to notify the local hot rodders in the 1920s, including John Shidler, when he was going to be patrolling over by the mill, so they could race their cars on still largely untraveled Sepulveda.
COURTESY OF LESTER E. STANLEY, JR.

Torrance saw ruin staring them in the face. But Judge Post, as president of the bank, lent financial support that not only saved his friends, but made the future safe for the city.

"There are men in Torrance today who point to his foresight, generosity and stern determination not to say quit as the only agents that operated successfully against financial disaster for themselves and the ruination of Torrance as a city."

In gratitude, the city of Torrance renamed Guadaloupe Avenue — the most expensive residential street in the city at that time and the one on which

Judge Post had resided — Post Avenue.

Judge Post's son, J. Wallace Post, had managed the family business, the First National Bank of Torrance, since his return from the battlefields of World War One. Some 42 men from Torrance served in the military during that war, including Post and Col. N.F. Jamieson But only Bert S. Crossland was killed in action, so the American Legion Post in Torrance is named for him.

Those who returned to Torrance after World War One, however, soon found themselves caught up in an era renowned nationally as the Roaring 20s,

"Where's the fire?" In an obvious promotional stunt, the Torrance Fire Department pulled up in front of the local movie house playing the 1926 M.G.M. release of *The Fire Brigade,* directed by William Nigh and starring May McAvoy and Charles Ray. State law prohibits smoking in the theater and that night, you can bet that law was enforced!

The proud men and equipment of the Torrance Fire Department are on display in this photo made in front of the city hall completed in 1923. The building housed not only city offices, but the police and fire department headquarters.

characterized by Prohibition-era bathtub gin or prescription alcohol "for medicinal purposes" and a period of flappers and unprecedented prosperity.

In Torrance, that prosperity came in a surprising and somewhat ironic form — discovery of a large oil field south and west of the city proper. Chanslor-Canfield Midway Oil Co., a Santa Fe Railroad subsidiary, brought in the first gusher in the Torrance field on Del Amo property in December, 1921. That discovery led to a stampede for oil leases and a boom in drilling and related equipment and employment in a town where manufacturing such equipment was already big business.

A forest of wooden oil derricks rapidly rose, as did the local excitment over the find. At the beginning of the oil boom, Karmee Dolley recalls, "Everybody closed up their businesses and ran down to see the gushers come in."

By June, 1925, oil — which even before the Torrance field was discovered, was

the main business of Union Tool and other Torrance firms — was clearly the biggest business in Torrance.

As late as 1938, you could build a wooden oil derrick in Torrance for $2,500. It took 54,000 square feet of lumber and 700 pounds of nails. It would stand 130 feet high, usually, and could drill from 3,600 to 5,600 feet into the earth. If it hit black gold, you could have it made for life. No wonder there were 582 producing wells in the Torrance field by June, 1925.

The last wooden derricks were removed during the early 1960s, though many old wells still pump today. The Del Amo Energy Co., a division of Great Lakes Properties, using an improved modern technique to force oil to the surface from old wells, continues major oil production on a tract of land north of Del Amo Fashion Center on Torrance Boulevard, not far from Torrance's first well. This secondary oil recovery project continues to help reduce U.S. dependence on foreign oil supplies.

The Pacific Electric Torrance shops included not only recreational facilities for employees, but even nearby company-owned houses. These cottages across the street and south of the shops were among the first, and as this photo shows, rose at a very early stage — perhaps as early as 1917 — in the development of the town.

94

The sturdy brick buildings of the Pacific Electric car shops stood from 1917 until 1984, though in later years they were used by Reynolds Metals for other purposes. Well-built of brick, concrete and steel reinforced to withstand the tests of time, the buildings fell to the wrecking ball instead. Bricks used in construction of the shops came from the Los Angeles Brick Co. in Los Angeles. The Torrance Historical Society offered authenticated bricks from the site as historical souvenirs at five dollars each.

PHOTO BY WM. FRIDRICH

This view from an aeroplane shows the Pacific Electric Co. shops in the right foreground with many electric railroad cars in the yard for servicing. Taken about 1923, the photo also clearly shows the forest of oil derricks that quickly rose to the south of downtown Torrance within a few years of the first oil strike here. Note the large expanses of undeveloped land, even in the major business and residential sections of the original townsite.

The original Torrance well continued to produce until 1953.

Other oil-related companies drawn to Torrance during the 1920s and 1930s included the International Derrick & Equipment Co. of California, D & M Machine Works, General Petroleum of California, Shell Oil of California, Union Oil, Superior Oil, Standard Gasoline Co., Standard Pipe & Supply Co. and Jordan & Taylor, a valve manufacturer.

A series of annexations of land to the north, west and south of the original townsite followed the oil boom. The first, the Northwest Annexation on February 23, 1926, took city boundaries to 190th Street on the north, just below Sepulveda Boulevard on the south and established the modern western boundary, though excluding a section known as the Victor Tract between Torrance, Hawthorne and Del Amo boulevards. The second annexation took Meadow Park — then largely a Japanese community — and Hollywood Riviera on April 18, 1927, followed by the April 16, 1928 annexation of Walteria. Most of north Torrance was added by the McDonald Tract Annexation on June 17, 1930 and the southeast came into the city on June 27, 1931. The last

substantial tracts to enter the city were the Victor Tract, taken in on June 22, 1956, and the El Nido section, added December 26, 1956. Otherwise, the city achieved what are substantially its present boundaries by mid-1931.

During those heady boom days of the 1920s, the Torrance Woman's Club and men's service clubs both began to have a major impact on the community.

A solid force for civic good in Torrance for the past 63 years, the Torrance Woman's Club (singular, like the ladies themselves) has grown from a tiny Vista Highlands sewing circle with $4.95 in the First National Bank, to the thriving multifaceted club of today with its own clubhouse on Engracia and several hundred active members.

The ladies organized, in fact, before the city did. They added a firm, but feminine touch to the incorporation ceremony by discarding the tattered flag the county provided, and spending $10.50 for a new one to fly over the proud new city.

Under Mrs. C.W. Stock, their first president, club members became active in causes as varied as Near East relief and the condition of women inmates at

Though the fellow in the foreground seems to be manning an early water fountain, it seems clear from this posed photo that the men of Pacific Electric took their work seriously. They kept thousands of commuters rolling along in the era before the automobile emerged as by far the dominant form of personal transportation in Southern California.

Workmen at the Torrance Pacific Electric shops are shown here working on one of the 1200 series in a common 1920s-era scene. P.E. in that decade was one of the major employers in Torrance with as many as 530 men on the payroll. In the extensive machine shops and vast brick sheds, work on the electric railroad cars could be done all year without fear of Torrance's November to April rainy season. The monthly payroll at one time averaged about $77,000, meaning average workers earned less than $150 per month. But cigarettes were only two packs for a quarter.

FROM THE A.E. BARKER COLLECTION

Like a flotilla in harbor, three generations of Pacific Electric cars are lined up in the Torrance yard. The 331 on the right is a Birney Safety Car, built by the J.E. Brill Company in 1918. In the middle is 691, built by the St. Louis Car Co. in 1924. The 995 on the left is larger and more powerful, and was built later. Many of these sturdy workhorses had a taste of foreign adventure before they fell to the wrecker's torch; they finished their useful lives in Central and South America, a lot of them in the Argentine. On the other hand, some cars which P.E. used here came from a failed line in Portland, Oregon. Street railway cars led a very adventuresome life.

FROM THE A.E. BARKER COLLECTION

San Quentin. Through the early 1920s, they raised money for their clubhouse by putting on entertainments in the high school auditorium and fashion shows sponsored by Van Andles Specialty Shop and Sam Levy's.

They also sold stock with enthusiastic help from Judge Post, George Neill and W. Howard Kingsley. Isabel Henderson and Mrs. Hurum Reeve were among the first directors. Other help came from Brian K. Welch, who was a relative of Sidney Torrance, and from such Torrance firms as Columbia Steel, Ebys Dry Goods, Haynes Lumber, Huddleston Furniture, Rappaports, Reeve Hardware, Rossman Lumber, and Smith & Kesler Tile Roofing.

Here are the names of those earliest members taken from a 1925 newspaper article: the Mesdames Stock, Otly, Crossland, Gilbert, Mueller, Beckwith and Reeve; followed by the Mesdames

Gardner, Clark, Briney, Lancaster, Curtiss, Neff, Garner, Paige, Roberts, Zamperini, Sammons, Wooten, Leake, Sharps, Henderson, Wise, Howe, Steinhilber, Watson, Isenstein, Levy and Zahradnik. Joining at the same time, June 6, 1921, were Mrs. and Miss Byrnes, Mrs. Lucy Reeve and Mrs. H.C. Reeve.

The 225 members held their first meeting in the new clubhouse October 8, 1925. Over the next twenty years, a round of fund-raising bazaars, minstrel shows and lectures (one topic in the 1920s: "Why the Radio is a Real Service") made it possible to burn the mortgage in 1946.

Some changes took place over the years. Social meetings with husbands as guests were approved for the first time in 1939, under the presidency of Mrs. E.A. Miles. And from 1941 to 1943, under Mrs. C.B. Mitchell, night meetings were scheduled because so many members were busy with war work.

Some of the women who have played leading roles in the Torrance Woman's Club during the postwar years are Mrs. Margaret Jones, Mrs. W.J. Laughon, Mrs. S.V. Raus and Mrs. Dean Sears; others were Mrs. B.T. Whitney, Mrs. B.W. Roberts, Mrs. A.F.R. Ewalt and Mrs. Groover Van Devanter. Responding to community needs, under Mrs. Richard Rogers and Mrs. H.L. Mitchell in the mid-1950s, the clubhouse was used for adult education classes and the club took an active stand in favor of establishing a municipal court in Torrance.

An example of the club's gumption: in

大正二年六月十二日　人百余名生徒師範撮影

1963, they had pledged to provide a wheelchair for a needy local child. When the chair arrived, however, funds were low and the Kiwanis men said, perhaps a little patronizingly, that they would pay for it.

Well! Mrs. Dean Sears recalls that an emergency round of bridge parties was invoked. "For two afternoons and two nights, we played bridge. The door prize was a $5 bill and it was raffled off four times and the winners just didn't have nerve enough to keep it."

At the end of the fourth party, the ladies counted their take, including that hardy survivor, the $5 bill, and they paid for the wheelchair.

Men's service clubs in Torrance also got rolling during the 1920s.

Sinclair Lewis in *Babbitt* did about all the damage that can be done to that enduring American institution — the men's service club. So the fact that service clubs are still with us, still flourishing, still doing well by doing good, still held in reasonable esteem by their neighbors and their communities is a sign, it seems, that they meet a need not just for their members, but for the communities in which they flourish.

This is certainly true of Torrance, where Rotary was the first service club formed in 1924. The first Rotary club in the world had been formed in Chicago only 19 years earlier. There is now another Rotary in Torrance, the Del Amo club, formed in 1967. Both meet at the Velvet Turtle Restaurant at noon; the Torrance club on Wednesdays, the Del Amo club on Tuesdays.

When that first Torrance service club celebrated its golden anniversary in 1974, they put together a vivid, anecdotal, even irreverent, history of the first fifty years. Even though the records of the first thirty years had been destroyed, they were able to reconstruct the story by drawing on the memories of Dr. Robin Bingham and Charles V. Jones, both presidents of Torrance Rotary in the 1930s; Harvel Guttenfelder, long-time secretary; Henry Halverson, Jr., whose father had been active in San Pedro Rotary which sponsored the new Torrance club; and Don Hyde and Jack Watt. The history was compiled by Stuart Marsee.

When the club was formed November 24, 1924, Calvin Coolidge had just been elected President. There were 4,400 people living in Torrance, more than twice as many as lived here in 1921

北米合衆国加州羅府サンレート下の大松浦太郎氏の苺園の挑

The hard-working, happy life of the Japanese-American farmers and their families in the South Bay is epitomized in this picture shot in 1927 on the strawberry farm that Sam Omatsu's parents operated between Carson Street and Torrance Boulevard on Hawthorne. The Omatsus and Sam's brother, Bob, and sister, Marian, are in the middle of this picture, taken facing Hawthorne Boulevard. The Del Amo Financial Center bears a different fruit on this site today. Later, the Omatsus farmed farther west around Anza, which was just a dirt road then. Sam Omatsu, who loaned the Torrance Museum this picture, is a store owner in Torrance today.

when the city incorporated. Another sign of growth: volunteer firemen had been replaced by an "on call" corps, who were paid $7.50 a month and were required to respond to all alarms. The new club met for a year next to the bakery on El Prado. When membership increased to twenty, they moved next door to the hardware store.

Rotary has always made a point of identifying the business or professional classification into which each member falls, and of seeking to assure that a representative of every important facet of town life is a member. So, it's interesting to look at the list of charter members from sixty years ago.

The first local manager of the Bank of America, James B. Hines, was president. Wilfred Teal, in oil machinery manufacturing, was vice president. The two onerous jobs, secretary and treasurer, were given to the same man, Carl Hyde. As secretary of the Chamber of Commerce, he was to play a leading role in the annexation of Walteria. Some people in town thought he pushed too hard on that. He used to lament that it was as hard to get people to pay their Chamber dues as to pay their Rotary dues. Sam Levy, never absent when there was a chance to help

Torrance move forward, was sergeant-at-arms.

Other charter members were William L. Booth, steel; Phra A. Cristiance, oil distributing; druggist Harry Dolley; and land developer Donald Findley. Service station owner John S. Hanson, dentist Robert A. Hoag and lumber store manager Charles V. Jones, who in 1974 was the last living charter member, joined them.

So did W. Howard Kingsley, Grover Whyte's partner in the *Torrance Herald.* There was the Reverend Benjamin H. Lingenfelter, pastor of the First Christian Church, and retailers Roy A. McFarland (ice), John W. McMillan (oil machinery) and Lovelle Olt (meat). The other charter members were Rufus Page, real estate; Fred Palmer, tires; Fay L. Parks, plumbing; Hurum E. Reeve, hardware; and grocer Walter A. Penn.

You could buy a new Ford car that year for $290, without a self starter, of course. But Rotary, like all organizations in a new, struggling town, had trouble collecting its dues. Some charter members were lost because money was so tight.

Harvel Guttenfelder tells how he and Dr. Bingham addressed that problem: "We got the members to come back by just having to pay for their meals and one dollar on their back dues. Membership in 1933 was down to a low of 13 members. When the international convention was held in Pasadena, there wasn't any money to finance Bing's attendance ... until two doctors paid their dues in advance so Bing could go."

Dr. George Shidler was president in 1927 and was succeeded by his partner, Dr. Jesse Lancaster, who was Post's son-in-law. Dr. Shidler apparently became well-known in Rotary circles for a rousing speech he was wont to give on how American morality was being undercut by the shenanigans that went on in the back seats of the increasingly ubiquitous automobile.

The men in Rotary shared the hard times after the Crash of 1929 with the rest of Torrance. When the glass factory went broke, its downfall affected small businessmen like Charles Jones; it owed his lumberyard $1,300. Guttenfelder had just sold the glass factory a big order of storage batteries so they could cope with the frequent unreliability of Southern California Edison power in those days. Since he couldn't be paid, a stockholder

named Bisbee tried to give him a membership in a duck hunting club instead. Harvel turned it down — and notes wryly that all members made a fortune when oil was discovered on the club's land.

Rotary was already embarked on the round of activities which has characterized them over the past half century. When J. Wallace Post was president in 1929, they were already sponsoring Boy Scout and Sea Scout activity. On Sunday, they'd take the Scouts down to Portuguese Bend in their big touring cars.

One of the joys of service clubs like Rotary is their high-spirited anecdotage. Anyone who has ever stopped into Buffy's Coffee Shop on El Prado, just a few yards from El Prado Park, to hear Harvel Guttenfelder in his raconteur mode, knows that. Guttenfelder still starts his day there, just a brisk stroll from his home.

Here is one of his stories, which captures nicely the spirit of how things were done in small-town America a half century ago:

"Sam Levy went ahead to build the theatre and expected Wallace Post to

The Torrance Woman's Club clubhouse as it appeared after construction in 1926. The 58-by-140-foot lot cost $2,515; the 50-by-125-foot building cost $13,574 to construct; and furnishings were another $2,700. The first meeting of the Vista Highlands Neighborhood Club was held on March 18, 1921, and on April 15, 1921, the group changed its name to the Torrance Woman's Club and joined the Federation of Women's Clubs. Founding members were among the social elite of small-town Torrance. Through the years, the women had an occasional tense moment with their programs. They felt that they had to put out an emergency notice in early December, 1941, that the regular meeting would be held but that the program was cancelled. It was to have been "The Art of Japanese Flower Arrangements."

COURTESY OF THE TORRANCE WOMAN'S CLUB

honor his drafts. Along came the bank examiners and they said, 'You can't loan money on a one-purpose building.'

"Wallace said Sam was good for it. The examiners talked to Levy — said he had no collateral, couldn't have the money. Levy went to the insurance company and they wouldn't loan it to him. He had started the theatre and had dug it out and still didn't have the money.

" ... the examiners were looking down Wallace's throat. So Sam decided he would get this money from one of the loan companies. ... They told him to bring in the papers. ... Sam went in and he expected to get the money. The loan company said, 'Where's the earthquake insurance? We can't loan you money without earthquake insurance.'

"So he got it, and when the quake came in 1933, Sam Levy was the only man in town with earthquake insurance."

Other service clubs whose members have played an important role in moving Torrance forward are Kiwanis, the Lions, Optimists, Sertoma, and the Exchange Club.

Lodges and fraternal clubs in Torrance antedate even Rotary. The Torrance Masonic Lodge was founded in 1913, the Order of the Eastern Star in 1920, and Job's Daughters in 1921. Odd Fellows began here in 1920 as the Tri-City Lodge. A Lodge of Rebekahs followed a year later. The Loyal Order of Moose began here in 1925; Women of the Moose in 1935. Other fraternal organizations in Torrance include B'nai B'rith, Elks Lodge No. 1948, and the Sons of Italy.

Torrance was prospering in many other ways during the 1920s as well. Among the films shot in Torrance in the 1920s were Universal's *Bob Hill* series. Hendrie Tire Co. was used for a plot involving a lovely heiress with labor troubles and an opportunistic villain. In 1936, the plot was retreaded once again, shot at Hendrie again with May Robson, Fay Wray and Victor Jory in lead roles.

The "modern industrial city" also made

Torrance dignitaries spending a carefree afternoon on the El Paseo at the Redondo Beach Pier are all lined up and wearing ribbons, much like prize hams at the Los Angeles County Fair. Second from left is Sidney Moyse; fifth from left is Sam Rappaport; sixth is Harry Marx; seventh is Mayor George Proctor; ninth, a Mr. Ashley; and tenth is R.R. "Dick" Smith, a superintendent of Union Tool.

strides in attracting even more industry, though with the extensive contacts Sidney Torrance had, one can't help but wonder if even more major plants might have located here if he had lived long into the decade.

The firm of Eberle & Riggleman did a study of Torrance in 1928 that may have had a major influence in attracting industry during the last days of the Roaring 20s and the early years of the 1930s. It highlighted Torrance as an industrial site with significant merits and led to the Santa Fe Railroad investing in 800 acres, followed by forty more

During the first year that Mines Field — later Los Angeles International Airport — was Los Angeles' first airport, the great silver dirigible, *Graf Zeppelin,* made an around-the-world voyage and made Mines Field its West Coast stop after a trans-Pacific crossing from Japan. On August 25, 1929, the great airship arrived and traffic backed up for five miles around the airport as people from throughout Southern California went to rubberneck. Among those who got close enough to get a look were, from left, Torrance residents Irene Lawrence, an attendance officer at Redondo Union High School for 22 years; Karmee Dolley holding her son, Harry H. Dolley, Jr., age two; Carolina Stachowitz; and Janna Olsen. Of the two men with their backs to the camera, the one on the left is Harry Dolley, the other is not identified.

COURTESY OF KARMEE A. DOLLEY

August 25, 1929   Mines Field

The Graf Zeppelin

Sometimes a picture's historical value is so great that it compensates for the difficulty in reproducing it adequately. This group gathered at a Halloween party, or perhaps a "factory frolic," some time in the 1920s, on the top floor of the Murray Hotel. The four "bumpkins" in the back row are Mr. and Mrs. Thrall and Mr. and Mrs. Aurthur (sic) Hodge. In front of them, left to right, are George Neill, Dr. Neelands, Mr. and Mrs. Neelands, Mrs. Sullivan, George Proctor (the new city's first mayor), Charleen Dolley, Mr. Sweet and Dick Smith of Union Tool. In the next row are Mrs. R.R. Smith, Sam Rappaport, Mr. and Mrs. Dolley, Mrs. Sam Rappaport, Frank Steinhelber, Miss Baccus, Harry Todd, Mr. and Mrs. Baccus, Mrs. McKinley, Mrs. Greaves, Mr. and Mrs. Turner, Mr. and Mrs. Watson, Mr. Effinger and Mr. Harosta. In front are Mr. and Mrs. Kellogg, Mr. Anderson, Miss Wilson, Clara Barnett, Fern Wilcox, Lucille Durham, Wilfred Teal, Dorothy Dolley, Mrs. Harasta, Marion Greaves, Mrs. McManus, druggist Harry Dolley and Mrs. Effinger. Alas, the supremely contented gentleman in front remains unidentified.

COURTESY OF GERALD ALTER (ORIGINAL OWNER OF PHOTO WAS MRS. W.J. NEELANDS.)

companies. One — General Petroleum (now Mobil Oil Co.) — is Torrance's largest corporate taxpayer today.

Another contribution by Torrance to the world's industrial resources is the diamond saw. Dick Felker, who invented it, was a Torrance Planning Commissioner from 1921 to 1936. Tim Wayt, a resident since 1919 and a long-time member of the Torrance Historical Society, was also an inventor whose devices are widely used in the oil industry. Wayt, a major figure in California fiddling groups and competitions, died just before this book went to press.

The mood of Torrance until the end of the 1920s was a buoyant one. Symbolic of the proud booster spirit of the town is the fact that the scrappy little city even had an official greeter in 1929. Torrance's answer to New York City's famed Grover Whalen was Phoebe J.

Milburn, whose husband, James, worked at the Torrance Flat Glass Co.

Torrance at the end of the 1920s was a prosperous small town with no reason to expect anything but more prosperity from the wells, mills and shops at which its working men toiled. But when the stock market crash came in late 1929, the national Depression that followed hit Torrance people hard. Soon Rotary dues were not all Torrance folks were having trouble paying, and city government began casting around for ways to cut spending as taxes declined, too.

Perhaps that's why, in the shadow of Black Friday on Wall Street, at Torrance City Hall on Cravens Avenue in 1929, City Attorney Perry G. Briney asked the city fathers to reduce his salary from $150 to $125 per month. In return, they agreed that he needn't stop by city hall every morning to see if they needed him.

TORRANCE HERALD

TORRANCE on REVIEW

June 1911 — Silver Anniversary Edition — June 1936

INDUSTRY BUSINESS HOMES RECREATION SCHOOLS CULTURE

Celebrating The Dedication OF THE BEAUTIFUL NEW CIVIC STRUCTURES

TORRANCE CITY HALL

NEW TORRANCE CITY HALL

TORRANCE CIVIC AUDITORIUM

NEW PUBLIC LIBRARY

A REVIEW OF THE PAST

A VISUALIZATION OF THE FUT[URE]

A PANORAMA OF THE PRESENT

The Great Depression: Torrance fights back

Woman sits beside Torrance Boulevard
with hungry children while husband seeks work;
PWA funds new public buildings and the city rallies.

During the 1930s, the Great Depression hung like a cloud over Torrance, which still was a small town populated primarily by blue-collar workingmen and their families. It was a time when families and the things people do for one another in small towns were especially important here. Toward the end of the 1930s, darker clouds presaging the second world war also

But when the bottom fell out of everything in 1929, poverty came knocking on doors in Torrance, too. "I saw young, grown men ring our doorbell and ask to wash windows for a sandwich," Shidler recalls.

And though things were better for doctors than for the masses of the unemployed during the Depression, even

Payday in Torrance in 1938 brought this scene at the First National Bank of Torrance at El Prado Street and Cabrillo Avenue. Edward C. Nelson, cashier of the bank, is in the right foreground behind the counter. By 1938, stability had returned to the financial and economic scene. But there were still people so traumatized by the Crash, bank failures and even the Bank Holiday a few years earlier, that they were reluctant to become depositors again.

began to cast their shadows on the city.

In the age of bread lines with millions of workers unemployed nationally, when "Brother, can you spare a dime?" was a frequently heard refrain, the closing of the glassworks and other factories in Torrance, whether temporarily or permanently, brought misery to many families here.

Judge John Shidler remembers that his father, Dr. George Shidler, accepted produce and other farm products in exchange for his professional services during those fear-filled years. "The reason we came to Torrance in the 1920s," he says, "was because of the oil boom." Dr. Lancaster had too much business to handle then and invited Dr. Shidler from his native York, Nebraska.

they had it hard. With no federal or state programs and little private insurance to pay the bills for patients, a lot of a doctor's work in Torrance in the 1930s was done free.

One of his father's patients, Shidler recalls, paid one dollar or five dollars on his account whenever he could for 15 years.

"Most of the people couldn't pay their doctor bills and 50 percent of the doctor's work was not paid. And so generally at Christmas, they would send them a card and just tell them, 'I know you can't pay this bill,' and cancel it off."

Shidler distinctly recalls the hardships imposed upon the town when major factories like the Columbia Steel plant

This special edition of the *Torrance Herald* had a lot to celebrate. The young city's downtown was being radically transformed, and right in the midst of a worldwide depression. What a Fourth of July this would be!

PHOTO BY WM. FRIDRICH

would shut down for awhile in the slackened economy of that decade.

While he attended law school during the early 1930s, Shidler says, his father's influence was the only way he got a summer job as a mechanic's helper, and "I worked for 39 cents an hour."

"People were very hard up in the Depression in Torrance," he says.

Karmee Dolley recalls seeing a woman with three young children sitting on a blanket under a roadside tree just

times. The group was founded by librarian Isabel Henderson, so Mrs. Dolley went to see her that day. Together, they packed sandwiches and milk for the roadside family and Mrs. Henderson arranged a place for them to stay the night.

"Every time she would find a case like that," Mrs. Dolley recalls, "she would get very upset and work very hard to take care of it."

But soon the problem got bigger and

In March, 1936, the new Torrance City Hall rises on Cravens Avenue adjacent to the old city hall, which had served not only as headquarters for the fire department but the police and city government as well. The concrete and steel structure was designed by Walker & Eisen, architects, and was a Public Works Administration project.

Civic Auditorium Torrance Calif
Photo by Haig & Haig

The Torrance Civic Auditorium on El Prado and the Chamber of Commerce building on Post Avenue were two other "federal-style" buildings built during this period, and dedicated on the same day as the library in 1937. The auditorium was the scene twenty years later of the banquet which celebrated the city's "All-America City" award from Dr. George Gallup, the U.S. Municipal League and *Look* magazine. The Chamber of Commerce was next to the present site of D & H Carpets.

outside town about 1932. She stopped to ask the woman if she was all right. "We're just staying here for the day because my husband's trying to find a job," the woman told her.

The Relief Society of Torrance was one way the people of the small town — then still only about 5,500 residents — helped one another through those hard

bigger, as President Herbert Hoover sought reelection, promising "Prosperity is Just Around the Corner" and Will Rogers quipped that America was "the first nation in the history of the world to drive to the poorhouse in an automobile."

When drought and famine were added to the curse already upon the land,

106

City Hall Torrance Calif
Photo by Haig & Haig

refugees from the dust bowl that the Midwest had become began to pour into Southern California in search of jobs or at least a more hospitable climate in which to starve. Torrance saw its share of these desperate families. They came in such numbers that an attempt — later declared unconstitutional — was made by the authorities to close the borders of California to those not already residents here.

"They just kept coming in swarms, all of these people from the Dust Bowl," Mrs. Dolley recalls. They lived in "Hoovervilles" wherever they could throw up temporary shacks, or slept under the stars or anywhere else they could find. "I know one family lived in a chicken coop," Mrs. Dolley says.

Her husband, a prominent druggist in Torrance who owned an oil well during the heady days of the 1920s' boom, now lost his well and found his business in financial distress because he wouldn't withhold needed drugs from sick people who couldn't afford to pay for them.

"We lost it and we lost our home and I went back to work," Mrs. Dolley says. In 1934, Dolley was broke and they moved to another small Southern

William T. Klusman, mayor of Torrance 1932-33, was the only Socialist ever to hold that office and consistently failed to find enough votes on the city council to sustain his positions. His top hat and political views were viewed as oddities in the small town that was Torrance during the early 1930s, but those were desperate days deep in the Depression and the voters turned to Klusman to see what he could do for them. Ultimately the experience was a mutually disagreeable one.

Many new public facilities were erected in Torrance during the 1930s, including the public library pictured here, designed by Walker & Eisen. For the first time in American history, municipal civic works were being federally funded, and Torrance was getting its share of the aid.

Many schemes to provide economic security for the elderly, the poor or the unemployed swept America during the 1930s. One, the Townsend Plan, threw senior citizens into a flurry of organizing and petitioning for guaranteed incomes for seniors under the slogan "Youth for Work, Age for Leisure." Torrance sent delegates to the Townsend national convention in Los Angeles in 1938. Delegate and visitor badges are shown.

PHOTOS BY WM. FRIDRICH

California town in search of a new start. "There were terrible and rugged days," she says.

The Dolleys' experience with their oil well may or may not have been typical. But by the Depression years, the heyday of the Torrance oil field was over.

The earliest well — a dry hole sunk to 2,600 feet at a location described as two miles south of Redondo Beach and two miles inland — was drilled in the Torrance area on the Palos Verdes Ranch in 1910. Another dry hole was sunk to 3,400 feet about 500 feet north of what was then known as the Wilmington-Redondo Road — now Pacific Coast Highway — opposite the Weston Ranch house. It was begun in October, 1919, by Traders Oil Corp. and abandoned in September, 1922, by the McQuigg Investment Co. Commercially productive oil was not found by either of these ventures, so it was not until 1921 that a real oil strike was made in the Torrance area.

The Petroleum Development Co. drilled its first well, Redondo No. 1, in the area 1,000 feet south of Redondo-Torrance Road — now Torrance Boulevard — and just west of Earl Street. In late 1921, at 3,035 feet, a production test yielded 25 barrels per day. On December 21, 1921, that well was being deepened and at 3,118 feet blew out, sending skyward a flow of natural gas — a dramatic 15 million

cubic feet per day. The explosive flow wasn't capped until a full week had passed.

Redrilled to 3,500 feet, on June 6, 1922, initial production of the well was measured at 300 barrels of crude per day with no water content. The well, taken over by Chanslor-Canfield Midway Oil Co., a Santa Fe subsidiary, was renamed Del Amo No. 1 and C.C.M.O. started to drill three more wells right away, with General

Signs visible in photo: WALKER & EISEN ARCHITECTS — FEDERAL WORKS PROJECT Nº 1175-R PUBLIC WORKS ADMINISTRATION — Torrance LIBRARY BUILDING — CRAVENS AVE. 1300 BLK. — POST AVE. 1300 BLK.

This is 1804 Gramercy Street, where the Torrance Public Library system began. From January, 1922, until 1935, it was part of the county library system. In 1935, finding itself hard-pressed for revenue to pay for the service, the city began contracting with the county for library services.

Torrance's first librarian, Isabel Henderson, is shown in the first public library — her living room at 1804 Gramercy Street — in Torrance in 1913. She issued the first library card to a boy — Albert Isen, later mayor of Torrance — who lived across the street. The library moved to a school building on Cabrillo Avenue in 1917 when the school moved to the site of Torrance High School. The library moved to "temporary" quarters in a white cottage at 1317 El Prado behind Newberry's for 14 years, until the federal Public Works Administration project of 1936 constructed a new facility at 1345 Post Avenue, which served the reading public for more than 40 years.

Petroleum (later Mobil), Union Oil and Standard Oil all rushing into the region to start test drilling, too.

As a result of this flurry of interest by many oil companies, the Torrance field's limits were clearly delineated by 1925. It was the largest in area in the Los Angeles basin — seven miles long by one mile wide, covering just over 4,000 acres and stretching from Redondo Beach on the west to Wilmington on the east. The field as a whole produced considerable gas with crude oil, the oil including a healthy percentage of lubricating oil. The wells yielded a low percentage of water and — particularly in the central portion of the field around Carson Street and Madrona Avenue — gasoline content was high.

The main oil zone was at a depth of 3,200 to 3,600 feet in the Lower Pliocene or Upper Miocene stratum of brown shale. In the first half of 1923, the average well, in a field of 240 wells, produced 222 barrels daily, with about one percent water. During the last half of 1924, the average Torrance field well — with 463 wells — yielded 125 barrels, with water 2.2 percent of gross fluid.

Drilling was almost entirely by rotary rigs. Some wells were producing within 35 days, though 70 was about average, and some took as long as 100 days.

Due to sandy conditions, particularly at the west end of the field, "operators as a whole have considerable trouble keeping wells on production," the California Oil and Gas Supervisor

109

In the early days of trading stamps, the lure was often more direct than it later became with Blue Chip Redemption Centers. In the 1930s, these Fox-McCown stamps were "the same as money in our store when your book is filled." Someone was in such a hurry to fill this page that the last two stamps are upside down. The page represents three dollars in purchases.

PHOTO BY WM. FRIDRICH

reported in September, 1925. "It has been found more profitable to keep the wells pumping continually by pumping moderately, maintaining a certain fluid level above the oil sand, than to pump to their full capacity. Less oil per day is recovered, but the extra oil which could be obtained would not pay for the added cost of pulling rods, cleaning out sand, or redrilling work."

The cost to an operator with at least a dozen wells to pump crude oil from the Torrance field was estimated in 1925 at 11 to 15 cents per barrel. Peak production for the Torrance field came in May, 1924, when the average daily production from 345 wells was 72,000 barrels of crude. The greatest single day production per well came in November, 1923, at 403 barrels. During the first four years of Torrance field production, a total of 26.8 million barrels was

This holiday season view looking southeast on Sartori from El Prado shows the Sam Levy Department Store, Safeway, Cornet 5-10-25 cent store and others, to the Torrance Theatre at Marcelina Avenue. Levy began as a tailor and added appliances and furniture over the years. He also was a leading businessman influential in the life of the young community. He remained in business in downtown long after the area had faded as the city's leading retail center in the 1960s and 1970s. The department store continues to this day under his daughter, Ella Schwartz.

The Torrance Theatre, flanked by Christy's Soda Fountain and Mountain View Dairies, featured *Ladies in Love* with *Three Married Men* in this Christmas time scene from the 1930s. The theatre and other businesses were on Sartori Avenue, then the city's leading business street.

Looking northwest on Sartori Avenue from El Prado during the 1930s, Roberts Cut Rate Stores, Adams clothing store, Rees Family Shoe Store, the J.J. Newberry Co., Western Auto Supply, J.C. Penney Co. and the Star Department Store are among the business establishments catering to the local Christmas trade.

extracted from 562 wells. Olaf P. Jenkins, the state geologist, reported that through 1940 about 100 million barrels were produced in that field from 1,200 wells. On September 1, 1941, the 656 wells still operating were producing 9,277 barrels per day.

It was not until July 22, 1936, that a deeper oil zone, at 4,887 feet, was found in the Torrance field by C.C.M.O.'s Del Amo No. 23. But that zone was later determined to be of limited extent and productivity. By 1943, production in the Torrance field was a mere shadow of the former geysers of black gold — the average yield per well was only 14 barrels per day, with six barrels of water per day.

Eugene Davis, chief of the production of the State Office of Petroleum Coordinator, reported that the boom days of the Torrance field were long since gone. "The field is of secondary importance commercially," Davis said. "Operations have been rather unprofitable due to low productivity, small demand for the crude produced, and high maintenance costs.

"Present low production, 14 barrels per day per well, is due to depletion and bad mechanical condition of the well casings. Collapsed casing in the oil zone is very common."

But the Depression was clearly hard on people as well as on oil wells in

Torrance. During the period of continued economic doldrums, many people were looking for answers to the dilemma of poverty and want in the most prosperous nation in the history of the planet, and — in particular — their own privations. Three years after the mighty crash of Wall Street, it was becoming obvious to many that Herbert Hoover could not deliver when he promised that prosperity was "just around the corner."

Just before the 1932 election, Torrance Democrats mounted a torchlight parade of 1,000 people. William Jennings Bryan, Jr. was the speaker that night. He seems to have inspired his listeners to carry the torch for the Democratic standard-bearer, New York Governor Franklin Delano Roosevelt. "F.D.R." carried

need of gasoline, meals, milk and bread. It also provided 529 free haircuts to vets.

Times were so bad, and the spirit of pulling together so strong, that city employees voted to donate 3.5 percent of their pay to Torrance relief.

Evidence of strain in the social structure was all around. A man named G. Allison Phelps maintained a colony for homeless men at 230th and Figueroa. The Ku Klux Klan posted handbills warning police to fight a variety of vaguely described threats to the American way or be "unmasked." Scrip as opposed to real money was circulating, the proposed City Charter

Torrance 1,730 to 1,048. And 117 Torrance residents voted for that perennial Socialist candidate, Norman Thomas. That election was the Democratic Party's first victory in Torrance since the founding of the town.

In his inaugural address, Roosevelt said, "We have nothing to fear but fear itself," in efforts to revive the national economy. But Roosevelt also saw one-third of the nation "ill-housed, ill-clothed, ill-fed" and Torrance people knew firsthand the fears associated with those difficulties.

The Veterans Relief Association at 1528 Cravens was another way Torrance people tried to help one another. During 32 weeks in late 1933 and early 1934, the association helped 2,829 families in

was defeated two to one, and a show called "The College Flapper" was presented in the American Legion Hall featuring local men dressed in outlandish women's clothes.

As if there were not enough shakeups under way, on March 10, 1933, a severe earthquake centered in Long Beach also shook Torrance. Merchant Sam Levy, who had been required by bank officials to get earthquake insurance to cover a construction loan, is recalled by some old-timers as the only man in town to have such insurance to cover his damage.

Karmee Dolley recalls that her husband didn't lose expensive perfume bottles in his drugstore because he had put a small piece of chewing gum on the bottom of each to hold them firmly on the shelves. She also recalls, with a laugh, that quake day was her daughter's third birthday, and for several years afterward, the child couldn't understand why there wasn't a quake in her honor every March 10.

Alice Taylor Koutny of Torrance recalls that her family came to Torrance during the 1920s and lived at 903 Cota Avenue. The house was one of many built by Pacific Electric for their employees. "The railroad financed the homes, and during the Great Depression of the 1930s, homeowners could skip

During the mid-1930s, federal public works projects gave Torrance a new city hall, a new public library and a new auditorium — all dedicated on the same day.

But there were many who did not think the efforts of government went far enough. Politics in Torrance tended to be more personal, more "down home," more flat-out eccentric in the 1930s, before the pervasive eye of television sent every candidate to charm school to learn about charisma and projecting the right image.

Take William T. Klusman, for example. He was a feisty, opinionated man with the courage of his unusual convictions. Politicians in that era of despair really had platforms — often strange ones, perhaps, but at least you knew what Upton Sinclair, Huey Long, Dr. Townsend or Norman Thomas stood for.

During the early days of Torrance, doctors were not the only ones who made housecalls. A wide variety of merchants peddled their wares or provided their services door-to-door. These photos suggest the wide range of services available during the 1930s. The Torrance Plumbing Co. truck responded to emergency calls about rising water; the Greater Torrance Market delivered groceries, Rocky Venable & Sons delivered rock, sand and cement to your door; King's Nursery carried greenery; the Torrance Ice Co. truck cooled home ice boxes; and the Torrance Laundry & Dry Cleaning Co. truck hauled away dirty laundry.

payments without losing their homes."

A stone chimney on the left side of the house was a casualty of the 1933 Long Beach earthquake, she says. But a towering palm tree out front today is the same one that was about four feet tall when she was only two years old and about three feet tall herself.

One of the many debts Torrance owes Sam Levy is that after the 1933 quake he fought city hall to save city hall. The combination city hall, police headquarters and fire station on Cravens Avenue was so severely damaged, it was to be condemned. But cutting through red tape and charging only one dollar per month for his services, Levy spearheaded a successful rebuilding instead.

And if you lived in Torrance in the early 1930s, you knew what Bill Klusman stood for. In fact, he told you in the pages of a quirky newspaper he called the *Torrance Independent*. He not only wrote and published it himself, but he personally passed it out door-to-door. Basically, he talked socialism with populist overtones, criticized the local city council frequently, and advocated solutions for the Depression, unemployment, labor unrest and bank failures.

A one-term member of the council, he was elected mayor by his council peers in 1932. He promptly demanded but failed to get the resignations of all city department heads, and at a council meeting could find no support for his position.

A native of Oldenburg, Germany, his trademark was a high silk hat, which he wore to council meetings. Judge Shidler also recalls that Klusman's false teeth "bothered him when he was eating," and "he used to take his teeth out and put them on the table at a banquet."

As a gadfly member of the council, Shidler suggests, Klusman made his fellow councilmen so annoyed "they finally elected him mayor to shut him up."

Though Klusman affected the high hat, he had to make a living, and though he listed himself as an "engineer" in city directories and worked for National Supply Co., his holdings included a chicken ranch in Lomita. For council meetings, he sometimes would go from

"Faith in Banks" Sunday.

But when Prohibition ended in 1933, Torrance people seemed less enthusiastic. Perhaps it had something to do with the fact that Torrance was a "dry" town from its founding, with restrictions on the original deeds from the Dominguez Land Co. which provided that any property owner found to possess alcoholic beverages would lose his property. It would simply revert to Dominguez Land. In any case, the Sartori Liquor House & Winery at 923 Sartori in 1934 is the first such store listed in city directories. Jean Rebadow was the proprietor. She and her husband, Harold, lived at 730 Portola. He was an employee of the National Supply Co.

Graduated with high hopes in 1928, but soon facing the grim realities of the Great Depression that held the nation under its pall for more than a decade, were these "chums" at Torrance High School. From left, they are Margaret Tiffany, Mildred Raymond, Rose King, Doris Skoon, Marie Boyd, Winnefred Nickerson and Robinette See.
COURTESY OF ROSE PAIGE KING

the house he shared with his wife, Katherine, on Carson Street in Torrance to his ranch. Then he'd arrive at city hall for council meetings just on time, a little breathless, wearing overalls and his tall silk hat.

It's easy to poke fun at Mayor Klusman. He hadn't the remotest idea of how to keep political fences mended, and he was soon out of office. Many years later, he committed suicide during a serious illness. But the records show that he was the guiding force behind the development of Alondra Park, which continues to bring pleasure to thousands of Torrance residents every year.

President Roosevelt, to end a panic which was closing banks throughout the country, announced a bank holiday. And in Torrance, St. Andrew's Episcopal Church observed a solemn

Another of the family businesses that has played an important role in Torrance over the years is Lovelady's Hardware at 1967 West Carson Street. Vern and Wayne Lovelady run it now.

Their father and mother came to the South Bay from DuPree, South Dakota, in 1927 and bought the store in 1933, not exactly the best year in American history for starting a small business.

For many years, the big family — four boys and three girls — were lucky they lived on a two-acre farm at 257th Street and Western Avenue. "We could take poultry in payment for hardware," Vern recalls. "Lots of our customers just didn't have ready cash."

Their building was so damaged in the 1941 earthquake, which was centered near Torrance and did more damage

"Old Main" at Torrance High School was constructed in 1917 and is the first building in Torrance to be placed on the National Register of Historic Buildings. A Torrance Historical Society plaque to the right of the entrance marks the building's significance.

Fred A. Lincoln, Sr., a second cousin to President Abraham Lincoln, brought his family to Torrance from Texas in 1917 when he took a job with the Union Tool Co. He later established his own business, the Lincoln Machine Shop, engineering specialists in tool and die making, which he operated until his death in 1976. The Lincoln children took part in the cultural life of Torrance during the 1930s by playing in their school and church orchestras. The girls were active in Job's Daughters and all were involved in scouting. They also enjoyed beach parties with swimming and wiener roasts on the sand, traveled by streetcar to Redondo Beach to take what they recall as "serious" swimming lessons at the Redondo Salt Water Plunge, and enjoyed the amusements of Redondo's El Paseo. In this 1931 photo, from left, are Fred Lincoln, Jr., Marian, Millicent and Marguerite.

COURTESY OF MARIAN LINCOLN DANCE

here than the 1933 quake, that it was condemned for use until extensive renovation was carried out.

Vern was a charter member of the Torrance Junior Chamber of Commerce in 1953 — Howard Percy was charter president — and Lovelady was president in 1955. Others active in the Chamber of Commerce in the 1950s were Charles Jones, *Torrance Herald* publisher Grover Whyte, Fred Hansen, investment counselor Marvin Getch, Doug Horlander who now owns Van's Belgian Waffle Shop in Redondo Beach, Jack Phillips, and later, George Post.

There are third generation Lovelady descendants active in the family business now, and 14 grandchildren, two named Lovelady, living here or nearby. Families like theirs, or the Posts, or Pueblo patriarch Andres Alvarez, with fourth and fifth generation descendants living

and working in Torrance, are reminders that even a wealthy, fast-growing city gains strength from the stability and continuity of its citizens' families.

But some families had more advantages than others in the 1930s. A 1934 Torrance High School graduate, Alice (nee Burger) Frankin, recalls during the 1930s her Sunday School class from the Torrance Methodist Church tried to go swimming at the Plunge in Redondo Beach, but one member of the class was of Japanese ancestry.

"We tried to have a party and go to the Plunge in Redondo," she says, "but they wouldn't let Japanese in, so the class didn't go in."

Mrs. Frankin also recalls riding her bicycle along Torrance Boulevard to the Plunge. "There was only one place along the way. It was a little, tiny restaurant

D.H. "Chris" Christensen, then 18, was working summers at Columbia Steel in Torrance when he posed for this photo in 1937 with, from left, Rose and Katie Ortman. The Ortman sisters ran the Ortman Inn on Cabrillo Street during the decade whose slogan became "Brother, can you spare a dime?" For a modest sum, they provided guests with immaculately clean, furnished rooms, complete with hearty breakfasts, bag lunches to carry to work, and hot dinners. Not far away was the McKinley Inn at 1417 Cota, another boarding house where some city council sessions and civic dinners were held.

COURTESY OF CHRIS CHRISTENSEN AND DOLLY SMITH

Work in the steel mills always has carried an element of risk: superheated metal, often in a molten state; noise, which can suppress the warnings of risk; corrosive chemicals, vital to pickling, annealing and other processes. So every proper mill had its well-trained and equipped rescue squad. This was the Columbia Works' squad in 1938. We can identify most of these men, beginning second from the left: Dick Connors, H. Cook, Al Elder, Bill Kurts, John Garner, Harold Woodman, Jess Cowan, Al Tracy, Carl Benner, William Sykes; then, skipping the young man in the front, Howard Prouty, Whitey Volhert, Gene Shaefer, one more unidentified, then Eddie Alstrom and a gentleman named Harney. A few years later, busy times would return to the Columbia Works with a vengeance when America entered the war; the mill closed forever in 1979.

tearoom and the gal would read tea leaves."

She also recalls visiting the 1932 Olympics in Los Angeles. "We saw 'Babe' Didrikson break a bunch of records," she says.

Mrs. Frankin also recalls that between Torrance Boulevard and 190th Street on Cedar Avenue — now Crenshaw Boulevard — the road was so quiet in the 1930s that "it was a great parking place; it was sort of a lovers' lane."

Louis Zamperini of Torrance was a formidable miler in an era of increasingly great mile runners. The world interscholastic record (4:21:2) he set as a junior at Torrance High in 1934 stood until 1954. His national collegiate record set at USC a few years later stood for ten years. (The present world record is 3:47:33, set by Sebastian Coe of Great Britain at Brussels in 1981.)

This little button is a reminder of those days when the right of working people to organize and bargain collectively with their employer had not yet been firmly established. Prosperity had not returned to America by 1937, though the New Deal's social legislation had, most historians agree, averted chaos or revolution. The National Labor Relations Act, which would give a structure to the dialogue between workers and their employers, was not yet in place. So the job of a union organizer, especially in California which had a strong pro-management tilt, and in a town like Torrance where everyone including shopkeepers was relying on the payrolls from a few big industries, was a challenging one. Writers like James Farrell, John Steinbeck and John dos Passos made this struggle come alive in fiction; decades later, the Academy Award-winning film *Norma Rae*, starring Sally Fields, caught the spirit too, though it was about a later struggle in the South.

This was the cream of the kegler crop at the Columbia Steel mill during the late 1930s. On the plant bowling team in the back row, from left, are Slim Watson, Nick Pevovich, Jack Moore, Bill Walton and Lou Greenman. In the middle row, from left, are Tony Chakowski, who'd lost an arm in a sheet mill accident; Vic Berry, John Hanks, an unidentified man and Orville Haefeli. Kneeling are Nick Chakowski, Carl Benner, Bob Wilson, Ralph Morgan and Clarence Richardson.

Another outstanding Torrance High School athlete of the 1930s was William Russell Stewart, known to many as "the man who could fly."

An outstanding broad jumper and high jumper, he once held the world high jump record. And just for fun he was known to leap unassisted over parked cars, running straight toward one, gathering himself about five feet away and sailing over it like a gazelle.

"His friends recall him as being built like Superman, with very large shoulders and a tapered body," a latter-day Torrance High student, Marina Herbert, reported in a research paper prepared for a city history and government class taught by Torrance Mayor Jim Armstrong during the late 1970s.

Stewart set many track records before his graduation in 1939, attended USC and competed in amateur athletic events. He achieved national recognition as a young man on the way up in a Long Beach high jump competition when he out-jumped all the well-known athletes. In official competition, he was the first man in history to jump 6'10".

Though he already could "fly," Stewart enlisted in the U.S. Army Air Corps less than a month after the Japanese attack on Pearl Harbor. In February, 1944, his Martin B-26 Marauder went down over the North Sea while trying to return to England after a raid over Europe. The aircraft, painted with a curvaceous female nude reclining on its fuselage, had been nicknamed "Heavenly Body" by its crew. At 22, Stewart was listed as missing in action, and his body was never found.

T.H. Wright of Torrance was a world-renowned pioneer in orchid growing. Beginning in a greenhouse on 190th Street in 1907 and continually

experimenting, by 1936 he had cut producing time from ten years to five and was getting four crops a year instead of one. He raised his orchids on artificial foods, heated them artificially, refrigerated them the same way and even watered them with artificial rain.

The Hollywood Riviera section of Torrance, an exclusive tract overlooking the sea, had been launched with great hoopla in the last years of the Roaring 20s, but most lots remained vacant through the Depression decade and through World War Two.

"If the Depression hadn't come along," says Judge Shidler, "maybe a lot of people would have built."

Two people who could afford to live in the Hollywood Riviera during that period were daughters of the late President Woodrow Wilson: Mrs. Eleanor Wilson McAdoo, whose

husband had been a U.S. Senator from California, and Miss Margaret Wilson.

The year 1938 was notable for at least two reasons in Torrance. For one, F.M. Andreaui, a former Los Angeles Port Commissioner, tried to resurrect a plan Jared Sidney Torrance had seriously advocated in 1912. Andreaui wanted to dredge the Dominguez Channel from the inner harbor at San Pedro to establish the Port of Torrance. His advocacy of the proposal was probably the last time the idea surfaced in anything approaching serious conversation.

Radio, the wonder of the age, brought Torrance into the worldwide information society in 1938 when Columbia Pacific built a 490-foot tower east of Hawthorne Boulevard and north of 190th Street to broadcast KNX Radio at 1050 kilocycles, later 1070, on the AM dial, with 50,000 watts of power.

Also in 1938, the Townsend Plan,

Badges have been important to working men since their use first began in the Industrial Revolution. What color was yours? How low a number did you have? Did the first digit indicate the department in which you worked or was that spelled out, as on the National Supply badge from the 1930s and the Union Tool badge from an earlier period?

PHOTOS BY WM. FRIDRICH

These 82 men were among the fortunate with good jobs during the Great Depression of the 1930s in Torrance. They worked in the National Supply Co.'s welding department here in early 1938. The firm continues to operate in Torrance as a division of Armco Steel Co. The plant was the first built in Torrance, established in 1912 as the Union Tool Co's new facility. Union Tool was a manufacturer of oil well drilling and production equipment. The firm won an Army-Navy "E" Award on May 9, 1943 for outstanding production. In 1949, National Supply advertised itself as the "largest completely integrated machinery manufacturing facility in the West." It made oil well equipment and aircraft ordnance steels. Some of the welders are wearing their protective aprons and goggles.

Another major federal construction project putting men back to work during the 1930s was Hoover Dam. Not only was Boulder City, Nevada built on a plan modeled after Frederick Law Olmstead, Jr.'s street layout for Torrance, but the International-Stacey Corp. of California at its Torrance plant fabricated structural steel used there in the construction of Hoover Dam. That hydroelectric project continues to provide electric power to Southern California. These gentlemen, posing with the first structural bridge units before they were shipped by rail to the contruction site, apparently were Stacey executives.

"Youth for Work, Age for Leisure," swept America's oldest citizens into a flurry of organizing and petitioning for guaranteed incomes for seniors. Torrance sent delegates to the national convention in Los Angeles in 1938. The growth of Social Security, wartime prosperity and Franklin D. Roosevelt's inexhaustible popularity caused the organization to dwindle thereafter.

Other 1930s' movements included Father Coughlin's Social Justice, Huey Long's "Every Man a King," Technocracy and the America First organization. Norman Thomas' Socialist Party was also a strong factor locally and nationally in the early 1930s.

Mrs. Carol Brown of Torrance was a member of the nearby Inglewood Townsend Club. Her 1938 Townsend

songbook contained rousers like this, to the tune of "Auld Lang Syne":

The Townsend Plan, it will succeed
To make prosperity,
For all the people now oppressed
By lack of currency.

The nation's folk of sixty years
Will guard our country's health,
For they'll become the purchasers
of all the nation's wealth.

The 1930s was an age of unrest and uncertainty, but it was also an era of growth for the major local repository of unpopular ideas — the public library.

Like another great entrepreneur, Andrew Carnegie, Sidney Torrance loved books and actively promoted public libraries. One of his first orders of business for

his new town was to persuade his cousin, Mrs. Isabel Henderson, to move here in 1913 and open a 300-volume library in her home at 1804 Gramercy Street. A widow, Mrs. Henderson had been a schoolteacher in New York before coming West in 1912.

She held the post of Torrance librarian for 22 years, when her daughter, Mrs. Dorothy Jamieson, took the post, which she also filled for 22 years, until 1957. Mrs. Henderson died in 1936. Her daughter died in 1983 at the age of 93 at home in the house on Gramercy.

During Mrs. Henderson's tenure, the ever-growing library moved to the school building on Cabrillo that had been vacated in 1917 when the Torrance High site opened on Carson Street, then to the Dominguez Land Co.'s former office at Cabrillo and El Prado, and in 1922, to a cottage on El Prado. In 1936, it moved into a grand new Public Works Administration-built structure at 1345 Post Avenue, which now houses the fine displays and collections of the Torrance Historical Museum.

In 1967, the voters of Torrance passed a 2.35 million dollar bond issue to support a city library system independent of the county library system, which had operated Torrance's libraries under a contract with the city since 1935.

Today's 57,500-square-foot main library at 3301 Torrance Boulevard was built in 1971. There are eight branches, one appropriately named for Isabel Henderson. There are now more than 350,000 books available, 600 periodicals, and a wide variety of audio-visual and artistic materials as well.

Happily, through the years, efforts to impose minority opinions concerning what constitutes literature suitable for the public in Torrance have always failed. The Torrance library system is a fine, modern one of the sort which would have made an inveterate bibliophile like Jared Sidney Torrance smile.

Out of even the worst of times, some good things come. If it had not been for the hard times of the Depression and the public works projects initiated by the federal government to put the unemployed to work during the 1930s, the most important library building in Torrance, which served for more than thirty years as the central library and an intellectual stimulus to generations, might never have been built.

Flooding after heavy rains continued to be a problem in Torrance in the 1930s, when these pictures of wash flying on a line above a flood area and a chicken sailing atop a guitar were made. Large areas of Torrance in the Walteria area and elsewhere had to be drained before they could be built upon in the 1950s and 1960s. Some continue to have problems with settlement and foundations on adobe and other fill.

Torrance's original hose cart and its most modern firefighting equipment were displayed in the early 1930s in front of Fire Station No. 1 on Cravens Avenue. The hose cart, drawn by strong-backed volunteers who manned the first volunteer fire department formed in Torrance in 1913, is currently on permanent display at the Torrance Historical Society Museum, 1345 Post Avenue, Torrance. The department of that day was a far cry from today's 164-man department, with five stations, seven fire engines, two fire trucks, four paramedic units, four reserve trucks and fifteen cars.

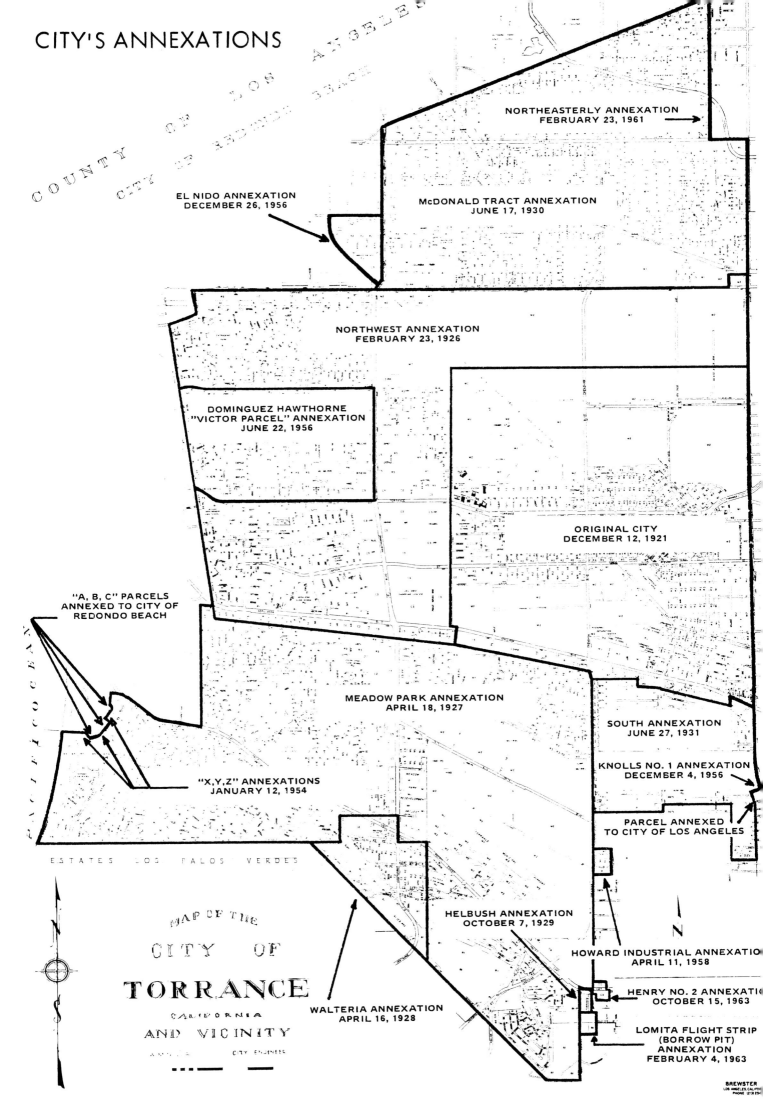

CITY'S ANNEXATIONS

NORTHEASTERLY ANNEXATION
FEBRUARY 23, 1961

EL NIDO ANNEXATION
DECEMBER 26, 1956

McDONALD TRACT ANNEXATION
JUNE 17, 1930

NORTHWEST ANNEXATION
FEBRUARY 23, 1926

DOMINGUEZ HAWTHORNE
"VICTOR PARCEL" ANNEXATION
JUNE 22, 1956

ORIGINAL CITY
DECEMBER 12, 1921

"A, B, C" PARCELS
ANNEXED TO CITY OF
REDONDO BEACH

MEADOW PARK ANNEXATION
APRIL 18, 1927

SOUTH ANNEXATION
JUNE 27, 1931

KNOLLS NO. 1 ANNEXATION
DECEMBER 4, 1956

"X, Y, Z" ANNEXATIONS
JANUARY 12, 1954

PARCEL ANNEXED
TO CITY OF LOS ANGELES

ESTATES LOS PALOS VERDES

HELBUSH ANNEXATION
OCTOBER 7, 1929

MAP OF THE

CITY OF

HOWARD INDUSTRIAL ANNEXATION
APRIL 11, 1958

TORRANCE

CALIFORNIA

HENRY NO. 2 ANNEXATION
OCTOBER 15, 1963

AND VICINITY

WALTERIA ANNEXATION
APRIL 16, 1928

LOMITA FLIGHT STRIP
(BORROW PIT)
ANNEXATION
FEBRUARY 4, 1963

CITY ENGINEER

BREWSTER
LOS ANGELES, CALIFOR
PHONE (213) 29

A good city is the sum of its neighborhoods: here are three

*A grand dreamer's vision of a Southern California Riviera;
a neighborhood grows around a vanished lake;
a lively center of family life carries on a rich heritage.*

Dedication day for the Hollywood Riviera section of Torrance in 1928 included musical entertainment, and drew an enthusiastic crowd lured by the prospect of getting in on the ground floor of a glamorous movie colony neighborhood built by Clifford Reid as a variation on his vision of the French Riviera. But the film stars did not buy and the landscaped parkway Reid envisioned to Hollywood from the coastal development was never built. Arrow indicates Fred W. Marlowe, one of Reid's best salesmen and later himself the developer of Westchester.

Torrance in its early days was of a mind to annex and grow. It moved north and west in 1926 to bring in Del Amo land, then south in 1927 and 1928 to enfold Meadow Park and Walteria. The last big move was to the northeast, the McDonald Tract, in 1930. Thereafter the boundaries were "squared off" with the Victor Parcel and El Nido in 1956, and with acquisitions along the Lomita border through 1963. A tiny town which, in 1921, had incorporated itself hurriedly while looking nervously over its shoulder at land-hungry Los Angeles, thus entered the 1970s with 21 square miles within its borders, a municipal power to be reckoned with in Southern California.

The annexations of 1926-31 laid the groundwork for Torrance to become a city of many residential neighborhoods. Not only was there downtown Torrance, but the Pueblo, Hollywood Riviera, Walteria, North Torrance, Meadow Park, Southeast and other areas.

The population boom of the 1950s and 1960s in Torrance would reinforce this

trend and bring it to full flower with regional homeowners associations that are represented today by such mainstays of civic activity as the Olde Torrance Neighbors, the Riviera Homeowners Association, the Southwood Homeowners Association, and other groups. These groups arrange meetings and social functions for their neighborhoods and often monitor and lobby city government for action favorable to their sections of town or their philosophies of government for the entire city.

It is perhaps a measure of the success of city government that the neighborhood associations are not more strident or more influential than they are, since the formal machinery of government considers and acts upon a broad view of the interests of its citizens in all parts

of town, and only rarely has been perceived as neglecting any particular section.

There are too many neighborhoods in Torrance to treat each one in depth here. Suffice it to say that the Olde Torrance Neighbors have been active in efforts to rehabilitate a business and residential area that was showing signs of its age until new residents began a "gentrification" process in the late 1970s. They have moved into and restored to former splendor what were, in the earliest decades of the city, the finest homes in town.

And Meadow Park is a vanished neighborhood, once predominantly Japanese and later declared a near-slum at the west end of the Torrance airport and razed to make way for the Skypark Industrial Park.

But within Torrance's 21 square miles there is still room for a diversity of places and a variety of heritages and lifestyles.

Let us consider the people and places of three neighborhoods: the Hollywood Riviera, Walteria and the Pueblo.

If ever a community was the living embodiment of its founder's vision, Hollywood Riviera was it. And Clifford Reid, prince of subdividers, was the man who made it happen, against the adversities of the Great Depression, World War Two and the vagaries of the marketplace.

He was born in Oregon, and after a brief venture in real estate in Portland,

came to Southern California in 1925. His first efforts here were in the San Fernando Valley. Then he struck a deal with the ubiquitous Henry Huntington to develop the one square mile of coastal hill land which lay tucked against the ocean at the northern edge of the Palos Verdes peninsula.

Reid and his wife had traveled in Europe and a vision of the French

The Clifford Reids of the world have seldom received their due. "Real estate developer" just doesn't have the ring to it that "statesman," "financier" or "merchant prince" do. But developers are more important in shaping everday life. And how different was Reid from Henry Huntington or Sidney Torrance? Their goals, like his, were to persuade people to subscribe to their vision of the South Bay. They succeeded; Reid did not. But looking at the Hollywood Riviera today, it would be hard to say he failed. Foster & Kleiser took this picture of their billboard in July, 1930. The location, at Western Avenue and Sixth Street, was adjacent to Reid's realty office in Los Angeles. The well-known watering hole, Blarney Castle, is there now.

Riviera — Nice, the Grande Corniche, Cap d'Antibes — was part of what was in his mind when it came time to name his development. A firm, if quixotic conviction that he could persuade the luminaries of the film industry to move here was the other element in his equation.

Voilà, "Hollywood Riviera" and it would be linked by the Palos Verdes to Hollywood Parkway to the distant Culver City and Gower Street studios,

where these artists toiled. A noble concept, the first element of which was actually built and is Palos Verdes Boulevard today.

Marshall Stewart, Clifford Reid's nephew, recalls that sales were "fierce" from 1928 to 1934, though precious few were ever made to Hollywood types. Marian Davies, John and Ethel Barrymore, Clara Bow and Gary Cooper visited the Reids — but didn't buy. Louis B. Mayer is reputed to have tried

Hollywood Riviera Beach Club
REDONDO BEACH
CALIFORNIA

Hollywood Riviera Beach Club

LUNCHEON DE LUXE 85c

CHOICE OF
Fruit or Seafood Cocktail

Soup du Jour

Salad

CHOICE OF ENTREES
Grilled Loin Lamb Chop (One), Glazed Pineapple
Creamed Chicken a la King
Steak Minute, Riviera
Omelette with Shrimp and Crab Meat, Poulette
Broiled Fish with Lemon Butter Sauce

Fresh Vegetables   Potatoes

DESSERTS
Vanilla or Choco
Apple Pie De Luxe   Italian Prunes   Pr
Orange Sherbet   Butterscotch or Chocolate Sundae with

DRINKS
Coffee, Tea, Milk or Butterm

SPECIAL HOT LUN

Soup and Sala

ENTREES
Ravioli with Sp
Individual M
Spanish or Den
Scrambled Eggs, P
Special Hot Roast

SPECIAL CO
Soup
Molded
Molded
Chicke
Sliced Cold

Vegetables

She

Hollywood Riviera Beach Club
Dinner De Luxe
$1.25

APPETIZER
TOMATO JUICE, SHRIMP, CRAB MEAT OR FRUIT COCKTAIL
CELERY EN BRANCHE   MIXED OLIVES
SOUP DU JOUR

SALAD
FRUIT, HEARTS OF LETTUCE OR VEGETABLE
WITH MAYONNAISE OR FRENCH DRESSING

CHOICE OF ENTREES
SPECIAL CHICKEN SAUTE SEC, RIVIERA CLUB
GRILLED LAMB CHOPS WITH BACON PARISIENNE
FILET MIGNON, MUSHROOM SAUCE
BROILED FISH, LEMON BUTTER SAUCE
COLD SLICED BREAST OF CHICKEN WITH CHEF GARNISH
FRESH VEGETABLES   POTATOES
HOME-MADE HOT BISCUITS WITH HONEY OR JELLY

DESSERTS
PIE WITH CHEESE
BUTTERSCOTCH OR CHOCOLATE SUNDAE
VANILLA ICE CREAM   SHERBETS   COOKIES

DRINKS
COFFEE, DEMI TASSE, TEA OR MILK

Special $1.00 Dinner
CHOICE OF COCKTAIL
SEAFOOD, FRUIT OR TOMATO JUICE
SOUP AND SALAD

ENTREES
GRILLED OR FRIED FISH, LEMON BUTTER SAUCE
RIVIERA MINUTE STEAK
DICED STEAMED CHICKEN A LA KING
IN CASSEROLE, WITH GRAVY
DISJOINTED FRIED CHICKEN, SOUTHERN STYLE WITH GRAVY
GRILLED LAMB CHOPS WITH GLAZED PINEAPPLE
GARDEN VEGETABLES   POTATOES

CHOICE OF DESSERTS
FRESH FRUIT OR CHOCOLATE SUNDAE
SHERBET OR VANILLA ICE CREAM WITH COOKIES
PIE

CHOICE OF DRINKS
COFFEE   TEA   ICED TEA   MILK

to buy, only to be deterred by disapproval, perhaps a manifestation of anti-Semitism from the newly formed landowners' association. His brother, Rudy Mayer, in company with a man named Kenner, developed the top of the Riviera in the immediate postwar years.

Stewart's father, Roy, moved into the Riviera in 1929. This allows Marshall to claim to be the resident who lived there first. He lived elsewhere for some time before returning to build in 1956. Mrs. Daisy Odom Geary, who has lived on Via Estralita since 1930, is the longest continuous resident of the Riviera.

Roy Stewart managed the Hollywood Riviera Club on the cliff above the beach west of Paseo de la Playa at the

Looking seaward and south from the Riviera Club in the 1930s. During World War Two, anti-aircraft guns would be emplaced on the beach, "scaring the whales and the dolphins when they fired practice rounds." Cliff Stewart recalls that the battery included half a dozen guns and ran all the way down to the far edge of Torrance Beach.

COURTESY OF MARSHALL STEWART

Who among us does not enjoy browsing through a menu from bygone years to marvel at both the unrelenting sumptuousness of the fare and the ludicrously low prices? Here are the choices Riviera Club members were presented a little more than half a century ago, when Clifford Reid, Roy Stewart, Fred Marlowe and Newt Bass were using the club as a lure to bring prospective homeowners down for a look at their grand dream.

Aspects of the good life at the Hollywood Riviera Club in the 1930s. Not visible in these pictures, but present in members' minds, was the boundary line separating Torrance from Redondo Beach. It ran right through the clubhouse, and because the two cities had different licensing regulations, it sometimes dictated to people where they should congregate if they wanted to be served a drink. One of these pictures was shot from one of the nine guest rooms the club maintained, two of which were in the tower.

COURTESY OF MARSHALL STEWART

A private dining room at the Hollywood Riviera Club in the 1930s. After the first few years, Riviera sales slowed because of the international Depression. But developer Clifford Reid and his brother-in-law, Roy Stewart, who managed the club, kept the flag flying as long as they could. Sold to outside interests in the 1940s, the clubhouse burned in 1958. The site is now Miramar Park, a county park. Riviera residents rallied to defeat a 1960s' proposal for a high-rise condo, topped by a restaurant.

COURTESY OF MARSHALL STEWART

127

foot of Calle Miramar from June 27, 1931, when it opened with a sort of desperate hoopla (the nation was in the throes of the Depression) until it ceased to be a private institution in 1942. Residents were automatically members, and paid dues which gave them swimming privileges and the right to host events there. The general public was always admitted to the dining area.

The whole "tilt" of the community was toward nearby Redondo Beach. "We never thought about going shopping in Torrance," Stewart recalls. But Torrance had always been the more resolutely acquisition-minded of the two cities, and in 1926 annexed the desirable residential area before Redondo did.

It was not all that exciting a conquest for many years. Sales lagged in the 1930s in spite of the efforts of Reid and of such persuasive sales aides as Fred Marlowe, who later developed Westchester, and Newt Ross, who went on to develop Apple Valley.

A leading academician at USC, Dr. Hans Nordewin Von Koerber, bought

here. So, briefly, did Paul Muni. But many of the houses went for taxes, and bargains, incredible by today's price standards, could still be had as late as 1970.

During World War Two, as prosperity returned, there was a brief sales flurry from 1939 to 1942. Then America's entry into the war brought anti-aircraft batteries emplaced beside the clubhouse on Torrance Beach, waiting for the roar of approaching Japanese bombers that — mercifully — never came.

Home construction halted. The club closed. It reopened as a public facility in the late 1940s and George Post, now president of Torrance National Bank, was a lifeguard at the pool there.

The Huntington Land Co. sold its interests to other developers in 1947. Clifford Reid continued to live in the magnificent 6,700-square-foot house he had built in 1928 on Via Monte d'Oro until he died in 1957. (It takes 14 furnaces to heat the home.) His wife died six years later. Stewart's father, Roy, died in 1982.

The 640-acre Hollywood Riviera development had laid out some streets and built about a dozen houses when this aerial photo was taken from above Palos Verdes Estates, looking north along the coast to Manhattan Beach. Modern photo shows the view today.
MODERN PHOTO BY WM. FRIDRICH

The grading of what probably was Palos Verdes Boulevard is under way in this scene. Developer Reid proposed a grand parkway that would link his Hollywood Riviera with the real Hollywood, but like other aspects of his vision of a playground for the stars, the plan would soon be scaled down by the economic reverses of the time and the many roadblocks set up by the jurisdictions through which the road would have to have passed.
COURTESY OF MARSHALL STEWART

You didn't need 3,000-foot paved runways to have a viable airstrip in 1928, when this picture was made in the Hollywood Riviera. In the early 1930s, the Riviera also was the international headquarters of a glider enthusiasts' organization. Today, just a few miles away, Torrance Airport (Zamperini Field) is the twentieth-ranked general aviation facility in the nation.

There are four middle-aged gentlemen in the South Bay who are just going to have to resign themselves to some friendly ribbing about this picture, taken 52 years ago on the beach at the Hollywood Riviera. From left, which is also from youngest to oldest, they are Patrick, Clifford, Marshall and LaMar Stewart, the sons of Mr. and Mrs. Roy Stewart. Their father was Clifford Reid's chief aide and managed the Hollywood Riviera Club. Patrick now lives in Rolling Hills Estates and is active in the highly regarded Stewart Film Screen Co. with his brothers, Marshall and LaMar. Marshall still lives in the Riviera; LaMar in San Pedro. Brother Cliff lives in Monrovia and is a potter. "Health and happiness on the beach" is how the *Riviera Review* captioned this picture. Harry Hopkins, then chief of police in Redondo, took this 1932 picture.

COURTESY OF MARSHALL STEWART

Spence

Some of Marshall Stewart's early memories of the Riviera include the old mule camp which Peter Bartmus ran, up Palos Verdes Boulevard against the tree line. All the curved streets in the Riviera were carved out by mule teams. Bartmus, he recalls, had nine children, and later moved to Arizona. Much of the land in the Riviera was farmed extensively in the early days.

There was a competition glider field in the Riviera in the 1930s too. It was on Via Monte d'Oro, the extension of Via Alameda, by the tree line. Glider pilots would bring their machines there by truck and assemble them. Then they'd be towed west by a car and, if lucky, catch the famous Palos Verdes uplift and soar for hours. Stewart remembers a flying family, the Buxtons, from Inglewood. "They'd land their two-seater at Mines Field (now LAX) and come down here to glide. If the wind was right, they'd glide right back to LAX."

Powered flight was even sometimes attempted off Torrance Beach. Once it was done for a Tim Holt film, and Stewart remembers the plane landing crosswind on the beach.

And, yes, it was true about the city boundary between Torrance and Redondo Beach going right through the old clubhouse and causing imbibers and late night revellers to shift their base of operations a few feet to legalize their activities at certain hours of certain days. This persisted when the club was in outside hands, as a public bar, until it burned in the 1950s.

Though not strictly in the Riviera, another transitory but dramatic element from the old days at the south end of Torrance, Lake Walteria, is gone forever. When it rained, the lake would appear, encompassing whole blocks around Pacific Coast Highway and Crenshaw. Then in a few weeks, it would be gone.

Though originally promoted as a swank Mediterranean-style home and playground for wealthy film stars and executives, the Riviera saw its most rapid and dramatic development during the 1950s post-World War Two baby boom. The vacant lots began to fill with comfortable homes for white-collar professionals, many of them employed in the South Bay's burgeoning aerospace industry.

Through the 1960s and early 1970s, the Riviera was a middle-class family kind of place, mostly Caucasian but with a smattering of families whose heads were well-educated individuals of Oriental descent. It was not until the 1970s that real estate prices began to soar in the Riviera section — with its obvious advantages of ocean breezes, hillside lots with ocean views, good city services and fine schools. The Riviera became such an affluent neighborhood that the

This 1965 photo shows the Chapel Theatre when it was located in Walteria adjacent to the Palos Verdes Bird Farm. The production the community theatre group was doing at the time was *The Fantasticks,* a musical comedy review. Another Walteria landmark, the Begonia Farm, has been located adjacent to the Bird Farm since 1941.

Torrance's "sometime" Lake Walteria, an annual and exciting occurrence when the rains overwhelmed the area's legendary poor drainage. "Belly deep to a horse" in some places, it made rowboat travel possible, even necessary in spots. Long before this, at the turn of the century, there was something like an inland waterway through Lomita and Walteria, from San Pedro and Wilmington to Redondo Beach. In the middle of the picture is the Palos Verdes Bird Farm on Pacific Coast Highway east of Anza, and also a building occupied in the 1950s by the Chapel Community Theatre which has since moved to Lomita. Above and to the left of that grouping, one can faintly discern the screen at the Torrance Drive-in Theatre at Torrance Boulevard west of Palos Verdes Boulevard. Better drainage has made the lake no more than a memory now.

PHOTO BY PAUL COMON

The diatomaceous earth mine, up Hawthorne into the hills from Pacific Coast Highway and above Newton Street, was Torrance's lone entry in that important field of endeavor — mining the earth. Begun in 1917 by Sidebotham, it had fallen into dangerous disrepair by 1965 when this picture was shot. This rickety old outbuilding was demolished soon thereafter. There was a sheer cliff there, too, looking into the worked-out excavation — dangerous to stand on, but providing a view for miles straight up Hawthorne Boulevard into the heart of the new South Bay.

PHOTO BY PAUL COMON

Truckloads of books at the old firehouse library in Walteria at Neece Avenue and 242nd Street. Opening day was not far away.

Mollie Dowd in front of the old firehouse library before it opened in Walteria in 1962. Note the truckload of books behind her. Mrs. Dowd taught scores of adults to read and taught hundreds of children to use the dictionary and the encyclopedia. She was the victim of a vicious assault in the late 1950s because of her zeal to protect the library. She had turned narcotics she discovered in the library over to police. A few nights later as she left, she noticed the lone overhead porch light was out. (It had been unscrewed.) She tripped over a nearly invisible wire and was severely injured. The criminals were never apprehended.

Pacific Coast Highway, between Hawthorne and Anza, looking northwest in the 1960s. As home-building flourished in the Hollywood Riviera and Walteria sections of Torrance, this empty arterial began to fill with shops and restaurants. South High, from which one of the authors graduated in 1963, opened in 1959 to serve the needs of this growing area. Attorney Douglas Brown, a Torrance council member in the 1970s, was also a member of one of the earliest graduating classes. His mother was one of the earliest librarians at South High. The round, wooden structure, with the ferris wheel visible behind it, is the merry-go-round of Rideland, operated in the 1950s and early 1960s by the Kiddieland Corporation at 3860 Pacific Coast Highway. Mr. and Mrs. A.Z. Zirbec ran it.

average Californian could not afford to live there.

The status of the Riviera became such, in fact, that at one time in the late 1970s four of the seven Torrance City Council members called it their home. Actress Rosemary De Camp and her husband, Judge John Shidler are long-time residents. Upgrading of existing properties in the Riviera continues, and prices of houses — a few still under $200,000 — continue to rise.

Much of the section continues to have Redondo Beach mailing addresses, a survival from the section's early

This is the unusual-looking old Walteria Lumber & Building Co., which stood on Park Street between 244th and Newton. Parties and public meetings were often held in the open area in front. It stood until after World War Two. Sharp-eyed readers may note the sign to the left of the open door grumps "No Dogs Allowed."

orientation toward the coastal town, viewed by some as a more prestigious address than Torrance.

Proposals over the years to improve the minimal street lighting provided by Torrance in the Riviera, or to install public sidewalks, have generally been opposed by Riviera residents as too costly and real threats to the atmosphere of the neighborhood.

Betty Stewart, Marshall's wife, finds one other change in the Riviera especially poignant. "Parkway School closed in the last few years." A French language private school now occupies the site. "At one time, there were 800 to 850 kids enrolled there (at Parkway), including our children.

"When it closed, there were only 400. Kids here now go to Riviera School. The Riviera's still a wonderful place to live, but we miss the children."

□ □ □

Mrs. Mollie Dowd has had a unique vantage point from which to watch Walteria grow for the past half century. From 1937 until 1967, with a few years away in World War Two as a registered nurse, she was county librarian in the little community. There were about 600 residents when she came.

She met the doyen of South Bay librarians, Mrs. Isabel Henderson, just a few months before Mrs. Henderson died. And she worked many happy years for Dorothy Jamieson, Mrs. Henderson's daughter, for whom she had great affection and respect. One of her proudest memories is that, working enthusiastically with young people, she was able in 1958 to "outcirculate" the main Torrance branch.

Mrs. Dowd confirms that Walteria is named after Captain Walters who maintained a lodging house there about the turn of the century. It was always good farmland too; when Lake Walteria would recede in the dry season, people like Mr. Venable, and later Japanese-Americans, would farm the low, flat land between Pacific Coast Highway and Sepulveda, and from Crenshaw to what would become in the early 1960s South High School. In the rainy season, ducks, mud hens and sea gulls frequented the lake. Petroleum tanks would be tended in rowboats, and Mrs. Dowd recalls the water was "belly deep to a horse."

Mrs. Evelyn Schooley, the granddaughter of Walteria pioneer Charles Quandt, has no trouble remembering the date when her mother married Charles Dunn. It was April 15, 1912, the day that "the great ship

Andres Alvarez, 93, is the patriarch of the Pueblo. He and his wife, Agapita, have lived here since 1931, raising eight daughters and six sons who, in turn, have presented them with more than 68 grandchildren and 70 great-grandchildren. As did many in the community, the Alvarez family came originally from Purepero in Michoacán. Mr. Alvarez worked in the rolling mill at Columbia Steel for 30 years, retiring only a few years before the mills shut down. Mr. and Mrs. Alvarez have been married 70 years. His grandmother, he recalls, lived to be 110. Visiting him the day this picture was taken were three daughters: Frances Colin of Redondo Beach, Irmalinda Villalobos who lives here, and Helena Savina of Sacramento.

PHOTO BY WM. FRIDRICH

(Titanic) went down." Her grandfather Quandt was also the developer of Meadow Park. He died in 1951.

Mrs. Schooley, who has been married fifty years, eloquently expresses a view which is typical of Americans who had to start a family during the Depression: "My husband worked for 41-and-a-half years for National Supply as a machinist here in Torrance. I thank God for the job. I used to thank God for the job

every April 14 (their anniversary). Some people don't, but I do."

They bought their first home at 2517 El Dorado in 1938 from Don Finley of the Torrance Investment Co. "There were only a dozen houses west of us in 1938."

Elsewhere in Walteria, there was an old, large and even famous chicken farm south of Newton and west of Hawthorne as late as 1936. This was soon after

Many of the leaders of community organizations in the Pueblo gathered with two of the parish priests in St. Joseph's social hall in 1948. In those days, the affairs of the local congregation were administered by Our Lady of Guadalupe Parish in Redondo Beach. Now they are a part of Nativity Parish in Torrance. The man third from the right in the rear is Andreas Alvarez who, at 93, still lives a few doors away from the church, as he has for 53 years.

PHOTO BY RUBEN V. HERNANDEZ

Torrance annexed Walteria. The area had possessed its own city charter for a brief period, but lost it, Mollie Dowd recalls, because of "squabbling."

The little community was served by Kato's and Tanaha's markets in the 1930s. When the relocation shame affected Walteria, these families didn't return from Manzanar. People named Dunn operated a market on Kato's site later.

Other old settlers whom Mrs. Dowd recalls were the Lockridges, the Buchinghams and Mrs. Della Armstrong, a realtor and an artist. "Then there were two families, William and Victoria Adolph, and the Codonas, all aerialists from the Barnum & Bailey Circus," says Mrs. Dowd. "Adolph and Los Codona streets are named after them."

One of the Walteria area's favorite stories a half century ago was of a bloody massacre supposed to have taken place two hundred years ago at the old turret at the top of Hawthorne. Mollie Dowd loves a good story. She's a professional librarian and they are the keepers of legends. But she agrees that this one is apocryphal, and, like Topsy, it "just growed."

A list she has kept of the first shipment of books into the new branch in July, 1937, gives an interesting look at what people thought might be a "good read" in those pre-television days.

Fiction included Willa Cather's *My Antonia* and Campbell's *Rose of Los Angeles*. Joseph Conrad, Conan Doyle and Dumas were represented. So were Mark Twain and George Eliot. John Galsworthy and Rider Haggard were apparently in demand. So was Rudyard Kipling, and there were three titles by the great romanticist, Raphael Sabatini. Booth Tarkington was still popular, as was P.G. Wodehouse.

Juvenile fiction included Blackmore's *Lorna Doone* and Wiggins' *Rebecca of Sunny-Brook Farm*.

The nonfiction ran heavily to travel — Burton Holmes and Richard Halliburton — and memoirs of the Great War, like Eddie Rickenbacker's *Fighting the Flying Circus*. Model aircraft manuals and Howard Pyle's wonderful pirate yarns were also represented.

□ □ □

From the Riviera and Walteria to the Pueblo, the distance is more than miles. It is the distance between two cultures.

In the earliest days, the Pueblo was known as the Mexican Village, and the first city board of trustees put pressure on the owner of the section to improve services. The section was originally outside the town and specifically designated as "foreign quarters."

To travel the road to the Pueblo, long-time Pueblo residents Ruben and Irene

Four generations of the Ordaz family, long-time residents on Del Amo Boulevard, are spanned in this photograph, shot in the front yard of Ruben Ordaz' home. His great-grandson, Steven Guerrero, stands beside Mrs. Ordaz; beside her is her sister, Celia Grajeda; Ruben and his son, Ruben, Jr., a long-time employee of the Torrance School Board and a leader in the Del Amo community, stand behind them. The Ordaz family have lived on Del Amo, a few houses apart, since 1925. Of all the family names mentioned in the very first census of the Pueblo in 1922 (Gabriel Garcia, Encarnacion Gonzales, Julio Lopez, Angel Navaro, Selvera Rios, Modesto Ruiz and Pablo Terazas), only the widowed daughter-in-law of Mr. Rios still lives here. "Many of the others," Ruben Ordaz, Jr. says, "moved to Gardena or Redondo."

PHOTO BY WM. FRIDRICH

The ladies of the Pueblo assembled for a Mother's Day ceremony 30 years ago at the Del Amo Pueblo Center. Many of the families which live there are now in their fourth generation of residency in Torrance. For all these years, St. Joseph's Church has been the beloved center of activities for these scores of families. In 1968, the community itself raised the money for a new recreation hall by holding a series of carnivals.
PHOTO BY RUBEN V. HERNANDEZ

Ordaz remember that before World War Two there was only a dirt path from Del Amo to 190th Street. They recall that the older generation of residents worked in the fields, or for Columbia Steel or Pacific Electric.

"We all remember some Yaqui Indians who worked for Columbia," Ordaz says. "They were very strong men, able to stand the heat of the blast furnaces better than anyone else."

"Lots of the people who lived here were from the same little town in Mexico," Ordaz recalls. "It's called Purepero, in the state of Michoacán about 200 miles west of Mexico City."

Much of the social life of the community focused in the 1970s around Pueblo Park. Until 1984, the city leased it for one dollar a year from American Standard. Some of those who were

instrumental in getting the park for the community were Robert Flora, a former Air Force officer and his wife, Wanda, Barbara Weir, Pat Groscup, former Mayor Isen, and council members Don Wilson and Ken Miller.

Another focal point was, of course, the church. Built in 1916 by the parishioners themselves, it has recently been served by pastors from Nativity Church. Father Patrick McGuiness was a particularly beloved pastor in the 1960s. On holy days, the congregation would move in procession from the church along the length of Del Amo between Crenshaw and Van Ness, under the giant shade trees.

The procession would usually be the start of a day of family togetherness.

A strong sense of family and community still pervades the Pueblo area. Ruben

The second lady from the left in this procession is Julia Ordaz, Ruben Ordaz' mother. The family has lived in the Pueblo for 59 years. A Head Start program now operates in the church social hall. The parishioners of St. Joseph's Roman Catholic Church love processions, and the children learned quickly to take their part in these community events. The children of Greenwood Avenue School are proceeding down Del Amo on a December 12, the Feast Day of the Virgin of Guadalupe, in the 1950s. Del Amo was widened and the center divider installed a few years later.

Another colorful activity in the mid-1950s was the crowning of the Pueblo Catholic Youth Organization Queen and this parading of her through the downtown Torrance streets on a flower-bedecked float, proudly flying the flags of Mexico and the United States.

Ordaz is proud of the fact that while, like all American communities, there have been some problems with young people and drugs, there are no gangs. As other ethnic groups — Vietnamese, Filipinos, some "Anglos" — move into the area now, the Pueblo absorbs and makes room for them all.

New corporate construction such as the Honda complex and the leveling of the old Pacific Electric shops will revitalize this old and valued neighborhood. Past injustices like Torrance's original racial restrictions on home ownership and residence will become historical footnotes, never to be condoned but now happily outgrown.

□ □ □

The Riviera, Walteria and the Pueblo are just three of Torrance's neighborhoods. There are many others

and all are constantly changing, constantly becoming something else. The Riviera population is aging, Walteria is no longer under water, and the Pueblo's residents have made great strides in recent years.

Sections that were once dairy farms are now tracts with names most residents have already forgotten. But in many neighborhoods there is still a strong sense of community, of connection with Torrance friends and neighbors, of faith in the processes of local government and the effectiveness of programs like Neighborhood Watch, in which neighbors look out for one another in an effort to reduce burglaries and other crimes.

Throughout Torrance's neighborhoods, too, there continues to be the feeling expressed by many that Torrance, after all, is still a pretty good place to live.

Torrance goes to war again: the city changes and grows

Torrance rallies behind its Japanese-American citizens; its factories work to support the war effort; city airport, local schools and city charter prepare for postwar growth.

In the decade of the 1940s, Torrance began to outgrow its small-town beginnings. As the population rapidly increased, a new city emerged.

At last Sidney Torrance's prediction of more than a quarter century before was fulfilled. Torrance finally passed the 20,000 population mark in 1950, recording more than 22,000 residents,

would add two elementary schools before the end of the 1940s.

Torrance at the beginning of the 1940s was the sort of place where Beacon Drugs at 1519 Cabrillo Avenue offered reservations on American, Pan American, TWA or Western Air Lines. And it was the sort of place where there were only five new car dealers.

The Pacific Electric shops were an important part of the Torrance industrial scene from 1917 until they were closed. The final phase in their demolition was going on even as this was written. Camaraderie flourished in the workplace then as now, and this group of some 40 men and three women — all employees with 20 or more years on the job — assembled cheerfully for this photo two months after the end of World War Two. All of the sturdy "track stars" we now affectionately remember as "the big red cars" passed through the Torrance shops many times before returning to the far-flung lines that stretched from San Bernardino to Long Beach during Pacific Electric's reign as one of the world's earliest and best interurban railway systems. Frank Thompson is fifth from the left in the top row. Of the five men in the upper row on the right, Carl Gramling and Jake Groscup are third and fourth from the left.

up dramatically from 9,550 in 1940.

The population increase of the 1940s was evidence that more people were discovering the joys of suburban living in Torrance. The period also was one in which many Torrance residents did their part to win a world war, those of Japanese descent were herded into "relocation camps," a wartime draft board and a Torrance ration board held sway, and the local labor union movement emerged as a force to be reckoned with.

The 1940s was an important decade for Torrance schools as well. It was a time in which the Torrance system was created and separated painfully from the Los Angeles City School District. To a district with one high school and four elementary schools, the Torrance district

As a transportation alternative, the city was served by the Torrance Municipal Bus Lines founded in 1941, Greyhound and Union Pacific Stages. Union Pacific phased out its services by the end of the 1940s. Torrance Transit maintained a terminal in downtown Los Angeles until 1959.

In 1941, Tom F. McGuire, personnel director of the National Supply Co., was mayor of Torrance and saw no conflict in also serving as chairman of the-city planning commission. In 1949, the position of mayor was held by Hugh J. Sherfey, Jr., manager of Stone & Myers Mortuary, but the mayor's job had been reduced in importance.

Down the road — Sepulveda, to be exact — was a distinctly rural recreation facility — Attebery's Recreation Barn —

These are the medals for valor, and for being wounded in combat, which were won in World War Two by William Russell Stewart, "the man who could fly." Left, the Air Medal with four oak leaf clusters; center, the Purple Heart; finally, the Distinguished Flying Cross. Stewart was a B-26 pilot, age 22, when his plane failed to return to its base in England in 1944. It was his thirty-seventh mission. His medals are now in the care of the Torrance Historical Museum, symbolic of the loyal service rendered the nation by Torrance men and women in World War One and Two, and in Korea and Vietnam.

PHOTO BY WM. FRIDRICH

139

where there was barn dancing beginning at 8:00 p.m. every Saturday night.

Interestingly, as the population of Torrance more than doubled during the 1940s, the number of dairies operating in the city also increased. Seven of the thirteen in Torrance in 1949 were not present in 1941. Apparently the cows, too, had discovered greener pastures in Torrance.

Some of the other businesses active in Torrance 44 years ago, as war clouds began to gather over the country, were Sam Handler and Harold Tuck's Live Poultry & Egg Market ("our poultry dressed under fresh running water") on Cravens, Marge's Beauty Shop on Cabrillo, Grubb's Market on Carson Way, and Leslie Prince's Beacon Drug Co. on Cabrillo.

And because war already had begun in Europe, the British War Relief Department was open at 1530 Cravens Avenue. Mrs. Ed Neese was in charge.

Prices then? Well, according to *About Town,* Vic's Cut Rate Drugs & Liquors at 1911 Carson was selling two packs of cigarettes for a quarter, three candy bars for a dime, and "wine 10¢ a bottle."

The Bal Tabarin at Redondo and Western offered three revues every night, a seven-piece orchestra, and steak or chicken dinners for one dollar.

On November 14, 1941, an earthquake inflicted $350,000 damage in Torrance, which was close to its epicenter.

Guests fled the three-story El Roi Tan Hotel, one of the Irving Gill-designed structures. The sharp temblor brought a shower of bricks and large chunks of cornice work thumping to the ground. Ledges shaken from buildings nearly filled some alleys in the business district, which was primarily of brick construction. The roof of a vacant store collapsed into the building and plate glass windows were shattered on more than a score of businesses.

The 1941 quake was probably the most severe to ever hit Torrance, but no lives were lost. Even so, the aftershocks were barely over before nature's surprises were outdone by another devised by man.

On December 7, 1941, a sleepy Sunday only a few weeks before Christmas, the forces of imperial Japan attacked the U.S. Naval Base at Honolulu, Pearl

The November 14, 1941 earthquake doesn't occupy the same place in California seismic lore as San Francisco in 1906, Long Beach in 1933, Tehachapi in 1959 or San Fernando in 1972. But it wasn't for lack of trying, as these pictures shot in the aftermath show. Jim Fitzgerald and Wilma Schreiber begin the cleanup on El Prado, between Sartori and Border, while a scene inside a local grocery store shows more of the same random nature of the upheaval.
COURTESY OF MRS. A.J. FITZGERALD

Harbor. In a few hours, virtually the entire U.S. Pacific Fleet was disabled or destroyed, though the extent of the damage was withheld from the American public. President Franklin D. Roosevelt declared December 7 "a date that will live in infamy."

Draft Board 280, the Torrance board headed by Carl D. Steele, an employee of Columbia Steel, was already at work at 1327 El Prado, and draftees from Torrance were soon on their way to war.

Torrance, like the rest of the West Coast, braced for a Japanese invasion that never came. But on February 25, 1942, the antiaircraft guns guarding the Greater Los Angeles area roared into

action in the predawn hours of what came to be known, somewhat tongue-in-cheek, as "The Battle of Los Angeles."

The *Daily Breeze* reported that hundreds of South Bay residents "were roused out of a sound sleep" by the firing. A reporter was dispatched to 190th Street and Vermont Avenue near Torrance in a fruitless search for an enemy bomber reported downed in a strawberry patch.

Throughout the South Bay, air-raid wardens and volunteer police scrambled to their posts in fear the war had come home. But what menace the guns were firing at that night, if any, was never clear.

Some property was damaged by a few misplaced shells but that was not the only sacrifice made for the war effort on the homefront. There were shortages of paper goods, scrap iron, tires, gasoline and other strategic materials. And the Torrance Ration Board had the power to dispense ration coupons which would permit citizens to obtain many items taken for granted during the normal peacetime course of life.

Mrs. Ruth Woodcock, an employee of the office during the war, compiled a scrapbook that includes letters from citizens variously pleased and irked by the wartime rationing. Mrs. Woodcock called the book "Little scraps from the Big Scrap!"

Albert W. Adams wrote the board that he was worried that he was unable to declare his oversupply of sugar — for which he could be fined — because "I am 83 years old, have a broken back and a lame foot and it is not easy for me to get around."

Jack H. Lane wrote on August 14, 1945 that "the reason why I had to apply for gas early is because my car gets very poor mileage. It is a big Nash!"

John E. "Pop" Jones, who had been a watchman at Soule Steel on Border Street, was chairman of the Torrance Ration Board.

Harry B. Groom, a resident of Mobile, Alabama, wrote to thank Jones personally for help in obtaining gas that Groom needed to return from California to his Alabama home.

"I am sure," Groom wrote, "that there is not another office that compares with the Torrance office for just all-around good fellowship, business attitude and horse sense in their dealings with old Jawn Q. Publix."

But not all fared as well at the hands of bureaucrats during the war. Though many had been farming the land even before the city of Torrance was founded, Japanese-Americans born and raised here and elsewhere along the West Coast were treated like second-class citizens or even enemies.

One of the best sources for the early history of Japanese-American families in the South Bay is *Rafu Shimpo*. This Japanese-American newspaper published annuals in the 1930s which included subscribers' names, listed by city.

In 1938, there was a Japanese school, "Keystone," here. The Blue Diamond Market was on a rural delivery route, Nagui Grocery was at 231 Arlington and Quality Supermarket was at 2171 Torrance Boulevard. Cherry Blossom Chop Suey was at 1314 Sartori. There were about 115 subscribers to *Rafu Shimpo* in the city. Remember, in all of Torrance then there were only about 9,000 people.

The Nisei (second generation born here) had made considerable efforts to become a part of the American scene, following the example of other ethnic groups — Irish, Slavic, German and Italian — before them. They were already at the stage where they had Japanese chapters of Occidental clubs and charitable groups: YMCA, Thalians, Boy Scout Troops, the American Legion, and the Epworth League.

The next generation — the Sansei — could be expected, following American custom, to move into the larger community. It was not to be. Pearl Harbor was bombed in 1941.

And Japanese-Americans as a group were *not* interned or relocated from the Hawaiian Islands. But on America's West Coast, it was otherwise. Lt. Gen. John L. DeWitt, the Army officer in

LOCAL BOARD NO. 280

CARL D STEELE CH.
EARL JACOBS
HOWARD E HUTTON

charge of deciding whether relocation was called for, seems clearly to have been a racist, from documents obtained in the last few years under the Freedom of Information Act. Some people's economic interests were served by relocation; John Victor Carson talked with scorn 30 years later of the men who came in, claiming that in a few hours a day snatched from a high-paying defense job, they could work a farm which a Japanese family had lavishly cared for seven days a week.

One way the massive war effort was financed by the federal goverment was through the issuance of U.S. War Bonds. A variety of methods was used to persuade the public to buy the bonds, including these matchbook covers patriotically emblazoned with the U.S. Eagle.
PHOTO BY WM. FRIDRICH

Newspapers were cowed or quiescent. Civil libertarians looked away in embarrassment, pleading ignorance of what constituted military necessity. Churches were silent while they sent parishioners off with prayer to restore democracy and the rule of law abroad.

And in the South Bay, as throughout the West, the trains for Manzanar and Tule Lake began to fill up. Land and property were sold for a pittance, or put in the care of those who misappropriated or neglected them.

The experiences of the Nisei who were relocated followed a pattern: first on Pearl Harbor day — shock, horror and anger that an enemy had attacked their country. Added to that, was their understandable concern for their parents, the Japan-born Issei. It seemed wrong that they should be punished for not being citizens when citizenship had been specifically denied them under alien exclusion acts — but this was war.

As the tempo of repression mounted from February through June, 1942, it became clear that Nisei were not to be spared. Curfews, permission needed to travel more than five miles from home, and exclusion orders were made binding. Ironically, on June 2, 1942, when only 17,000 were already in camps, the

When Torrance Draft Board 280 was in session, this handmade sign was hung out. Carl Steele, a Columbia Steel employee and union leader, presided over the agency that selected local boys sent off to fight the battles of World War Two. The office location, 1327 El Prado, is Hope's Jewelry Gift Shop today.
PHOTO BY WM. FRIDRICH

government doomed another 93,000 harmless old aliens and their citizen children to years in the desert and the destruction of the property rights on the very day that the Nisei were rejoicing with their fellow Americans over the great victory at the Battle of Midway which had ended forever the threat of a Japanese invasion of Hawaii, much less of the mainland.

A remarkable book just published by Random House, *And Justice for All*, edited by John Tateishi, is a collection of interviews with those who went through the camps.

Yuri Tateishi had been raised in Torrance but was living in West Los Angeles when relocated to Manzanar. Her fatalistic attitude was typical of many of the relocated.

"When I think back on the relocation, that's something you'd like to erase if you can, but it's a fact. We went through it. I'm unhappy about it, but I don't think I was really bitter. ... They tell you; you go or else. You just had to go. You hurt. Everybody was at the point of just getting out of the Depression and then all that happens."

Others like Donald Nakahata have become bitter over the years. "We went along with it, because we knew we were second-class citizens. It was an emasculation. That's why nobody would talk about it."

Paul Shinoda had a degree in horticulture from the University of Illinois. He had built greenhouses in Torrance in 1939 on ten acres. He had associated with *Hakujins* (Occidentals) in business all his life.

"Of course," he says "there was nothing social for us, because organizations like Kiwanis weren't open to Japanese then." He felt he could rely on "American fair play — being an American citizen and learning all this at school.

"Then they put the curfew on," he recalls. "I stayed in Gardena." But then it turned out that those of Japanese descent from Gardena couldn't cross Western Avenue anymore.

"I couldn't go to the nursery in Torrance anymore. So the next day we packed up and left." He finished the war as a voluntary evacuee in Idaho. He was able to reclaim and enlarge the Torrance Nursery after the war.

His thoughts are a mixture of bitterness, understanding and regret: "We were going too much like sheep. We should have sat still and been taken one by one by bayonets. They hauled a lot of Issei away, but not the Germans and Italians. If they picked just the Japanese for evacuation again, I'd raise holy hell and I'd sit there until they pretty well shot me up before I'd move.

"The people who lived next to us in Gardena knew that the Japanese were patriotic ... but those bastards that didn't know anything about us made the decision. We lived just like they did, and we went to work everyday and came home. And Mom stayed home and took care of the kids, and we went to church on Sunday. They knew it; they could see us as well as we could see them. But nobody came out, and nobody went to the trouble to ask."

Luckier than most Japanese-Americans in Torrance, Sakumatsu Omatsu and his wife Hanayo were able to move

classmates at Fern School asking him, "What do you have to move for?" And, he says, "I couldn't answer them." His father, in fact, was an honorably discharged veteran of World War One military service, and hence already a U.S. citizen.

When they returned in 1945, they farmed again, this time at Del Amo and Hawthorne boulevards. "There was nothing else there then but a dairy and a dog pound," Sam recalls. They farmed until 1949 while he went to Torrance High. Then they began cultivating flowers nearby until 1959 when they started Holiday Liquors.

Sam Omatsu's brother-in-law, Lou Miyamoto, was a member of the famed 442nd Infantry Battalion, the Nisei

hearts of some Japanese-Americans. Their desire to love and serve their country — the United States — was always being countered by their awareness that justice was simply not being done to them.

"*Shiataganai* (It can't be helped)," said the older Issei with weary resignation.

But for those born here the injustice was obvious. Among them were 63 Nisei who served three years at McNeill Island Penitentiary for refusing to register for the draft unless their parents were released from the camps first.

"Where the hell is the democracy we learned in school?" asked Jack Tono, one of the 63. "Hey, if I have to give up my life for democracy, I want to see the damn thing first."

One bright note of calm and a decent regard for the American way in the midst of federally sponsored racism and hysteria was sounded by the Torrance City Council.

before the relocation to Fresno and then to Brigham City, Utah, for the duration. They had been leasing a field at Carson Street and Anza Avenue to grow strawberries. Even so, Sam Omatsu, 54 now, remembers his

battalion which carved its heroic niche in history in the Italian campaign and in the Vosges Mountains of France from 1943 to 1945.

Perhaps the ultimate evil of the relocation was the rage it set up in the

At their December 12, 1941 meeting, less than a week after the terrible events at Pearl Harbor, Mayor Thomas McGuire said, according to minutes of the city council, he felt that "Council should go on record to recognize the American-born Japanese people in this vicinity as American citizens and to express to them by resolution of the Council the confidence of the Council in their loyalty to the United States of America, copies of the Resolution to be mailed to the various Japanese-American

These temporary shacks were constructed along Western south of Carson in 1944 and 1945 to house workers in the nearby mills and foundries. Western hadn't been cut through to Pacific Coast Highway yet. Some of this critically needed housing was very "no frills" indeed; tents, tar shacks and the ubiquitous "Chic Sales" outdoor plumbing.

PHOTO BY PAUL COMON

If you want to encounter the generation gap at its widest point, try telling your teenage friends about ration books in World War Two! This was Paul Johnson's, issued in October, 1942. Each family member had one, including little Richard who was 23 inches long, weighed 11 pounds and was two months old. And there were coffee, sugar, gas and meat coupons too. The whole nation accepted the statement of President Roosevelt, printed in each book: "We cannot have the things we want if our boys over there are to have what they need." The Johnsons still live on Acacia as they have for 44 years. Little Richard, mentioned above, is still a Torrance resident too.

PHOTO BY WM. FRIDRICH; BOOK LOANED BY DOROTHEA JOHNSON

associations in this area," and made a motion to this effect.

Councilman Lawrence V. Babcock seconded the motion, which was unanimously carried. Councilman James E. Hitchcock suggested that copies of the resolution be forwarded to the schools to be read to students. It was further suggested that the city of Gardena be informed of the action taken by the city council of Torrance.

Torrance might have had more of an excuse for succumbing to war hysteria than most cities, because it had quite a substantial Japanese-American population. Out of a total population of at most 12,000, there were 408 Japanese aliens and 781 Japanese-American citizens.

But Torrance didn't succumb and, in fact, went on public record in a forthright and courageous way. In succeeding weeks, the city received expressions of gratitude from several Japanese-American associations to which it had sent copies of the resolution.

☐ ☐ ☐

Some organizations have been a vital part of the Torrance story for almost the entire period of our city's existence. Now there may well be second and third generation family members playing roles in the organizations, as did their parents and grandparents before them. Rotary, the Woman's Club, and the Chamber of Commerce are three such organizations. Another is the American Legion, Bert S. Crossland, Post No. 170.

Crossland was the only Torrance man killed in action in World War One. After surviving the blood bath in the Meuse-Argonne and at St. Mihiel, he was slain at Waargehem in Belgium on November 1, 1918, just eleven days before the Armistice. (There were 41 other Torrance men who served in World War One. Jules Van was part of the strangest and coldest campaign American soldiers ever fought — the Expedition to Siberia in 1919.)

Bert Crossland's death stirred his hometown. William Klusman, who was to be mayor briefly a decade later, joined civic leaders George Proctor and H.M. Tolson. They enlisted the support of Isabel Henderson. A public subscription was held, and a memorial flagpole for Crossland was erected. Soon thereafter, the veterans themselves met in the old Campbell Hall on El Prado. The Torrance Legion Post was formed there with James Wallace Post as president.

A lot on Border Street was bought from the Dominguez Land Company at a giveaway price. The First National Bank loaned the post $500 and the charter was granted to the Torrance post in January, 1920. The charter members were Nelson H. Reeve, Edward J. Whilamb, Forrest J. Young, Claude E. Talcon, Clarence R. Long, Kenneth T. Paige, Mather A. Russell, Vincent F. De Tour, Everett E. Brandt, William J. Cormey, Lawrence V. Babcock, Exter C. Hughes, Arthur E. Burmaster, James W. Post and Edward B. Stevens.

In 1924, the post sold its first building on Border Street and acquired the lot on Carson on which it built a new headquarters. The men of the post that year also had the chance to hear from "Comrade Miss Greenland" about her service in France with the Signal Corps.

The post's minute books reflect a wonderful cantankerousness and

disrespect for Robert's Rules on occasion. For instance, December, 9, 1924: "This meeting was not adjourned. Everyone just walked out." Another notes that an errant member was "fined two bits for not keeping the records in good shape."

A charming note from the minutes of December 27, 1927, shows the Legion at its amiable best: "After the meeting, the Post serenaded Post Commander Robert J. Deininger at his residence, with bugles and drums. He was recently married."

By that time, too, the post had established a solid tradition of sponsorship for scouting activities in Torrance, as well as Americanism rituals. But the year 1929 began inauspiciously for the Torrance Legion. (It wasn't a very good year for the country either, of course.) There was no profit on the auxiliary's annual dinner, and "the turkey shoot was not a success and the post had to ... reimburse the woman who ran the hot dog stand $4.75."

By 1931, there were more than 200 members in the post. They were, in the midst of burgeoning unemployment, becoming very direct in their dealings with city officials. ("That a resolution be sent to the city council sponsoring a

There is little left at Manzanar to remind the older among us and to inform the younger of the sad and unsettling thing that happened here forty years ago. So that it is not entirely forgotten, a plaque was erected in 1973 by the California Department of Parks and Recreation, the Manzanar Committee and the Japanese-American Citizens League. It reads: "In the early part of World War Two, 100,000 persons of Japanese ancestry were interned in relocation centers by Executive Order No. 9066, issued on February 19, 1942. Manzanar, the first of ten such concentration camps, was surrounded by barbed wired and guard towers containing 10,000 persons, the majority being American citizens. May the travesties and humiliation suffered here as a result of hysterical racism and economic exploitation never emerge again." Hugh Cherry, a long-time country music disc jockey and commentator, and now a teacher in Torrance, kneels beside the plaque.

An example of the housing into which bewildered, heartbroken or bitter Issei, Nisei and Sansei — a great many of them American citizens — were relocated in 1942. Alondra Park was a gathering point for the journey into the bleak desert. So was Santa Anita Track, where stables provided shelter. The sons of many of those relocated were soon to volunteer for military service. Some, at considerable front line risk from their fellow soldiers, became invaluable interpreters and intelligence specialists in the Pacific. Others joined the Nisei battalion which, fighting in Italy, amassed more medals and more casualties than any other Army unit in World War Two. Many came home to find their families' businesses destroyed. Compensation was not even thought of then, but it has become a burning issue in the past few years.

carried tons of food stuffs, clothing, blankets and wood to Long Beach, did traffic duty in Compton and Huntington Park, provided 94 beds for "refugees" and supervised Torrance Military Academy students and those from the high schools as guards at unsafe buildings in Torrance. One such was their own headquarters, which was severely damaged.

A few years later, as the nation girded for its second major war in less than 25 years, the Legion moved to its present headquarters on Van Ness Avenue. As Torrance grew, the role of service clubs and veterans' organizations inevitably diminished. But the Legion, and organizations like it, played an important role in building the sense of community which still prevails in Torrance today.

Though the removal of Japanese-Americans from Torrance had a negative impact both on the lives of Torrance residents and on their numbers, overall the war was to prove a boost to the city's total population.

Much of Torrance's population increase — it more than doubled during the 1940s — was spurred by World War Two and the strong activity at Columbia Steel and National Supply. Those firms put the slow and uncertain days of the Depression behind them and did their part in the national war effort. New firms began to emerge as employers in Torrance, too, including the Harvey Machine Co. — later Harvey Aluminum — at 19200 S. Western Avenue, and the Doak Aircraft Co., Edmond R. Doak, president, at 2321 Abalone Avenue. In addition, Torrance was becoming a bedroom community

public playground and that no alien labor be used in its construction.")

The post compiled an impressive record of service during the Long Beach earthquake March 10, 1933. Eighty-one legionnaires with five trucks and an ambulance reported for duty. They

One of the War Relocation Authority camps which took Japanese-Americans from Southern California was Gila River, Arizona, west of Tucson on the Gila Indian Reservation. More than 13,000 people were concentrated there, guarded by about 130 military police. This view is looking west from the water tower located in the M.P. camp. The residents produced tons of produce for their own use and to help feed the nation which most of them loved. A factory in one of the three Gila River camps even produced cargo nets for the U.S. Navy. Robert Metcalf, for many years now a resident of Torrance, and a teacher and counselor in the "driving under the influence" school at Southwest Driver Benefit Program here, was drafted out of high school in 1942 to be an M.P. at Gila River. He took this picture in 1943. Some of those he was guarding were former high school classmates.

PHOTO BY ROBERT METCALF

for the burgeoning aircraft and shipbuilding industries nearby.

Labor organizations had made some attempts to organize Torrance workers during the 1930s, but in the Depression climate of too few jobs and too many unemployed there was always another man willing to work if you went out on strike, so the organizers often failed to find much support. During World War Two, however, workingmen in Torrance began to seek not merely any job available, but jobs with good wages, benefits and humane working conditions. And they began, in the early 1940s, to create, join and otherwise support labor unions.

The story of labor in Torrance, of course, is complex — too rich to handle in great detail here — and spans the entire history of the city, beginning with Sidney Torrance's idea that workers should live so well in his model industrial city that they would not be interested in smashing capitalist industrialism as some radicals suggested, but would help to preserve it because it provided well for them.

There is, for instance, a plain one-story building at 1316 Border Street which harbors a goodly slice of Torrance labor history. Today it is the headquarters of Local 6700, United Steel Workers of America, formed in 1965 to organize Harvey Aluminum Co. But until 1980, it was the headquarters of Local 1414, chartered in 1942 to organize the Columbia Steel works.

When Columbia closed in 1980, No. 1414 returned its charter to the international. Local 6700 moved from rented offices in Gardena to take over the building for which the members of 1414 had raised the funds and done much of the interior finishing themselves. Retired members of 1414 — men like Art Vega, Marion Freeman, Hansell Anderson and Luciano Archuleta — are still welcome at their old stomping ground, where their charter, signed by both Phil Murray and David McDonald, still hangs on the wall.

Vega, born around Hawthorne and Del Amo boulevards, joined 1414 in 1943 and put in 37 years. Now he does security work, often at U.S. Honda, sometimes patrolling the razed site of the former Columbia works where Honda will soon build its U.S. corporate headquarters.

He started in 1943 at 76 cents an hour, and by 1980 he was making, as a shipping clerk, about $15 an hour, including incentives. But he didn't work during the three-month strike in the 1950s, he recalls. "I worked in a carwash then," he says. "But we won the strike."

Anderson, a former member of John L. Lewis' coal miners union in Kearney, West Virginia, came here in 1955. He worked with tow motors and forklifts for 25 years. He lives in Torrance now, as does Luciano Archuleta, who worked in the open hearth for 27 years from 1953 until the Columbia closing.

Marion Freeman, 77, comes to the hall a few times a week still, even though he retired in 1970 after 41 years in the jobbing mill and as a roller. He usually arrives on his 750cc motorcycle.

"We tried to organize in the 1930s," he recalls, "but we didn't make it until 1942. The international only began to help us in 1947."

He recalls that the local's full name was "The Milky Williams Lodge," honoring a legendary U.S.W.A. organizer back East. Always active in the local he helped to found, Freeman remembers when management wanted to fire the union president during the 1940s. They had discovered he was carrying membership applications into the plant in his lunch bucket. His name,

incidentally, was Carl D. Steele, the fellow who also headed Torrance's wartime draft board.

Nickolas Drale and Victor Benstead, members of the Torrance City Council during the 1950s, were both members of the steel local.

Local 6700 has had a colorful history, too. After 13 years of unsuccessful efforts to organize Harvey Aluminum's plant at 190th Street and Western Avenue, the U.S.W.A. succeeded in 1964 in winning recognition by 1,019 votes to 473.

Carlos Cordova, a young law student and son of Luis Cordova, a founding member of Local 6700, has written an interesting research thesis on the Harvey organizing battle and the strike that followed the next year, the most bitter in Torrance history. He makes it clear that the Harvey family, especially patriarch Leo Harvey, was antiunion.

But the local, he points out, was led by inexperienced men like Americo Argenta and Bill Feierabend. They had little capacity for the give-and-take of negotiations. They had no awareness of the international's strategy, which was to bring pressure to bear on the Harveys within the Democratic Party. (Leo Harvey's daughter, Carmen Warschaw, was a National Committee member from California.) And they had neither the ability nor any evident

Though there had been other beauty queens in Torrance before 1939, the Miss Torrance Pageant sponsored by the Torrance Moose Lodge at the Torrance Auditorium at Cravens and El Prado may have crowned the first Miss Torrance. Of a field of ten contestants, Leila Combs, a 14-year resident of Torrance who attended grammar school and high school on the Torrance High campus, was the beauty that carried the day. She was the kind of girl young men going off to war two years later would remember, would decorate their barracks and their bomber fuselages with. Now Leila Turner, Miss Torrance 1939 still lives in Torrance.

COURTESY OF LEILA COMBS TURNER

desire to restrain their own hotheads.

In the first strike vote, on April 5, 1965, the response in favor of striking was an overwhelming 1,194-to-23. A month later, the union rejected a Harvey offer, 864-to-5.

It was a bitter and sometimes ingenious battle. The union cut a 45rpm record, *From One Worker to Another*, which featured an anonymous worker and his wife. In tones that ranged from angry to plaintive, they contrasted the nonunion Harvey worker's lot with his unionized counterpart at Alcoa.

They circulated letters, with accusations about unsafe working conditions: "I am talking about saw blades breaking and flying out in all directions; trim presses double tripping (remember Charlie); mechanical presses falling apart and pieces hitting the foreman (remember James B.); hydraulic presses rocking and shooting parts out to mow the workers

When the boys came marching home again in 1947, some of them paraded along Sartori Avenue in honor of the annual Factory Frolic, and local merchants like Sam Levy offered "Bargain Days." This view looks southeast along Sartori toward the National Supply Co.

down like bowling pins (remember John R.)."

Management fought back with flyers that shouted: "Wanted! More dues payers by U.S.W.A. all power (sic) employees. We need your wages for our lush expense accounts, our union bosses' salaries, propaganda distribution..."

Violence erupted in July, 1965. The union accused the Torrance Police Department, especially Captain Joe Miles, of harsh and arbitrary actions, and compared the Torrance Police unfavorably to the sheriff's deputies who were involved on the other side of the plant. But Cordova points out that the Torrance Police had the duty at the point of maximum tension, the plant parking lot. Also, this was their first major strike and they were learning as they went.

There were, he thinks, "outside agitators" present, not invited by either the local or management. Some, like CORE, had a respectable agenda if no particular right to pursue it then and there. Others, including the Hells Angels, were simply looking for trouble.

So there was some excitement — 26 arrests and seven injuries — but eventually cooler heads on both sides prevailed. In fact, Governor Pat Brown brought state-suggested arbitration to bear. Even as some of the local's leaders languished in jail on contempt of court convictions for defying an injunction, the international signed an agreement for the local in early 1966. About 1,300 of the 1,900 workers had struck; about 1,100 returned, their jobs secure, their wages and working conditions bettered.

There was another strike three years later. One year after that, Leo Harvey sold the plant to Martin Marietta. Local 6700 and Martin Marietta have enjoyed an almost trouble-free relationship for 14 years now.

Local 6700, under President Thomas Collins, serves as the focal point for several other unions in the area. These include No. 8722, Joe Batty, president, and No. 14407, Sarah Strights, president. Barbara Lee is vice president of No. 6700 and Jonnye T. Hewitt is secretary.

It's clear that for the men and women of Torrance trade unionism — people like Marion Freeman, who helped found No. 1414 and lived with it till it died — there's no argument. A steel mill was a

149

TORRANCE HE

ESTABLISHED 1914 · · · · FOUR SECTIONS — 32 PAGES

TORRANCE, CALIFORNIA, THURSDAY, DECEMBER 12, 1946

32nd YEAR—No. 50 · 12

ZAMPERINI AIRPORT DEDICATED . . . Torrance city government officially assumed control of the Army-developed Lomita flight strip Saturday morning and dedicated the airport to the favorite son of Torrance, Capt. Louis Zamperini, athletic and war hero. Pictured during the ceremony which completed the first step in the city's acquisition of the field as a Torrance municipal airport are those appearing in the picture above, left to right, Mrs. J. Hugh Sherfey Jr., Anthony Zamperini, Mrs. Leslie Scholar, Mrs. Anthony Zamperini, Mrs. Louis Zamperini, Cap'. R. L. Lewellen, Miss Virginia Zamperini, Reed H. Parkin, chairman, Aviation Commission, Capt. Louis Zamperini, Mayor Sherfey, Pete Zamperini, Councilman G. V. Powell, Lt. Col. H. G. Reeder II, Rep. Cecil King, Col. Tom Scott, Mrs. King (partially hidden by Bear flag), Martha Vickers, Mrs. Parkin, Col. R. Q. Williams, Ed Doak and David G. Logg. Complete details of those attending the affair are contained in an adjoining news account of the ceremony. (Torrance Herald photo.)

THAT LUCKY ZAMPERINI . . . Captain Louis Zamperini poses with his bride, Cynthia (right), and Miss Martha Vickers (left) before an Army AT-6 following the dedication ceremonies Saturday at Zamperini Field. "The lovely Cynthia ought to be in pictures," quoted the camera man as he shot the above scene. Miss Vickers, recently elevated to stardom on the Warner lot, was guest of the Zamperini family during the ceremonies. She is currently being seen in the Warner Bros. pictures "The Big Sleep" and "That Way About Women." (Torrance Herald photo.)

ZAMPERINI FIELD CEREMONY MARKS CITY'S ACCEPTANCE OF ARMY-DEVELOPED AIRPORT

In a colorful ceremony Saturday morning, Torrance Municipal Airport came into being and officially was designated as "Zamperini Field."

Participating in a program at the former Lomita flight strip which saw as many newsmen and photographers gathered as have been found in one gathering at one time in Torrance for many a year were government officials, movie stars, Torrance leaders and aviation enthusiasts who joined members of the Zamperini family in creating a fitting climax to an athletic and war career such as has been experienced by no other son of Torrance.

Capt. Louis Zamperini, who made international fame as a long distance runner and whose fame lead to extra severe punishment by the Japanese following his capture after 47 days on an open raft in the South Pacific, was the center of interest as the City of Torrance formally accepted the 89 acres comprising the flight strip itself and named it for Zamperini. The 89-acre piece, heart of the 480-acre airport, was granted to Torrance by the Federal Public Roads bureau on a perpetual permit pending the acquisition of the balance of the field from the War Assets Administration, proceedings for which now are being drawn to a successful conclusion.

Captain Zamperini, his bride, the former Cynthia Applewhite, of Miami, Fla., and members of his family, shared the spotlight with Rep. Cecil King and Mrs. King, David G. Logg, airport disposal engineer for the Civil Aeronautics Administration, H. L. Henkel, assistant to Logg, Martha Vickers, Warner Bros. star, Torrance officials and friends in bringing to a conclusion one phase in the long campaign to acquire and dedicate the multi-million dollar airport built on the Weston ranch property by the Army Air Forces as an auxiliary field for training of pilots and crewmen for duty in connection with World War II.

Long before the airport was declared surplus, Ben Weston and members of his company officially declared that their

(Continued on Page 4-C)

Mayor Sherfey's Dedication Talk Published Here

Mayor J. Hugh Sherfey Jr., dedicating Torrance Municipal airport as "Zamperini Field" Saturday at 11.25 a.m. spoke as follows:

"Five years have passed since that Sunday morning in December, 1941, when Pearl Harbor suddenly was changed from a scene of sabbath stillness to one of flame, fury and chaos.

"The wreckage of the great battlewagons still was smoldering when the shout arose, "Remember Pearl Harbor." That became the rallying cry around which our war effort was centered. We remembered Pearl Harbor. We remembered the thousands who were killed and wounded in that attack. We remembered the vicious treachery of the enemy. We remembered how close we had come to complete disaster.

"These things we kept before us nearly four years later when what the Japs started at Pearl Harbor we finished in Tokyo Bay.

"Now the war seems long past, and Pearl Harbor a tragic event of history. But out of the stunning blow of Pearl Harbor have come many lessons—lessons which will always help us to remember Pearl Harbor.

"One of the heroes of the war which Pearl Harbor thrust upon our nation is a son of Torrance who had made his

(Continued on Page 5-A)

Most Torrance Stores To Stay

POPULAR SUBSCRIPTIONS ASSURE CHILDREN OF CITY CHRISTMAS PARTY DEC. 21

Yes, kids, there will be a Christmas party in Torrance this year.

Spearheaded by the Torrance Lions club, a Yule celebration, complete with Santa Claus, a Christmas cantata by the First Christian church children's choir, a band program and presentation of the motion picture "Child of Bethlehem," will be held in Torrance Civic auditorium on Saturday afternoon, Dec. 21, starting at 2 o'clock.

The Christmas party will feature presentation of fruit, nuts and candy by Santa Claus to Torrance area youngsters, and it is anticipated that from 1,500 to 2,000 children will attend.

After hearing the announcement that the regular party sponsored each year jointly by the City of Torrance and the Moose lodge would not be held this year, members of the Lions club took up the appeal for the affair.

Presenting a resolution to the City Council Tuesday night, they found that the City Dads, as a body, could do nothing

year, are asked to send in their donations to the Children's Christmas Party fund, in care of Allen's Cafe, 1413 Cravens ave.

The committee in charge of the affair for the Lions consists of the Rev. Ronald J. Menmuir, pastor of the First Christian church, and Dale Riley, superintendent of City Recreation department, program; Albert Isen, attorney, H. C. Allen, Allen's cafe, Frank Dominguez, of El Prado Furniture, John H. Ritchie, finance; Frank S. Selover, managing editor of the Torrance Herald, George P. Thatcher of Walteria and W. T. Greene, jeweler, publicity and arrangements.

Louis Zamperini learned to run like he had the devil at his heels here at Torrance High School and because of his prowess was a member of the U.S. Olympic Team that went to Berlin in 1936. What dramatic times these were for American athletes and sports fans! Eleanor Holm, later to marry Broadway producer Billy Rose, was kicked off the swimming team because — horrors! — she drank champagne en route. Louis did well — he finished eighth worldwide. He particularly won the hearts of his countrymen when he "requisitioned" this very swastika from in front of Hitler's *Reichskanzlei* one night. It was a bad time for Hitler and his Nazi proponents of race supremacy — the magnificent runner, Jesse Owens, won his Olympic Golds there in the heartland of "Aryan philosophy." When the authors asked Zamperini to don his Olympic participant medal, blazer and hat, and bring the swastika with him for this photograph, we made the mistake of not calling ahead. Understandably, we had some explaining to do before being allowed to proceed.

PHOTO BY WM. FRIDRICH

This clipping from the *Torrance Herald* (December 12, 1946) tells some of the Louis Zamperini story. One of America's top milers in the 1930s, Zamperini — noted for hijinks in his schoolboy days here at Torrance — was a U.S.A.A.F. bombardier in the Pacific in World War Two. He was shot down in 1943. After 47 days on a raft, he and one crewmate drifted ashore on a Japanese-held island. Zamperini survived more than two years in a P.O.W. camp. Converted to active Christianity after the war by the Rev. Billy Graham, Zamperini now is a lay minister for the Presbyterian Church and runs Victory Camp for young boys in the Antelope Valley.

Mrs. Anthony Zamperini, 88, with her sons, Pete (left) and Louis, in the garden of her home on Sonoma Avenue in Torrance. An early member of the Torrance Woman's Club, Mrs. Zamperini recalls vividly her boys' athletic accomplishments at Torrance High in the 1930s and the town's excitement over Louis' 1936 Olympics participation. She remembers most, of course, the sorrow of hearing Louis was missing in action in World War Two, and the joy the town shared with her and her family when he was discovered alive years later in a Japanese prison camp. Pete recently retired as athletic director and track coach at Banning High. He was his kid brother's first trainer in the early 1930s.

PHOTO BY WM. FRIDRICH

good place to work, they say, but only if you had a strong union to fight your battles for you.

But the bonds between workingmen in Torrance were not the only ones strengthened during the war. In 1943, the *Torrance Herald* produced a small book called *Gone Forth to Serve*, a "compilation of the achievements of the graduates of Torrance High School."

By April, 1943, there were already Gold Stars to be noted: John Junior Fess, and missing in action Army Corporal Louis Madrone, Class of 1938. Captain William C. Keefer and Lt. Louis Zamperini had already been awarded medals for bravery or meritorious achievement in aerial engagements. Addison Smith and Robert Emerson had also already been cited for bravery.

The book contains fascinating insights into the circumstances in 1943 of the earliest graduates of Torrance High. Betsy Byrnes, Class of 1918, had been a voice teacher in Honolulu and Long Beach, and was then with the U.S. Engineers in Glendale. Marguerite Paour Nuckles, from that same first class, already was the first alumna to have a child — June Nuckles, Winter of 1940 — to graduate in turn.

There were no graduates in 1919. Of the two students who graduated in 1920, Geraldine Laven Satchell was an officer with Torrance National Bank and Polydore Rubo had died. Again, there were no graduates in 1921.

Thereafter, the graduate roll swelled. Mary Jessome Vonderake, 1923, was the editor of the Women's Section of the

151

Torrance Herald in 1943. Albert Isen, 1924, was an attorney as he is today. In the 1950s and 1960s, he was to serve many years as the accomplished albeit controversial mayor of Torrance. Harry Kiyomura, 1925, was working for Kress Wireless. Garnet Cook Sidebotham, 1926, died just as the book was going to press in the spring of 1943. Floyd Chandler, 1927, was with the California Highway Patrol; his classmate, Thomas Dougherty, was with National Supply and was an organizer for the AFL-CIO U.S.W.A.

Mildred Pannier Sherk, 1928, had become a nurse and in 1942, a prisoner of war in the Philippines. Phyllis Knoss, 1930, had graduated from USC and was now teaching at Torrance Elementary School. Her classmate, Olive Robinson, was a policewoman in Torrance. Dullas Danford, 1931, was a band leader and music arranger. Pete Zamperini, 1932, had graduated from USC and taught several years at Torrance High; now he was a chief petty officer in the Navy.

Valerie Tucker, 1933, was married and was secretary to the city clerk of Torrance. La Vern Jones, 1934, was the mechanical superintendent at the *Torrance Herald* and helped produce *Gone Forth to Serve* for his fellow graduates. George Arakawa, 1935, was in the diplomatic services in Washington, D.C.

The occupations of the graduates of more recent classes, 1936 to 1942, held few surprises. Many were in the armed services; others working for Columbia Steel, National Supply or in the shipyards. Lucille Stroh, 1936, was desk sergeant for the Torrance Police Department; her father, John Stroh, was chief from 1938 to 1954. Weston Leech, 1938, was a bomber test pilot.

The book closed with a quote from graduate Harold Stevenson that sums up the spirit of those exciting, even dangerous but straightforward and unambiguous war years:

"When this is all over, I would like to visit dear old Torrance High and talk to the gang that has been fighting with the old red and gray spirit on a team that has no substitutes or time outs, but that is a SURE WINNER."

When the war was won, Torrance welcomed home its own authentic war hero. The December 12, 1946 ceremony in honor of Captain Louis Zamperini also marked the twenty-fifth anniversary

of the incorporation of the city, and the beginning of Torrance Municipal Airport.

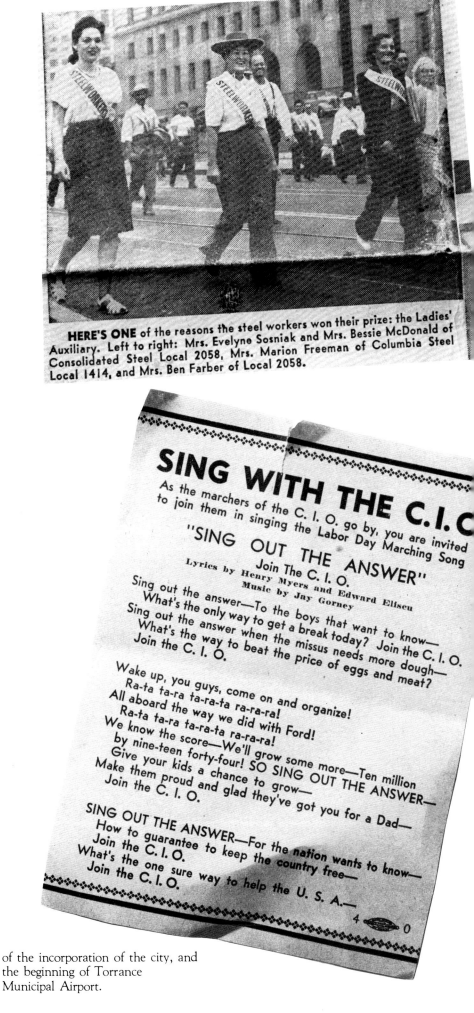

HERE'S ONE of the reasons the steel workers won their prize: the Ladies' Auxiliary. Left to right: Mrs. Evelyne Sosniak and Mrs. Bessie McDonald of Consolidated Steel Local 2058, Mrs. Marion Freeman of Columbia Steel Local 1414, and Mrs. Ben Farber of Local 2058.

SING WITH THE C.I.O

As the marchers of the C.I.O. go by, you are invited to join them in singing the Labor Day Marching Song

"SING OUT THE ANSWER"
Join The C.I.O.
Lyrics by Henry Myers and Edward Eliscu
Music by Jay Gorney

Sing out the answer—To the boys that want to know—
What's the only way to get a break today? Join the C.I.O.
Sing out the answer when the missus needs more dough—
What's the way to beat the price of eggs and meat?
Join the C.I.O.

Wake up, you guys, come on and organize!
Ra-ta ta-ra ta-ra-ta ra-ra-ra!
All aboard the way we did with Ford!
Ra-ta ta-ra ta-ra-ta ra-ra-ra!
We know the score—We'll grow some more—Ten million
by nine-teen forty-four! SO SING OUT THE ANSWER—
Give your kids a chance to grow—
Make them proud and glad they've got you for a Dad—
Join the C.I.O.

SING OUT THE ANSWER—For the nation wants to know—
How to guarantee to keep the country free—
Join the C.I.O.
What's the one sure way to help the U.S.A.—
Join the C.I.O.

4 ◆ 0

Reminiscent of *Norma Rae,* the ladies of the United Steel Workers in the Los Angeles Labor Day Parade in 1946. Third from the left is Bertha Freeman, wife of Marion Freeman, a founding member of Local 1414 here in Torrance. Marion, 77 now and retired for 14 years after 41 years working in the mill, recalls fondly that his wife, who is now deceased, "was a good union lady — matter of fact, she was on strike when I met her." When this picture was taken, the Torrance local was only four years old.

COURTESY OF MARION FREEMAN

At a time when trade unions are either taken for granted or regarded with the same skepticism accorded other entrenched American institutions, it's interesting to go back 43 years to when unions were relatively new and organizing a local was part of a great adventure. The C.I.O. — Congress of Industrial Organizations — had brought new energy and militancy to the struggle for collective bargaining. One way they kept up their members' morale was with "pep songs" like this.

COURTESY OF MARION FREEMAN

Four decades of Torrance economic history are spanned in this picture of Local 1414 founding member Marion Freeman, 77, with the 1942 charter signed by Phil Murray and Dave McDonald. He's in the front of the local's headquarters at 1316 Border Street, occupied since 1980 by Local 6700 which represents the Martin Marietta workers. Freeman retired in 1970 after 41 years in the mills. He still comes to the hall, where 1414's retirees are always welcome, usually riding his 750cc motorcycle.

PHOTO BY WM. FRIDRICH

During the war, a 480-acre airport had been built on Weston Ranch property in southwestern Torrance by the Army Air Corps. It served as an auxiliary field for training pilots and crewmen to fly military aircraft, and had the advantage of being close to Fort MacArthur and to the coast, but sheltered by the Palos Verdes hill in such a way that it rarely was fogged in.

On the twenty-fifth anniversary of the city's formation, a solemn ceremony was held at the airfield to mark the turning over to the city of an 89-acre parcel, the heart of the airport. Ben Weston, the original owner of the land used as a training field by the federal government during the war, and the Federal Public Roads Bureau both abandoned any further claim to that portion of the airport.

Because of its proximity to Lomita on the east, the airport had formerly been known as the "Lomita Flight Strip." But on that day in 1946, Torrance Municipal Airport came into being and in honor of Captain Zamperini was designated "Zamperini Field."

Zamperini had survived 47 days in an open raft in the Pacific after his plane crashed during a bombing mission. He was harshly treated in a Japanese prisoner of war camp and returned to Torrance more than a year after he was officially declared dead by U.S. authorities unaware of his capture.

Quicker action was expected, but the federal War Assets Administration did not turn over a quitclaim deed to the balance of the airport land until March, 1948.

Almost immediately, bulldozers began carving out a new, wider entrance to the field and the city began drafting permanent leases for the flight schools, aircraft repair shops and other businesses already on the site.

The city that now had its own airport was ready to fly in a figurative sense as well — from the Los Angeles School District. Torrance voters elected in August, 1946, to create a separate Torrance school system with its own superintendent hired by an elected five-member Torrance School Board, beginning with the fall term in 1947.

When Torrance opted out of the Los Angeles district, Los Angeles tried to strip the schools of furniture and supplies and even transplant several bungalows at Torrance Elementary.

Thanks to Fay Parks, Judge Shidler, Attorney S.V.O. Pritchard and the *Torrance Herald*, Los Angeles' fit of pique was thwarted. They even had to return two bungalows which already had been spirited away. ("Stop that bungalow!")

Obviously, the split was not without pain on both sides. To actually create the new district, Torrance not only had to sue the Los Angeles district, but had to impose a special tax to operate the schools, then attended by 1,991 children. State aid in the amount of $180,000 which would have gone to Torrance-area schools operated by Los

Angeles went to the Los Angeles district instead, because the new Torrance district had no record of average daily attendance in the previous year. Money was raised by public subscription to carry on the victorious legal fight.

All five of the public schools in Torrance when the district was formed already had active PTA organizations. Those groups got together on July 18, 1947, at the new office of the Torrance Board of Education to create the Torrance Council of PTAs. J.H. Hull, Torrance's founding superintendent of schools, was present, as were these local PTA presidents: Mrs. A.C. Turner of Torrance High; Mrs. E.S. Moon of Torrance Elementary; Mrs. B.J. Michels of Walteria Elementary; Mrs. V.T. Vanderpool of Fern Avenue Elementary; and Mrs. A.B. Cowie of Perry Elementary School.

After approval from the First District PTA, the council was formally organized on December 9, 1947, at a meeting in the Torrance High auditorium.

By 1949, there were seven schools in Torrance; Seaside and Casimir elementary schools had been added. The phenomenal growth of Torrance in the 1950s brought that total to 32 by 1959, including two new high schools: North, added in 1955; and South, opened in 1957. Reflecting the post-World War Two baby booms, the Torrance district opened its thirty-ninth and fortieth schools — Levy and Wright

Some of the continent's top industrialists, publishers and politicians gathered in Torrance in the mid-1950s for a U.S. Steel Board of Directors meeting. In the front row, left to right, are Alex C. Nagle, president of the First National Bank of New York; George Sloan, publisher of *Southern Agriculturist*; Matthew Miller, general counsel and former governor of New York; Arthur Andersen, vice president of J.P. Morgan & Co. and later founder of one of the "Big 5" national accounting firms; Cason Callaway, director of Chemical Bank & Trust; Enders Voorhees, chairman of the U.S. Steel finance committee; Ben Fairless, president of U.S. Steel; chairman of the board Irving Olds; former president Will Irvin; Phillips Clarke, president of Federal Securities; International Nickel of Canada's president Robert Stanley; and a local boy amidst all those eastern luminaries, James Black, president of Pacific Gas & Electric. Behind them, the second team, left to right, are Al Puetz, Torrance works auditor; John Osmers; H.P. Dotson; J.G. Cummings; Gus Nanert; Carl Wittenberg; Frank DeLong; A. Averell Brown; Lee Pringle; "Pop" Gray; W.A. Ross, president of Columbia Steel Co.; O.A. Kresse, general superintendent of the works; T. Marshall Ohris, superintendent of the rolling mill; T. Carlisle McDonald; and Lee Sharp.

A dramatic reminder of how far the once mighty American steel industry has fallen: 29 years ago, in the early days of television, the *U.S. Steel Hour* gave its Torrance employees a feeling of pride and of belonging to a nation-wide family. Originally the Llewellyn Iron Works, constructed in 1916 when three brothers from Wales accepted Sidney Torrance's invitation to build here, it was acquired by West Coast-based Columbia Steel in 1923. U.S. Steel took over the Columbia works in 1930.

— in 1966. But thereafter, the school age population began to decline dramatically.

Just three years after the last two schools were built, the Torrance district began a conservative program of campus closures by shutting down Madison School. By 1979, there were only 33 member schools in the Torrance Council of PTAs.

Over the years, the Torrance Council of PTAs has had a history of political activism. Six bond issues and tax overrides were approved by Torrance voters between 1948 and 1967 with the active support of the Torrance council, and they often won by stunning 10-to-1 margins. In 1982, the Torrance Council of PTAs was honored by the California State PTA as the outstanding council in the state.

Torrance schools, too, have a long-standing reputation for excellence. All are fully accredited, and have long been noted for offering quality education. Torrance students generally are above average in national tests and gather more than their share of National Merit scholarships and other awards.

Torrance was starting off in new directions with its airport and its new school district during the 1940s. But an even bigger step in getting ready for the truly explosive growth ahead was revamping the form of city government. In 1946, a city charter was proposed and approved by the Legislature. It was not until 1948 that Torrance voters approved the document as well.

Until then, Torrance had been governed by a mayor and city council, and the mayor usually wielded considerable power, though he and the council were part-timers with other jobs, often with the major industries in town. The new charter established a paid, full-time professional city manager as the prime city administrator, with the mayor and council in policy-making roles.

But if Torrance was making big changes during the 1940s to prepare for the future, it also was still carrying on at least one continuing small-town tradition: the Factory Frolic.

Thirty years after she served as the reigning monarch at the Factory Frolic, Miss Industry 1948, Tallulah Nagy, was recalling how she earned that title.

"My mother kept nagging me to. Just to please her, I did it. That's the only contest I've ever gotten in."

Tallulah, 17 at the time and a Torrance High student, sold 54,000 tickets at 25 cents each to get the title. In 1978, she lived in Costa Mesa, was married and had two children.

She recalled that her prize included "a nice trip to New York." She flew from the fledgling Torrance Municipal Airport on Arrow Airways to New York.

In New York City, a General Petroleum Co. official showed her the sights. She dutifully tried to deliver a small keg of nails from Columbia Steel's Torrance works to Mayor Wm. O'Dwyer of New York, but ended up turning them over to an aide in an outer office instead.

She was keeping in touch with her former Torrance High School classmates in 1978, and through her many moves during three decades, was still carrying with her a box containing scrapbooks recalling that special Factory Frolic. It was the sort of event only a small town with great pride in its large factories — the strength of industrial America — would carry on.

There is some evidence that there were a few more Factory Frolics. But even in 1948, it was clear that Torrance was growing dramatically, had already outgrown many of the trappings of its small-town past, and was ready to grapple with the big changes ahead in the 1950s.

10 YEARS AS A COUNTERSPY... BY BORIS MORROS

LOOK

20¢ NOVEMBER 26, 1957 ★

A bustling California city earns an All America City Award for keeping ahead of its problems

STARTLING EXPANSION has been the story of this small city south of Los Angeles, since it was founded in 1913. Beginning as a planned community of 300 persons, by 1947 it had a population of 13,000. In 1957, it is a model combination of major industry and small homes with a population of over 92,000. Such rapid growth could have been expected to lead to all kinds of housing, school, traffic and crime problems, but they simply don't exist

in Torrance. When the city's dedicated mayor, Albert Isen, submitted his community's case for an All America City Award, he could report that his city had never had organized crime, vice or corruption. The award sponsors — LOOK and the National Municipal League — found that Torrance has grown and prospered without ever needing a cleanup. For such an outstanding record, Torrance is one of 11 recipients this year of All America City Awards.

TORRANCE: Growth without strain

City Manager George Stevens, in office nine years, credits members of City Council for much of Torrance's record. He cites their high standards of public service and their work in behalf of equitable tax rates and long-range improvement programs for the community.

continued

Torrance takes off: is voted "All-America"

Workers, homeowners and anti-war demonstrators make themselves heard; explosive growth gets awards for minimum strain.

Though it looks like a scene in downtown Berlin in 1945, this is actually the Kaiser Steel plant in Fontana in May, 1951, as a long line of Pacific Electric 1200 series cars from the Torrance shop are broken up for scrap. The automobile, especially as it became both cheap and reliable, and the paving of at least the main arterials had almost spelled the end of the interurban cars in the late 1930s. Then the war, gas rationing and a suspension in auto production gave them another decade's lease on life. The postwar boom and freeway construction — the Long Beach Freeway in the late 1950s, for example — finished the job. Unaware of how we would miss them, or how nostalgically we would recall their merits, we consigned the streetcars to the wreckers in scrap yards like these.

FROM THE A.E. BARKER COLLECTION

Torrance won the honor of being named as an "All-America City" in late 1956, but it was not until November, 1957, that *Look* magazine, then a major national weekly magazine, made good on a promise to profile the town. Torrance's fantastic growth in the previous decade was trumpeted, along with its claim to have achieved that growth without strain. And city manager George Stevens, who administered city government through the period, was shown in proud profile, though he was careful to credit members of the city council for Torrance's achievements.

PHOTO BY WM. FRIDRICH

Growth was the watchword of Torrance in the 1950s and 1960s. The city even won awards for "growth without strain" for thriving on a pace of growth which was truly phenomenal.

Beginning with 5,538 dwellings and 22,241 residents in 1950, by 1970 Torrance had 45,293 units and what may have been the city's peak

population to date of 134,584 residents.

Where there had been only 527 people per square mile in 1940, in 1950 there were 1,177 and in 1970 there were 6,568. On its way to suburbia, Torrance had become an urban place.

Why that residential boom came, how the South Bay aerospace industry contributed to it, and the ways the city managed growth are interesting subjects for exploration.

The 1950s and 1960s were the era in which downtown Torrance was far surpassed as the commercial center of the city by the shopping mall that began to rise at Del Amo, a period in which the social unrest of the 1960s reached to the quiet, well-manicured lawns of Torrance and echoed outside

the walls of its generally well-run factories. It was a period of growth, and growth is often painful.

To a certain extent, the story of Torrance's post-World War Two boom is the story of America in that age, when the veterans of that last popular war came home. Their plans were to marry the girls who'd sent perfumed letters while they were away. They settled down in suburban tract houses with lawns to tend; cars, appliances and furniture to buy; exciting new devices called televisions; and three children — and a dog — to raise.

Perhaps because of the nature of the aerospace industry, on the whole the new Torrance families were very young, and had above-average educations and above-average salaries with which to buy the pleasures of suburban living.

Some idea of the pace at which the city grew in those early years can be gained from special censuses taken in January, 1952, November, 1953, and September, 1955. They found 31,834 residents, then 44,014, and finally 67,459. There were 6,900 telephones in Torrance in 1951; two years later, there were 10,213.

Though we often talk of the early 1950s as the "postwar" period, there was another war on at the time that also helped to boost the economy of Torrance.

Douglas Aircraft, now McDonnell Douglas, opened facilities in Torrance in 1952 because of that Korean War. A 1.3-million-square-foot facility operated by Alcoa during World War Two stood empty after U.S. Steel bought it in 1948.

When Korea heated up, Douglas' El Segundo facility was building the powerful AD-Skyraider attack bomber for the U.S. Navy. The planes were highly effective, attacking the Korean mainland daily from Navy carriers offshore and carrying a load of bombs, rockets and torpedoes to equal anything the four-engine B-17 Fortesses delivered during World War Two. So to get the planes assembled more quickly, the Navy started condemnation proceedings against the site at 190th Street and Normandie Avenue and leased it to Douglas.

On August 18, 1952, just 21 days after remodeling began, the plant was ready to begin aircraft assembly.

By 1956, Douglas Aircraft Co. claimed to provide more jobs than any other firm in Torrance. About one-third of the undeveloped land in the city at the time was still zoned for industrial purposes, in accord with the original vision of the city as a balanced community with room for housing, factories and stores.

Other industrial firms that had found Torrance attractive by then were Rome Cable Corp., Carbide & Carbon Chemical Co., Reynolds Metals Co., General Aluminum Corp., Dow Chemical, Pittsburgh Paints, American Standard, Rubbercraft Corp., North American Aviation, Sheridan-Gray, Longren Aircraft, Hi-Shear Rivet & Tool, and Great Lakes Carbon.

By 1956, there also were more than 100 other small industries in Torrance, plus the giants which had been here for decades, including U.S. Steel, General Petroleum and National Supply.

And as the new suburban neighborhoods spread across the open spaces of Torrance, city government prospered as well. In 1956, the city already had a new central fire headquarters at Carson Street and

Crenshaw Boulevard. And a new civic center complex on Torrance Boulevard on 35 acres was under construction, with a new city hall, police station, county courthouse and community swimming pool — the Victor E. Benstead Plunge — as part of the initial phase of development.

A city directory of the day quaintly lists five dealers of "television apparatus," including the De Bra Radio Co. on Cabrillo Avenue. Also on Cabrillo Avenue near the heart of the business district was Ding How's Restaurant. And out on Hawthorne Boulevard at Torrance Boulevard, near the spot where the future main business district of Torrance would soon begin to rise, were open fields and a drive-in restaurant on the northwest corner called Mary's Little Lamb.

By 1956, the town had grown phenomenally, but there were still only two banks, Bank of America and California Bank, the former Post family bank which had been sold to a larger

When Torrance was honored by the National Municipal League in 1956 by being named as an "All-America City," it was partly due to the efforts of thousands of Torrance schoolchildren who were encouraged by Superintendent J.H. Hull to write letters explaining why they thought the honor was appropriate. In these photos, Mayor Albert Isen reviews some of the letters, and shares the letter announcing the city's selection with Gaye Wilson, then Miss Torrance, and assistant city manager Don Mansfield, who prepared the information required to complete the application form for the contest. Eleven American cities were so honored in 1956. Thus, the "All-America" designation was an allusion to football.

COURTESY OF ALBERT ISEN

158

branch banking operation. Two savings and loans had come to town, however, and one offered a whopping 3.5 percent interest and stayed open Fridays until 7:30 p.m.

The Palos Verdes Begonia Farm in Walteria, then the largest nursery at the south end of town, scolded that "a house is not a home until it is planted."

The suburban dream house with a well-manicured yard was a powerful lure in those days, and the real estate section of the Yellow Pages for Torrance in 1956 is one of the largest categories in the book. There are also lots of garden supply and equipment stores, and furniture stores, since a house is not a home without furniture, either.

Surprisingly, through the greatest portion of the explosive growth of the 1950s and 1960s, one man served as mayor. And though he presided over a city of newcomers, he was not a newcomer himself, having arrived in 1913 at the age of six. That man was Albert Isen, a member of the Class of 1924 at Torrance High School, an attorney who served as mayor of Torrance longer than any other man — from April, 1955 until April, 1970. Despite the city manager form of government, which tended to put most administrative power in the manager's

hands, Isen was a strong mayor.

When the rest of the city council decided to discontinue the municipal bus system, he refused to sign the necessary papers.

"The jails run at a loss, the police department runs at a loss," he says today. "It was one of the vital functions of the city. I can be awfully stubborn when I want to be."

He was so stubborn on that issue, in fact, that he carried the day. And plans for a new bus facility in the near future at the civic center complex call for naming that structure after Isen as a tribute to his foresight.

Isen was active in the founding of the Armed Forces Day Parade, persuading court authorities to locate a county courthouse in Torrance, and Sears, Roebuck & Co. and Broadway to build stores in a new shopping center on then-deserted Hawthorne Boulevard, just north of Sepulveda Boulevard. This was on the spot where J.J. Millard raised mushrooms from the 1930s through the early 1950s.

"If we didn't encourage the original Sears/Broadway deal," Isen says now,

It almost seems as though there is an inverse relationship between the pace of activity in old Torrance and the number of municipal admonitions felt necessary to direct its course. Graduation from an Evelyn Wood speed reading course was almost called for, if a driver were to be fully informed!

We wonder what Sidney Torrance would have thought of this photo, shot in the mid-1950s at Torrance Boulevard and Western Avenue. It was intended, presumably, to convey the impression of a city with plenty of open spaces, pretty ladies and ... oh yes, industrial opportunity. Our city's contribution to the national resources in the area of pretty ladies includes Bo Derek and Cindy Jordan, whose pictures are included in this book to prove that history need not be a dull subject.

Klink's Cabrillo Market at 2323 Cabrillo Avenue, operated by J. Robert Klink throughout the 1950s, offered "carots" for 11 cents for two bunches, watermelon at two-and-a-half cents per pound, and free delivery. The Klink family still maintains their home on El Prado in Torrance today. This photograph apparently was made prior to May 31, 1953, since both the sign on the then-popular "woodie"-style delivery Jeep and a sign painted on the window of the store advertise the phone number to call for delivery as 1682. The four-digit telephone numbers were used for operator-assisted calls in downtown Torrance and vicinity until May 31, 1953, when the Pacific Telephone & Telegraph Co. converted the area to a customer-dialed system and replaced the four-digit numbers with seven-digit numbers beginning with the prefixes DAvenport 6 or FAirfax 8. The new number for the Cabrillo Market was FAirfax 8-7574. FRontier was the prefix for the Riviera section of Torrance adopted at the time that automatically routed self-dialed calls were instituted. By 1969, the more colorful word prefixes had been abandoned.

PHOTO BY BOB ROBERTS

"they were going to Lomita. Then we would have had all the traffic and other problems without the revenue."

Isen also recalls battling against locally influential developers who wanted to create the first and only cemetery in Torrance. "I was against having a cemetery in town. They wanted to put it right next to New Horizons.

"I stood my ground," he says. "I thought I was right and I still think I was right." There is still no cemetery within the city limits today.

He also was involved in a fight to keep the Coast Freeway from being built in the general vicinity of Pacific Coast Highway during the 1960s, a project with three proposed routes that all would have done major damage to the Riviera and Walteria sections and other prime neighborhoods.

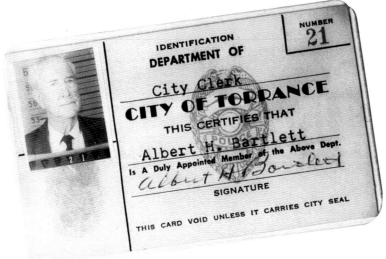

"I had fights every week," Isen says, "because the town was growing and we had honest differences of opinion. It was quite a period. It wasn't always fun."

He seems to have only two regrets about those 15 years. One relates to 1963, when the Congress of Racial Equality chose builder Don Wilson's Southwood tract in Torrance as a target for picketing on the issue of opening housing to all, regardless of race, religion or creed. Isen responded flippantly to a reporter who asked him at a mayor's conference out of town: "Do you really have a colored problem in Torrance?"

Isen's blithe answer went home and flashed around the world on international news wires: "No, because we don't have any (colored people)!"

But to this day he says with considerable embarassment: "I didn't mean anything at all by it."

Actor Marlon Brando led one parade in that protest that marched from the Del Amo parking lot to the tract's model homes at Anza and Calle Mayor. Though the police monitored the parade, "we weren't involved in the controversy at all," Isen says.

When the builder agreed to sell to all without discriminating, a check presented by a CORE-backed family that wanted to buy a house bounced. Isen says he was then convinced the whole thing was for media attention, not for fair housing in Torrance. "I don't think they wanted to settle. I think they wanted the publicity."

His other regret is that the city boundaries and the postal boundaries are not one and the same. Some Torrance residents have Redondo Beach addresses, others Gardena or Lomita. If all Torrance residents were given Torrance mailing addresses, he says, "I think it would be a unification factor for the city."

One accomplishment of which Isen is particularly proud is the All-America City Award Torrance announced in 1956, less than two years after he became mayor. It all started one night when he came home late from a Shrine gathering. His wife, Sarah, was angry about that. He had trouble sleeping, he recalls.

Downtown Torrance as seen from the air in October, 1957. This picture shows downtown looking southwest, with Western Avenue and Torrance Boulevard in the middle foreground. Some oil derricks still can be seen on open land between Carson Street and Sepulveda Boulevard.

"I got up real early and the *Times* hadn't come yet." So he sat down to read *Look* magazine, discovered a short notice of the All-America City competition and clipped it to suggest Torrance become involved in the contest. Assistant City Manager Don Mansfield prepared the response to the application and the city spent $600 to print a brochure about Torrance and another $600 to send Isen and his wife by train to Memphis.

Isen took the precaution of having eleven "Oh-So-Soft" inflatable seat cushions specially made at Rubbercraft in Torrance, with the city's name on them, to distribute to the judges from the National Municipal League. He rightly guessed they would be sitting on hard chairs listening to presentations for hours. Isen figured the cushions would help the judges "keep their minds on Torrance."

Unfortunately, he recalls, "they were blown up here (in Torrance) and then

they were sent airmail. And because of the altitude, the air was out of them and one was all torn up" when they arrived at the Peabody. So Isen and his wife had to blow up the ten surviving cushions all over again themselves.

After making the judges comfortable, Isen made a formal 15-minute speech extolling the wonders of the city manager form of government in managing Torrance's amazing postwar growth. Then when someone asked, among other things, what the city does about Southern California's most famous scourge, smog, Isen cracked: "We blow it to Pasadena!"

Another interesting aspect of the lobbying effort which Torrance carried out to become an All-America City was a schoolchildren's letter-writing campaign: 18,000 letters, from a student body of 21,000. Put another way, six out of every seven students wrote a letter. And, of course, they're wonderful to browse through 28 years later:

A gathering of Torrance city executives from the 1950s, left to right: Councilman George Powell; Ralph Perkins; Water Department head Angus McVicar; Building Superintendent John V. Russell; Fire Chief John Renner; Ladeen Chamberlin, secretary to City Manager George Stevens; Police Chief Percy Bennett; Parks and Recreation Superintendent Harry Van Bellehem; City Engineer Ron Bishop; Bus Superintendent Marshall Chamberlin; and Assistant to the City Manager, John R. Patrick.

"Torrance should be the All-America City for 1956 because it has more people come to it each and every year. Torrance used to be a little city until more and more people came and it grew to be a big city," wrote Gary Inman.

Here's an image to conjure up: "It's a nice city and the people are mice," another child wrote.

But for every letter that brings a smile, there's another good enough to be included in a Chamber of Commerce brochure.

"Over 7,000 people have moved here (since I did). They have found good jobs ... good schools for their children, fine places of entertainment and good shopping centers. I myself have enjoyed living in Torrance very much," wrote Judy McCully, an eighth grade student at Arlington School.

The Chamber of Commerce would have

beamed at this: "The shopping centers are clean and honest. The manufacturing plants are all equipped with modern machinery and able-bodied men to work them. ... The papers are not in Torrance's streets. They are in the cans provided for that reason," wrote Judy Rich, also of Arlington School.

Another student had a personal reason for touting Torrance: "They're fixing streets in front of our school so that when it rains children will not have to walk in puddles."

And Elizabeth Mason, a fifth grader at Seaside, expressed one of her reasons for living in Torrance with heartfelt conciseness: "The teachers are not grumpy, thank goodness!"

Many of the children's thoughts were echoed by *Look* magazine in its November, 1957 coverage of the city's accomplishments. They accepted Mayor Isen's claim that the city "had never

Little Company of Mary Hospital on Torrance Boulevard as it was being completed in 1962. It has 268 beds; Torrance Memorial on Lomita Boulevard has 325. Torrance now has two general hospitals and major medical office centers which have grown up around both of them.
PHOTO BY PAUL COMON

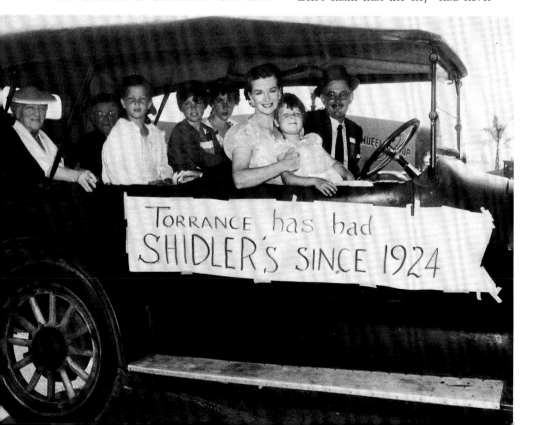

One of Torrance's most distinguished families is headed by Superior Court Judge John Shidler, now retired, and his wife, Rosemary De Camp Shidler, an actress who has starred on radio, television and in films for many years. In this photograph taken during the early 1950s, the Shidlers ride in a car of the sort Shidler's father, Dr. George Shidler, could conceivably have driven here from York, Nebraska in 1924. Those in the car, from left, are Rosemary's mother, Margaret De Camp, Shidler's mother, Mina Shidler, daughters Valerie, Martha and Margaret, Rosemary De Camp Shidler, daughter Nita and Judge Shidler.

When Torrance National Bank affiliated with Calbank in 1954, the father and son team on left and right here were active in the bank's affairs. James Wallace Post, left, was the son of Judge George W. Post who had come from York, Nebraska, in 1913 to join Sidney Torrance in building the new town and lending stability to its financial structure. James W. Post's sister, Mildred, married Dr. Jesse Lancaster, also from York. With Dr. George Shidler, father of Judge John Shidler, Lancaster was one of the town's first physicians. James W. Post's son, George, on the right, is now president of The Torrance National Bank. The charming ladies in the middle were tellers Camille Burt, Doris Royko and Lenora Gray.

had organized crime, vice or corruption."

They were impressed with a typical multiple-use accomplishment by City Manager George Stevens: "The city bought waste land, now sells sand from it, uses hole as city dump, will cover area for a park."

They showed School Superintendent J.H. Hull working on a nail keg seat in a converted store in 1947, and contrasted that with 1956. They pointed to the welcome given new industries like Duschak's Helicopter Rotor Service. (They're still here 27 years later, on Abalone Street.)

They noted how the whole community had rallied to help polio victim Fred Diesel. Fred, however, died in 1960 at

Population, which tripled between 1948 and 1960, was already nearing 100,000. But the citizens of Torrance seemed determined to act as if they all still knew each other. So they held a big block party.

There was a big city-wide general assembly in the Torrance High School auditorium. There was a reception in the American Legion Hall, a banquet for 400 in the Municipal Auditorium and then a dance at the Legion Hall. State Attorney General Pat Brown was the featured speaker at the banquet. Douglas J. Horlander was the chairman of the citizen's committee.

City Manager George Stevens and Chamber of Commerce director Dick Fitzgerald felt satisfaction at the way

the age of 21. The only child of William and Louise Diesel, Torrance residents since 1920, he contracted polio in 1952, before the Salk and Sabin vaccines were developed.

Isen says he believes the Look article really put Torrance on the map. "I'm convinced that industry came to Torrance because of this article."

The last rural free delivery route in Torrance, on Normandie Avenue, was closed in 1957, "due to increasing urbanization of the area," the post office announced.

But when Torrance celebrated its selection as an All-America City on January 25 and 26, 1957, it did so with a small-town flavor and zest which was ironic, even touching, considering that the award from Look magazine and the National Municipal League was for "the orderly handling of problems arising from phenomenal and rapid growth."

cooperation between the city and business interests had helped make it happen. Rev. Walter M. Stanton and Father P.J. McGuinness gave the invocations. And, of course, it was Mayor Al Isen's time to shine.

Cold weather and biting winds couldn't diminish the city's enthusiasm for the event. Why, there were three beauty queens riding in the parade, all bundled up against the weather: Barbara Cage, 17, of North Torrance for the Fuschia Society, though her float had hundreds of red and blue imitation roses instead of fuschias; Carol Morris, who was Miss Universe of 1956, and was sponsored by the Torrance First Christian Church, whose pastor was a close friend of her father; and Gaye Wilson, Miss Torrance, 1956.

The Torrance Youth Band played all over town, it seemed. The Adventurer's Club of the YMCA put 400 boys in the backs of dozens of trucks for

165

the parade.

And each of Torrance's schools had an official representative pupil in the parade. School growth — from 1,772 pupils in four schools in 1947 to 19,000 pupils in 20 schools in 1957, with four more scheduled to open in a few months — was one of the most dramatic elements in the Torrance story.

The pupils selected to represent their classmates were Carol Atkins, North High; Mary Yoshioka, Torrance High; Linda Appling, Casimir; Roy Dohner, Perry; Richard Hardesty, Walteria; Judy McCutcheon, Howard Wood; Tom Anders, Sepulveda; Les Eyestone, Arlington; Mason Wolpert, Evelyn Carr; Jo Anne Pabst, Crenshaw; Janet Moon, El Nido; Ronnie Campbell,

Fern-Greenwood; Jack Pierce, Hillside; Regina Larson, Madrona; Aggie Sampecio, Meadow Park; Sandra Douglass, Newton; Robbie Hall, Riviera; Kathy Miller, Seaside; Pat Biren, Carol Steele and Robert Weister, Torrance Elementary.

But overall, it was a weekend for celebration and Torrance made the most of it. Manuel Dominguez and Sidney Torrance would have enjoyed being there, too; they both thought the South Bay was a good place to turn dreams into reality.

As a footnote to the story of Torrance's 1956 All-America City Award, the city tried for a second such award ten years later, in 1966, but was not among the finalists.

A pleasant constant in Torrance for the past quarter century has been the sight of the young men and women leaving the Bishop Montgomery Catholic High School on Torrance Boulevard every school day afternoon, heading for home. George Montgomery, after whom the school was named in 1957 at its founding, was the first Bishop of the Diocese of Los Angeles. Patriotic exercises, like this flag-raising ceremony, have always played an important part in school activities.

Like all community organizations, the Torrance Area Youth Band has usually had to raise its own funds for expensive projects like this 1957 trip to a Chicago band clinic. Hence this album. A lot of nighttime tootling filled the air over Torrance through the years as band members practiced. Did you ever live next door to a novice tuba player? But a lot of parents' hearts swelled with pride later when the band played.
PHOTO BY WM. FRIDRICH

West High School in 1963 as it neared completion. Each of the four Torrance public high schools has carved out particular claims to fame over the years. West High's are the high caliber of its volleyball program and, more importantly, in 1984 it was recognized as one of the top high schools in the country in academic resources and in such criteria as faculty advanced degrees and teacher-to-pupil ratio.
PHOTO BY PAUL COMON

Also, by sheer coincidence, apparently, during the twenty fiscal years from 1949 to 1969, Torrance city government ran deficits in only two years: fiscal 1956-57, when the city won the All-America City Award for accomplishing growth without strain, and 1966-67, the year of that second, unsuccessful bid for the same title.

Failure to win a second All-America City Award was one of City Manager Ed Ferraro's few defeats in his twenty-year tenure. Until 1983, he presided over a bureaucracy (it needn't be pejorative) which gave Torrance its nation-wide reputation as a well-run, prosperous city.

Like Mayor Isen, Dick Fitzgerald saw Torrance in the 1950s from a unique vantage point — as manager of the Chamber of Commerce from 1955 to 1960. Isen is given credit by Fitzgerald for getting the Harbor Freeway to run near the southeastern edge of town.

Fitzgerald recalls some of the leading figures in town with affection: Sam Levy, "a hell of a man;" George Vico, a 1950s' councilman who worked for the Dominguez Water Co. and was a former ballplayer for the Detroit Tigers ("He hit a home run his first time up in the majors."); Jay Beasley, a liberal from Walteria known as "Buckskin."

He recalls that Torrance hadn't had a Rose Parade entry for many years, until participation was revived in the late 1950s. Ryan Aircraft built a "Spirit of St. Louis" to scale as the entry. "Then we got no cooperation at all from Charles Lindbergh, and we had a battle with the Tournament people because the word RYAN was on the tail in small letters, just like on the original plane."

Some other business leaders whom Fitzgerald remembers from the 1950s are Tommy Thompson, the Mobil plant manager; Don Hyde of U.S. Steel; Fred Mills of National Supply; Dick Pyle from the phone company; John Obbinghaus, Bob Plomert and Orville Trueblood. He holds Kenny Uyeda, involved with the planning commission in those busy times and into the 1970s, in high regard.

Among journalists, he recalls especially Reid Bundy, who used to edit the *Torrance Herald*, and now edits the *Peninsula News* in Palos Verdes, and Bob Currie, for years the publisher who made policy at the *Daily Breeze*.

If there is any snobbery among cities — and, of course, there is — one touchstone might be if a city has its own charter, which allows the governing body to write its own basic laws, or whether it is a "general law" city,

functioning under the general provisions of state laws. Torrance has its own charter, which provides for a council-manager form of government, with the council setting policy and the city manager administering the mundane but important daily details of practical government.

Torrance's charter was not easily achieved. Torrance was a general law city until 1946, when a charter ballot proposal carried 1,385-to-771. An earlier effort to achieve a charter in 1931 had failed. The 1946 charter made it possible, for one thing, to form an independent Torrance Unified School District. Such a district was initiated, of course, in 1947.

Torrance's mayor, incidentally, has no

affectionately and vividly.

He came to Torrance from Culver City where he'd been City Engineer and Chief Administrative Officer after World War Two military service. His friends in Culver City thought he was leaving an oceanliner for a rowboat when he came to Torrance. But with extraordinary prescience, Stevens "could see a future."

"They had the land and the jobs. The industry was here already. There was the desire to grow." These were his feelings when he started here January 1, 1948.

He thinks the City Council and the Chamber of Commerce weren't afraid of industry and weren't afraid to go after it. "I'm from Santa Barbara," he says,

Father Patrick McGuinness, center, at a colorful outdoor ceremony a quarter of a century ago at Nativity Church on Engracia Avenue. The congregation met as early as 1918 or 1919 in a school building on Cabrillo Avenue. Then the wooden church at Cota and Manuel was built and in 1922, the present edifice on Engracia. Father McGuinness was also for many years the pastor for the congregation at St. Joseph's, the church built on Del Amo for the scores of Mexican-American families whose breadwinners often worked for nearby Columbia Steel. Other early churches in Torrance were St. Andrew's Episcopal, First Baptist, First Methodist, First Christian and Central Evangelical. No provision for churches had been made in the master plan; worshipers were expected to pitch in and rent an office building for Sunday use, or pitch a tent, and then move through fund-raising to lot acquisition and construction. Which, of course, they did!

veto power partial or complete, as does the mayor of Redondo Beach, for example, who can kill or carry a 3-2 vote by Redondo City Council. Torrance's mayor is elected as mayor but thereafter — though he presides over council meetings — he is one vote among seven council members, all elected at large to overlapping four-year terms.

Amendments to the Torrance charter have been made over the years. One, in 1948, introduced the city manager system. Another, in 1966, prohibited the public display of female breasts.

Torrance's first city manager was George Stevens. Stevens was city manager of Torrance from 1948 to 1961, 13 years of rapid growth, including the year Torrance was an All-America City. Still hale and hearty, he lives with his wife in nearby Rancho Palos Verdes and remembers that hectic 12 years

"and you mention industry there and they bog right down."

Special censuses were required all through the 1950s to persuade funding authorities that the city was entitled to much more than it received just a few years before.

With city services strained to the limit, when a new city hall was built on Torrance Boulevard, Stevens and the council fought off criticism that they were moving the civic center to the outskirts of town. Some said, "And they'll never need all that space either." They acquired the parcel at Madrona Avenue and Torrance Boulevard from something called the South Bay Railroad Co. at bargain rates only rivaled by the terms of the Alaska Purchase.

In Stevens' time, El Nido Triangle, north of 190th and west of Hawthorne, was annexed. So was the Victor Tract,

Torrance people knew how to have a good time thirty years ago. This lively group, young and old alike, are watching cartoons at the 1952 Factory Frolic. The man wearing the hat in the left middle is Raymond J. Derloo, a beekeeper and amateur photographer. Jim Giacalone of Torrance Camera, active in the Kiwanis, is leaning across the counter. Harry Van Bellehem, Torrance's long-time Parks and Recreation Director, is on the far right. The whole town could still come out for such events, confident they'd meet friends and neighbors. But the period of rapid growth had begun and in less than ten years, population would exceed 100,000.

PHOTO BY PAUL COMON

The Armed Forces Day Parade has been a proud feature of Torrance life since 1960, when Mayor Al Isen, Chamber of Commerce manager Dick Fitzgerald, Bob Horlander and others organized it as a tribute to their friends and fellow Torrance citizens who served in the National Guard. It has grown over the years to be one of America's largest and most eagerly awaited demonstrations of old-fashioned patriotism and love of country.

a big gulch in county territory between Torrance and Del Amo boulevards, from Hawthorne Boulevard to the Redondo line. And the growing giant, Torrance, almost annexed the unincorporated peninsula, land that is now Rolling Hills Estates and part of Rancho Palos Verdes. Stevens thinks it was simple snobbery in the hills that motivated opposition to the plan, because all the economic factors favored it.

One of Stevens' vivid memories is of the

scrambling they did to provide services for a city that was growing sevenfold in 12 years. They needed a fire engine, and when they went shopping, they found two which some luckless municipality had ordered and now couldn't pay for. So they snapped up the "twofer" at a bargain rate, confident that they'd need the second engine soon enough.

It was during this same period that Stevens worked with Congressman Cecil

R. King to help Torrance get final title to the entire city airport.

After he resigned in 1961, George Stevens joined the State Department and served two terms as a senior advisor on municipal government in Turkey.

Stevens' tenure as city manager included the year the world's largest shopping center began in Torrance. As early as 1952, farsighted men like Realtor Gerald Alter could see that the downtown Torrance business district was not keeping pace with the growth of the rest of the city.

"Torrance actually has had such a remarkable and almost unprecedented growth in the past 12 years," Alter wrote in an article published in 1952, "that our business district has lagged behind in proportionate expansion for a city of this size. However, new buildings and an increase in size of those already here is steadily going forward to bring this downtown section in the future up to the size needed for a community this large. Torrance, actually, is now the

shopping center for a population area of more than 100,000."

Alas, downtown failed to rally to the challenge and ultimately suffered from the fact that it was now too far from the geographic center of the city as well. But it was to be six more years before Sears and Broadway began to build the first stores in an open-air mall on Hawthorne Boulevard between Carson Street and Sepulveda Boulevard. When they began to build in 1958, you could still get eggs at K's Poultry Ranch on Emerald Street, at the Knotty Pine Egg Ranch on 182nd Street, or at the Olding Egg Ranch on Newton Street. The *Daily Breeze* was published in Redondo Beach but kept a Torrance office at 1618 Cravens Avenue and Marina Federal Savings & Loan was paying four percent interest on savings. But the shopping center was just one of the many other changes in the air.

Radio, which had been the home entertainment king for forty years, was being displaced rapidly in Torrance living rooms by the television set. Where a 1956 Torrance directory listed

radio dealers and said "see television-radio dealers," the priorities were different by 1959, when there were no separate radio dealer listings. Under the radio heading, it simply said "see television and radio dealers."

And if the pace of change was too swift in Torrance in 1959, help was beginning to arrive, too. Psychologist Allan Schlaff was the first of his profession in town, offering his services at 1104 Sartori Ave.

When the Sears Del Amo store opened on September 30, 1959, the *Pacific Coaster*, a magazine published for Sears employees, reported breathlessly that the crowd at the door "seemed to be the most eager-to-shop group ever to face an uncut ribbon. Even though the dedication ceremony was a model of brevity, you could almost sense a feeling of, 'This is all very interesting, but I have an awful lot of shopping to do.'"

Emcee Bill Welsh of KTTV introduced Mayor Isen, County Supervisor Burton Chace and J.H. Paget, president of the Torrance Chamber of Commerce. On hand from Sears was John G. Lowe, the

Until 1965, the *Daily Breeze* plant on Wall Street on the old Redondo Beach waterfront was headquarters for the South Bay's most popular and influential local newspaper. In 1965, the *Breeze* moved to a new, modern offset printing plant and offices on Torrance Boulevard at Palos Verdes Boulevard, a move that symbolized the increased importance of Torrance as the "Headquarters City" of the South Bay. The old *Breeze* building in Redondo was torn down in 1967, part of a project that destroyed Redondo's old downtown business district to upgrade the waterfront there.

COURTESY OF THE *DAILY BREEZE*

store manager; A.T. Cushman, vice president of Sears' Pacific Coast Territory; and K.R. Barton, Los Angeles retail district manager for Sears. Jim Ameche, of KABC radio, broadcast live from the store.

The Sears store had six-and-a-half acres of floor space. Because the ocean was near, it had the largest selection of boats in a Southern California Sears store. "Also, this is an area of new housing developments," the *Pacific Coaster* noted, "so special attention has been given to the Garden and Pet Shop.

"Young married couples who are just starting to raise families are attracted to the residential areas surrounding Sears and Del Amo Center because of the uncramped housing and the large number of nearby beaches and recreational areas."

Obviously, Sears had done its market research well. Between 1950 and 1960, 78,000 new residents came to Torrance. By 1960, the citizenry was largely Caucasian with a small Oriental minority. Most residents were homeowners. The average adult had completed 12.1 years of school and many worked in the aircraft, missile and space industry plants throughout the South Bay. Their median income was more than $8,000, above average for all

of Los Angeles County at the time. In short, they had money to spend.

The year Sears and Broadway opened, the largest listing in the city directory under "department stores" was not an ad placed by either of those giants of retailing. It was for the Sam Levy Department Store on Sartori Avenue in downtown Torrance. The first line of the ad: "Since 1919!"

Levy was fighting a rear guard action. After the Del Amo opening, Levy's and its neighbors on Sartori — J.J. Newberry, Scottie's Department Store and Strum's Department Store — soon discovered they could not outdraw the big stores in the new suburban center.

In 1963, in response to the plight of downtown merchants, the city spent $100,000 on new street lights, parking, landscaping, center dividers and installation of a public address system to pipe music to shoppers outdoors in downtown Torrance. But even that did not help downtown compete with the charms of Del Amo, where there were soon more than forty businesses with parking for a total of 7,000 cars.

Del Amo quickly became the commercial center of the city, and

William Zappas was the crusading, flamboyant publisher of the *Torrance Press*. His weekly fought city hall and championed the little man with equal fervor. Here he is beaming with pride at some of his headlines in 1956. Torrance is now home to one national magazine, *Windsurfer,* some record labels, and an internationally known ad agency, Dancer-Fitzgerald-Sample.

Back when the Madrona Marsh lay like a bizarre but beautiful anomaly across the heart of Torrance, attracting myriad species of wildlife to remind us busy urban dwellers that we are a part of the great order of nature. Raymond Derloo kept bees at Maple and Carson in 1953, just a block from where the world's largest indoor shopping mall was soon to be built. Inset picture looks east towards still-busy derricks. The derricks, and the bees too, were to be gone by the mid-1960s.
PHOTO BY PAUL COMON

indeed of the South Bay. City government benefited significantly from that development. Sales and use taxes rose from $1.25 million deposited in city coffers in 1961 to $2.5 million in 1966.

For more than two decades, one major advantage Torrance retailers have had over others, particularly those in the beach cities, is that there is not a single parking meter in all of Torrance. Each of Torrance's many neighborhood shopping centers has free off-street parking. In the downtown district, a parking assessment provides revenue to the city in lieu of parking meters and fines, and some off-street parking has been developed.

As Torrance's commercial development moved forward in the early 1960s, the voters approved a $1,225,000 airport revenue bond issue and the federal government appropriated $400,000 for improvements at Torrance Airport, alias

Zamperini Field.

In 1966, the city initiated the Meadow Park redevelopment project to clear a housing tract by that name from the southwest end of the airport. The city described housing in the area at the time as "substandard and deteriorating" and "incompatible" with the airport. After a long legal wrangle, the area became a brand-new industrial park.

Also gone now are all of Torrance's dairies, which reached a peak in sheer numbers about 1960. Apparently as the local population soared, dairymen moved their herds in to be close to the rising demand.

In 1959, for instance, there was the Cream O' Farms Dairy operated by James McCandless on Cherry Avenue; the Hudson and Freitas dairies, both on Arlington; Emerald Glen on 166th Street; Morgan's Dairy on Earl Street;

On November 23, 1963, this minipark was already contemplated and designed at Sartori and Cabrillo in downtown Torrance. As did hundreds of other American cities, Torrance felt a need to memorialize its slain young President. It has been Kennedy Park ever since. Reflecting the vision of Sidney Torrance and of the Olmsteads, Torrance has been rich in parks from its beginnings.
PHOTO BY PAUL COMON

Sunny Crest on Spencer; Leendert and
William Verburg's place on Crenshaw;
Jake Zwaagstra's Palos Verdes View
Dairy on Hawthorne Boulevard; the
Mayfair Creamery at 20301 Western
Avenue; on Del Amo Boulevard,
Quinn's Dairy, operated by Lester and
Harriet Quinn; Roger Jessup's Colbrook
Dairy; and Inglewood Farms.

The latter, operated by the brothers
Stanley, Ralph and Al Voges, was open
to school tours for many years and as
early as 1951 boasted equipment capable
of bottling 40,000 quarts of milk a day.
An estimated 8,000 schoolchildren took
the Inglewood Farms tour that year. But
good farmland is usually also prime
property on which to build housing
tracts when the city grows that far.
Dairies are rather odorous neighbors. So
as the houses advanced, the dairies
disappeared during the 1960s and 1970s.

Through this period of astonishing
growth and change in Torrance, when

everything else around the old-timers
must have seemed to have gone topsy-
turvy, there was at least one constant at
city hall. As astonishing as it may seem,
in the 63 years that Torrance has been
incorporated, there have been only five
city clerks, and one man served forty of
those years.

Albert H. Bartlett was actually the
second city clerk, and had served 40
years to the day — Torrance's longest
incumbency in elective office — when
he retired on April 17, 1962.

Bartlett was born in Jamestown, New
York, on September 9, 1878 and lived
in Denver before arriving in California
in 1908 and Torrance in 1912. He
worked as a timekeeper for Union Tool
Co. and later as a cost accountant
there. He organized Torrance's first
insurance firm, the Torrance General
Insurance Co., was a founder of the
volunteer fire department, and helped
organize the Torrance Chamber

of Commerce.

He had been a member of the Democratic National Committee in 1915 and remained an active Democrat throughout his life.

Bartlett's retirement came only after ill health kept him from fulfilling the demands of his office. He was known to

By the end of the 1960s, it was clear that the groundbreakings had just begun. The *Daily Breeze* moved from its former headquarters in Redondo Beach to its new, modern offset printing plant on Torrance Boulevard at Palos Verdes Boulevard in 1965. The *Breeze* was founded in 1894 by Samuel D. "Doc" Barkley, a Redondo businessman whose career of public service included a stint

One of Torrance's assets during the past seven decades has been the willingness of its business leaders to take an active part in community affairs. Otto Kresse was manager of Columbia Steel's huge shops here in the 1950s and also served as president of the board of directors for Torrance Memorial Hospital. Union officials, too, played important civic roles.

Daily Breeze photo

Strikers Picket in Torrance

More than 1,500 picketers went to the Torrance plant of Harvey Aluminum Co. early this morning, and scores of Torrance and Los Angeles police had to be called to maintain order. Leo M. Harvey, chairman of the board at Harvey, was shot at. He suffered a minor hand cut from flying glass.

This clipping from the *Daily Breeze* illustrates the classic confrontation of a strike in heavy industry — pickets outside Harvey Aluminum's Torrance plant, April 19, 1965. The new union had voted to strike two weeks earlier, 1194-to-23. But inevitably there were those who felt impelled to cross the picket line, and the signs made it clear how the strikers felt about them. "God forgive scabs. We won't." Some families were split by the strike; one brother working, one picketing. "My brother and I just learned not to talk about the strike," recalls one man who struck. "And we haven't now for twenty years."

his many friends simply as "Bart." A local newspaper during his lifetime said "his office is friendly headquarters where courtesy rules and helpfulness is the foundation."

Bartlett's blue eyes, the paper said, "register consideration and he would rather help Torrance grow than be owner of Kimberly Diamond Mines."

Bartlett was 83 when he retired from the clerk's office. He died three years later, in April, 1965. The Albert H. Bartlett Senior Center on Cravens Avenue in downtown Torrance is named in his honor.

City clerks since Bartlett include Vernon Coil, 1962 to 1978, also a lengthy tenure; Sherie Nelson, 1978 to 1982; and Donna Babb, elected to serve 1982 to 1986.

as postmaster of Redondo. The move of the *Breeze* to Torrance was yet another acknowledgment of Torrance's central location and swift rise to preeminence in the South Bay.

The new Torrance Post Office on Monterey Street was dedicated on December 11, 1965. Bullock's Fashion Square broke ground in September, 1966, and eventually would add not only a Bullock's but an I. Magnin, a Desmond's men's store and others to the north side of Carson Street at Hawthorne Boulevard, laying the groundwork for the colossal center which 15 years later would bridge Carson Street to the Del Amo Center and create one gigantic enclosed shopping mall. And on the west side of Hawthorne Boulevard, the Financial Center tower rose by the end of the 1960s.

The heartbeat of Torrance from the very beginning was directly dependent on the steel, rubber and glassworks persuaded to relocate here by Sidney Torrance and his fellow entrepreneurs. Columbia Steel, the successor to Llewellyn Iron Works which opened here in 1916, was itself bought by United States Steel in 1930. Soon thereafter, a complete sheet mill moved from San Francisco to Torrance. Then the two original 40-ton open hearths were replaced by four 63-ton furnaces. This scene, shot in the Columbia mill in the mid-1960s, captures some of the matter-of-fact beauty, danger and excitement of the work done here. From 1949 to 1953, a nail-making line was in operation. In 1948, foundry operations stopped and in 1953, ingot mold facilities were discontinued. On April 30, 1954, the sheet mill permanently closed. The continuous caster was installed, on the other hand, in 1968. The Torrance works had the distinction of being the first steel mill in America to install electrostatic precipitators on its furnaces to comply with pollution ordinances. The plant grew, between 1916 and 1954, from 34 to 175 acres.

174

One survey at the end of the decade found more than 700 retail stores in Torrance then, with more than 150 manufacturing plants. And Torrance had become, in 1970, the third largest city in Los Angeles County and the eleventh in population in the state.

What was the lure of Torrance during those years of dynamic growth? A 1963 Chamber of Commerce study suggests that among the advantages the city offered was that Torrance was an "all-round, self-contained community with adequate school facilities, convenient shopping centers, diversified industry for job opportunities and municipal recreation facilities."

Torrance, that study adds, also has a climate with moderate temperatures year-round and westerly winds that generally keep the area smog-free. It also had a reputation for "clean city government," plus "a low city tax rate."

The 1963 study also found that many of the suburban stereotypes had reality here. Less than 16 percent of residents over the age of 20 had never married, for instance, and only one-third had no children. Most Torrance families had children then, with three the most popular number. Nearly three-fourths of the dwellings in Torrance were owner-occupied.

The study also found that more than 77 percent of Torrance adults were high school graduates, more than one-third had some college education and almost one-in-four had graduated from college. Amost half of all Torrance households had at least two cars.

At the time, before the 1965 Harvey Aluminum labor riots took the wind out of their sails on the issue of labor peace, the 1963 Chamber study suggested that "employees in the Torrance area have found a favorable labor-management atmosphere. There have been few strikes over the years, and those that have occurred have been

The Mobil refinery by night: stark beauty and great profit, too, for the city of Torrance, where it is the leading property tax payer. Most residents have become accustomed to, even perversely proud of, the strange odors which sometimes result from the complex processes which turn oil from the ground into gasoline and valuable petrochemicals. They seem content to accept the fact that municipal prosperity exacts an occasional price.
PHOTO BY PAUL COMON

of a nationwide nature. Further, while many of the manufacturing plants have unions, a great many of them do not."

That 1963 study also touted Torrance schools, which had a well-earned reputation for excellence. "The local schools to which these employees send their children are above average and this promotes the continued maintenance of an intelligent labor force."

A similar Torrance Chamber study in 1969 noted that Torrance had more than twelve times as much taxable wealth in 1969 as in 1947, when the Torrance Unified School District was inaugurated, but the student enrollment in the district in 1969 was more than 16 times the 1947 enrollment. Fortunately, that was the historic peak in enrollment and student population thereafter began to decline.

Torrance has played a major role in arming the United States and its allies in two World Wars and in the Korean and Vietnam conflicts. This C-137, workhorse of the worldwide Military Air Transport Service for decades, had substantial work done at Douglas' B-6 shops at 190th and Normandie. This gleaming behemoth is a far cry from the eccentric craft which valiantly struggled skyward from nearby Dominguez Hill only a half century earlier.

With the success of the Apollo moon landing in 1969 — Mayor Isen attended the blast-off in Florida as the city's official representative — aerospace budgets began to be cut, and employment in aerospace engineering and related fields began to level off. Since almost forty percent of the Torrance labor force was employed in

nine percent nationally, but Torrance chalked up an eight percent decrease.

"Statewide statistics show juvenile narcotics arrests increased by 34 percent, while Torrance showed an eighteen percent decrease," the report adds.

The Union Carbide plant in Torrance was pictured in this May 23, 1956, photo looking northwest from just south of Del Amo Boulevard, foreground. Hawthorne Boulevard is at left. Note the vacant lots between Del Amo Boulevard and 190th Street on the east side of Hawthorne, where the Old Towne Place shopping mall is today. The old railroad bridge at Hawthorne and 190th made it necessary for traffic headed east on 190th to turn left onto Hawthorne and right onto the eastern portion of 190th to continue along 190th. In the foreground is another business that added a pungent odor to the air in the vicinity of the chemical plant — Quinn's Dairy, at 4016 Del Amo Boulevard, operated by Harriet Quinn.

manufacturing then, "with electrical machinery and aircraft parts suppliers predominating," the end of NASA's most spectacular early mission had major impact here. It prompted many to move into second careers in unrelated fields or move elsewhere in search of work during the 1970s.

There was also a shift in community concerns by the end of the 1960s, a decade that saw the Armed Forces Day Parade picketed by anti-Vietnam War activists. The 1969 Chamber economic profile of the city was at pains to note that during the first six months of 1959, FBI crime statistics found major crime up

And if Torrance residents generally thought they lived well during the booming years of the 1950s and 1960s, they may have been right. In 1963, a secretary could average $432.50 per month in pay, and rent a one-bedroom apartment in Torrance for $45. Six years later, a secretary could average $552.50 and find a $95 apartment. Rent as a share of income had gone from 10.5 percent to a still reasonable 17 percent in 6 years.

And if that secretary had saved her money, in 1963, she could dream of owning a house in Torrance for $12,500 to $21,000, full purchase price; or as low as $18,000 in 1969!

Torrance area leaders are shown through the American Standard plant in the 1950s by general manager Henry Krieger. In the front row, left to right: Nick Drale, Fred Mills, Paul Diamond and Dick Pyle. Did men's clothing styles ever take a worse turn than they did in the "Happy Days" of the 1950s?

We look at Torrance today and speculate about tomorrow

"Recycling the land" as Honda and Marriott (and the Aga Khan) come to town; what might have been; the shape of things to come.

The end of an era, that of "high temperature" industry in Torrance, was the 1979 dismantling of the Columbia Steel Works on Van Ness, south of 206th Street. Steel had played a major role in the Torrance story since the Llewellyn brothers had accepted Sidney Torrance's overtures in 1916 to move their iron works here. Ironically, some of the stacks and superstructures seen here being dismantled had only recently been built or upgraded at great expense to comply with increasingly strict environmental rules and emissions standards. Completing the irony, the site will soon become the headquarters of Honda, USA where the sales of Japanese autos, made from Japanese steel, will be coordinated.
PHOTO BY PAUL COMON

Symbolic of the new white-collar, future-oriented emphasis of Torrance industry in the 1980s is this circuit board from a CADO Tiger ATS 32 business computer. CADO Systems Corp. was founded in 1976 and manufactures business computers at its facility on 190th Street in north Torrance, where design and testing are also under way. In January, 1983, CADO was acquired by Continental Telecom, a diversified "high-tech" telecommunications company. CADO's Tiger 32 allows 32 user stations, and models offering from 16 to 64 also are available for moderate-sized companies beginning to require the new electronic tools for word processing, data storage, bookkeeping and other applications.
PHOTO BY WM. FRIDRICH

After three decades of rising population, frenetic housing construction, and simultaneous commercial and industrial development, Torrance during the 1970s and early 1980s seems a relatively quiet spot. This period, the modern period, if you will, is one of harmony within city government. Parks are being perfected, a commitment to preserve Madrona Marsh for future generations has been inked

and attempts are being made to ease many aspects of urbanization by doing things like improving streets to speed traffic, or limiting operations at Torrance Municipal Airport to increase its compatibility with surrounding neighborhoods.

These are the years in which Del Amo Fashion Center bridged Carson Street to become the grandest shopping mall of them all. A recession in the early 1980s may have added a brake to what was already a relatively sedate pace for Torrance, but we remain a prosperous place, with a balanced tax base, a reputation for good government, fine places to work and shop, and good schools — altogether a pleasant place to live and work.

For the first time in its history, from

1970 to 1980 the population of Torrance actually declined. From its historic peak of 134,584 in 1970, it fell to 129,881 in 1980, the U.S. Census found. But prosperity continued. The median family income in 1980 was $28,600, which exceeded the national median by 44 percent, the state by 33 percent, and the Los Angeles/Long Beach metropolitan area by 34 percent.

And those of Asian descent in Torrance had median incomes in 1980 of $34,400 annually, exceeding the $30,600 median for whites. Hispanics claimed $26,400, while blacks had $20,500.

Though the total population declined, housing grew by 5,700 units from 1970 to 1980, bringing the city-wide figure to 51,000 and reflecting the decline in household size from 3.9 people in 1960 to 2.6 in 1980. In 1960, nearly three-quarters of the households were married couples with children under 18, but only 48 percent were in 1980. Reflecting that trend, the Torrance public schools in 1984 numbered only 29, down from 40 in 1966.

In 1980, more than two-thirds of the workers were in managerial, technical or sales jobs, and one-fourth of all

179

"Chuck" Curtiss, 90, has seen and played a major role in the history of Torrance for more than 60 years. He came here in 1920 after World War One military service, and worked for the Dominguez Land Corp. as an accountant. He recalls Jared Sidney Torrance vividly: "a fine, big man." His wife of 52 years, Katherine, seen here with him, recalls: "One day in 1912 I saw Mr. Torrance across from the post office. (Her father, Herman Burmaster, was the first official postmaster.) He pulled a sandwich out of a sack and stood there, eating his lunch. I thought it was strange that the man who started our town ate lunch like a workingman, but Dad explained that he had diabetes and had to be careful of what he ate." The Curtisses have lived in the same house on Engracia Street for more than half a century.

PHOTO BY WM. FRIDRICH

households had three or more cars. But where 80 percent of housing had been owner-occupied in 1960, by 1980 it was only 56 percent.

There also was a continuing trend toward multifamily construction instead of single family housing. In 1980, the proportion of single family houses to multiple units was 60-to-40, but the trend was toward apartment buildings and condominiums.

Governing the city during the 1970s was often a quieter task than it had been in the tumultuous 1960s. In fact, Ken Miller, a man who speaks softly and smiles and laughs easily, was mayor through most of the 1970s and says he tried to bring a new, harmonious style to city government.

"We got the council working together," he says. "We simply tried to avoid polarization. We really worked hard for a new image for the city."

Miller says he was always aware that though he had the title of mayor he still had only one vote. So, early in debate he encouraged other members of the city council to avoid positions that ruled out whatever he advocated, and later he tried to gently persuade them to move closer to his position. For a mayor to influence the council in Torrance, Miller says, "one thing he has to have is respect."

Miller was a member of the city council from 1962 to 1970, when he became mayor. He served two four-year terms and backed a charter amendment approved by the voters which limits all future Torrance mayors to a maximum of two terms.

The men and women assembled here were gathered to celebrate their 50 years of active participation in the Torrance adventure at the Charter Citizens party held May 13, 1971 at the Torrance Recreation Center. The addresses of those who signed the Charter Citizens roll that day are indicative of how people were willing to settle down and stay put, in the old days, once they'd found a good place to live. Arlington, El Prado, Post, Engracia, Andreo, Carson, Gramercy, Cota, Acacia, Madison, Greenwood, Fern, Sonoma and Portola addresses abounded.

Among the accomplishments he points to is the "land-banking" the council did during the 1960s and 1970s, when it authorized the purchase of more than 200 acres of land throughout the city for park land, though funds were not then available to develop those parks. Miller, a real estate broker, says he thinks that policy was wise and led to terrific buys for the city.

In the case of Wilson Park, for example, Representative Charles Wilson helped to bring the chairman of the House Armed Service Committee to Torrance as grand marshal of the Armed Forces Day Parade one year while the city was exploring the possibility of acquiring the surplus U.S. Navy facilities which

became the park. Wilson represented the northern half of the city for 18 years, from 1962 until defeated in the Democratic primary in 1980 after censure by the House for alleged campaign contribution irregularities. (Wilson died in 1984 as this book was going to press.)

"He told the Navy to strike a deal with us," Miller recalls. So the city got the park land for $5,000 per acre. "It was worth $75,000 to $80,000 per acre in those days."

In addition to Wilson Park, Miller mentions Columbia Park and Del Thorne Park as other land-banked facilities which are now developed.

Miller says he's proud that Prairie Avenue was opened through to Madrona Avenue with a bridge over the railroad tracks north of Del Amo Boulevard.

He also believes that his years in city government were years of "healthy-type growth" for the city as a whole, with a spectacular business expansion, creating solid tax revenue.

"We reduced taxes twice during the 1970s," Miller says, noting that Torrance's property tax rate was adjusted downward as sales tax revenues rose in relative importance.

He also notes the city's role in initiating paramedic emergency medical service. And Miller says he believes restrictions placed upon Torrance Airport and delay in developing commercial land there are benefiting the city. Clauses in documents transferring the airport to the city declare that the site would revert to the federal government if air operations there ever came to an end, Miller notes. Torrance Airport is the twentieth-busiest general aviation airport in the nation.

The only major disappointment during his years in city government, Miller says, was "not bringing Madrona/Prairie all the way to Lomita Boulevard." The lack of that portion of the street, he says, "compounds the traffic problems on Hawthorne and Crenshaw boulevards."

Looking back on his years of public service, Miller emphasizes his style of conciliation and compromise: "You've got to give a little and take a little. You can't win them all."

Miller's successor, Jim Armstrong, sits in his city hall office on a late afternoon, wearing a sports shirt like a sensible Southern California mayor. In the middle of his second and final term, he's sharing some thoughts about accomplishments during his two decades of political life in his adopted city; he was born in Los Angeles 54 years ago.

"Perhaps I'm most proud of Wilson Park," he says. Armstrong, an indefatigable Democratic activist in political campaigns before he became a nonpartisan planning commission member in the 1960s, a council member in 1972 and mayor in 1978, served as former Congressman Charles H. Wilson's field deputy from 1973 to 1978.

He's proud, too, of Columbia and Sur La Brea parks. He uses the latter as an example of how a couple of generations of concerned citizens and politicians are sometimes necessary to bring an idea to fruition. "It was conceived when Al Isen was mayor, carried forward by Ken Miller, and I was there when we finally dedicated it."

He takes pride, too, in successful efforts to get an exemption for seniors from the utility users' tax. He's optimistic that low income senior housing plans, at Cravens and El Prado, will be realized soon.

Armstrong is pleased with what has been accomplished in the Civic Center but impatient to see a Fine Arts Center (the architect is drawing plans now). The Group W cable television studio is going forward now too, of course. He

wants to involve the private sector in the theatre plans; and he thinks that perhaps it will take professional fund-raising efforts to bring this about.

He talks about "recycling the land" — the old Columbia Steel Works of the early twentieth century becoming the Honda corporate site of the twenty-first century. "See what American Standard is doing with their industrial park, how Reynolds Aluminum is expanding by tearing down the old P.E. shops. Look at what independent businessmen like

Mayor Ken Miller served in that capacity 1970-78, during a period of relative calm — after the explosive growth of the 1950s and the controversies of the 1960s. Miller's era was one of prosperity and continued orderly growth, which may explain why Miller's smile in this picture is as wide as his tie.

Torrance Mayor Jim Armstrong took office in 1978 and was reelected in 1982. He is a Torrance High School teacher who has long encouraged his students to cultivate an interest in the government and history of their city.

The Torrance Civic Center complex on the north side of Torrance Boulevard in this 1984 photo includes city hall, still flying flags for the 1984 Olympics in Los Angeles. The building on the left is the former police headquarters, currently undergoing remodeling for use as additional office space for the recreation department, data processing, central services and cable information staff. The city hall of the 1950s and 1960s is at right, now housing city staff offices including the planning department. In the main city hall building, the city council chamber and city clerk's office are on the ground floor. The top floor houses the mayor and city council's offices and offices of the city manager and city attorney. Other floors include offices for the finance and transportation departments.
PHOTO BY ROBI HUTAS

Harry Harper of Harper's Furniture on Van Ness have done by upgrading."

He wants the city to remain committed to saving downtown, and to restoring and upgrading it. He thinks the depot can be saved.

Armstrong gives Torrance Transit high marks. It's clear that he's proud of the city's professional staff, and the way they've grown into responsibility by moving up the ladder right here in

Torrance. City Manager LeRoy Jackson was former long-time manager Ed Ferraro's assistant for many years. Police Chief Don Nash has been on the Torrance force for more than 20 years.

Much remains to be done: alleviating "the agony of the airport," bringing Madrona Marsh into full use as a nature study center, solving traffic congestion,

with a return to interurban transit or even with grade separations at acute points like the Torrance/Hawthorne Boulevard intersection, reputedly the busiest in Los Angeles County.

Armstrong is quick to come to the city's defense, especially in historical matters, as befits a man who's taught American government and the history of Torrance at Torrance High for many years. He thought the authors were blanketing Torrance in their criticism of Caucasian apathy 40 years ago during the Japanese-American relocation. So he had an aide find the city council resolution from that time condemning the move.

He can't run again for mayor in 1986, of course, due to the two-term limit, but he isn't closing any doors on other directions his zest for politics and the art of governing may take. He clearly is tuned to what the people of Torrance want from city government: an absence of internecine warfare such as prevails in some nearby cities, efficiency, a willingness to push long-range projects, a commitment to easing the strains of life in urban society.

Elected to council in 1972 by the largest plurality ever afforded a candidate, he was elected mayor in 1978 with only an earnest young conservative, Richard Corsi, a South High senior, running against him. ("A nice young man," Armstrong says. "We played it straight.") In 1982, he received more than 90 percent of the vote in his reelection bid. His opponent, a pleasant and somewhat quixotic gentleman named Lloyd

Sorenson, lost a few more votes one time, Armstrong recalls, when he answered the query of a group of environmentalists about his plans for Madrona Marsh with a crisp "pave it!"

Among the issues Armstrong, Miller and their compatriots on the City Council have had to face in recent years, few were more controversial than efforts to preserve a boggy piece of land east of Del Amo Fashion Center for birds and wildlife instead of allowing it to be developed in more lucrative ways.

Saving at least 54 of the 182 acres between Crenshaw and Madrona, Carson and Monterey was long touted by S.T.O.P. (Stop Torrance Overdevelopment Plans) and the Friends of the Madrona Marsh in terms of preserving a natural and unique habitat, a fresh-water marsh.

Then an environmental impact report in 1974, complete with dated aerial photos, showed it at least possible that the marsh was almost wholly man-made and recent, the result of runoff from nearby construction after World War Two.

Still, it was many people's desire that the city preserve it, regardless of how and when it had been created. And Friends of the Marsh accumulated some impressive testimony from long-time residents, like Tim Wayt and Eva Snow, that the marsh was a long-existing phenomenon, albeit perhaps a recurring one.

Georgean Griswold notes that vernal marshes "are supposed to be wet in

Torrance has had a passion for parks since the very beginning 72 years ago. There are now 23 of them, or nearly one for every 5,000 residents. Columbia, at 190th and Prairie, 18 years in the acquiring, has 53 acres with a community garden area that includes this unique "Fujimihara" sculpture. At first, it looks like just a large steel cylinder with a semicircle band cut through the middle. But the elliptical cylinder casts a shadow that changes with the time of day and with the season. It's a gift to the city from the park's neighbor, Standard Brands Paint Co. Joslyn Center is a focal point for Torrance residents interested in painting, sculpture, and other fine and applied arts. The Parks and Recreation Department also operates neighborhood teen and senior centers, a nine-hole pitch-and-putt course, tennis courts and the Victor E. Benstead Plunge.

PHOTOS BY FORREST HUNT

Streets, curbs and alleys were among the amenities the Dominguez Land Corp. installed in Torrance during the decade prior to incorporation of the city in 1921. Shown here are three examples of early curbs and sideways that included the street names inscribed in concrete. Redondo Boulevard, reflecting the reversal in the relative importance of the two cities in the modern era, is called Torrance Boulevard today. Guadaloupe Avenue is now Post Avenue, renamed for Judge George W. Post, a banker and manager of the Dominguez Land Corp., who was credited by his contemporaries for being the second-most important man in the founding and preserving of the city of Torrance. The rising tide of street asphalt over the years is also seen on what was formerly 216th Street, now known as Sonoma Avenue.

PHOTOS BY DAVE GEIER

winter, dry in summer." She has also called to our attention a Gabrielino word for the area, PWINUKIPAR, which may mean "wet now, dry later" or, with slight change, "dry now, wet later."

But the marsh land was privately owned by Santa Fe Industries. Local developers Ray Watt, Guilford Glazer and Shurl Curci had plans for it; plans that seemed not unreasonable to many citizens and officials.

The scenario was complicated as revenue sources for acquiring the 54 acres became available, then vanished, all through the past ten years. The U.S. Army Corps of Engineers even got into the act for a while as a protector of the marsh. Then it had second thoughts and abandoned its veto over development.

The final resolution of this classic conflict between idealistic environmentalists and decent-minded but pragmatic developers came in August, 1983. Torrance Investment Co. and Friends of the Madrona Marsh agreed to a 10-year plan, which the city council approved 6-to-1 for 1,482 residential units, 850,000 square feet of office space, and extension of 223rd Street through the property between Crenshaw and Madrona.

The city in turn gets to buy the heart of the marsh — 43 acres — with money from two state environmental funds. The Park Del Amo development will go forward, though a new anti-development tilt to the city council after the 1984

After the 1983 storms, the Madrona Marsh remained wet almost all year and at the highwater mark flooded across Madrona Avenue, as this photo shows. The view is looking southwest to Sepulveda Boulevard. In this condition, the wetlands teem with Canada geese, mallard duck, godwall, pintail, green-winged and blue-winged teal, cinnamon teal, American wigeon, shoveler duck and canvasbacks. Avocets, stilts, sandpipers and yellowlegs feed on the spring mud flats. Tiny shrimp and other invertebrates abound, attracting songbirds. Late in the year, bittern, heron and egrets feast in the shallow ponds. Wrens, blackbirds and rails prefer the heavy tule-cattail vegetation.

PHOTO BY MICHAEL JUSTICE/INFINITY; COURTESY OF FRIENDS OF THE MADRONA MARSH

nature makes the whole world kin."

There are a few interesting entries, too, in the "what might have been" category for Torrance. The most grandiose and intriguing involved the plan, still alive as late as 1938, to dredge a channel from San Pedro to Torrance, so ocean-going freighters could dock on our east side.

Just think: Bon voyage parties at Carson and Cabrillo, quaint waterfront cafes along Arlington, mothers of high school girls warning their daughters not to let sailors turn their heads.

Another "near miss" was the consideration which Torrance gave in the 1920s to annexing Redondo Beach, which was then plagued by storms,

election will subject its actions to close scrutiny. The Friends will train docents and establish and maintain a nature park.

Even today the marsh is the habitat for 98 species of birds, several species of reptiles, amphibians, small mammals and numerous invertebrates, as well as 142 species of plants. Raccoons still fish on the marsh land.

One vital role the marsh will continue to play, of course, is as a stop in the

Pacific flyway for migratory birds enroute from Alaska and the Great Slave Lake to Mexico and Chile. It's important for predators, too. The great horned owl and the barn owl hunt small mammals in the surrounding drylands.

"Out in the tules" usually means far from civilization. But in Torrance, thanks to preservation of the marsh, it's only a short walk from the world's largest shopping center to a natural retreat. There it can happen that, in Shakespeare's words: "One touch of

eroding coastlines, gambling and a lack of industry. Plucky Redondo's comeback story is a matter of record now.

Finally there was the proposal in the early 1960s that Torrance become the site of a South Bay state college. The "All-America City" put together an impressive proposal. But the tremendous amount of land available and offered at Dominguez Hills in Carson carried the day for our neighbor city to the east.

By 1984, 72 years after Jared Sidney Torrance dreamed his incredible dream, what had Torrance become? A very wealthy city for one thing. But one which did not wear its wealth flauntingly, like some others north and south of here.

If our gross municipal product is compared with the gross national products of the 215 independent countries which make up the United Nations, Torrance would outdo two-thirds of them. In 1982, retail stores here outsold Detroit, which has nine times as many people. Taxable sales per resident are twice as high as in the rest of the South Bay and retail business rose 47 percent between 1970 and 1980.

Del Amo Fashion Center mall, the largest enclosed regional shopping center in the world, is responsible for much of that prosperity, of course. What Great

Lakes Properties Co., and later Guilford Glazer, accomplished here is impressive, even in dry statistical form.

There are eight major outlets (Bullocks, Robinson's, Wards, Sears, I. Magnin, J.C. Penney, Ohrbachs and Broadway) and 350 smaller stores, 2.65 million square feet, 6,000 employees, and retail sales of nearly $400 million. And promotions which range from the dignified through the zany (e.g., One day feline fanciers were offered the chance to prove that their cats were the ones featured in a newspaper page full of cat photographs. The resultant cataclysm was not catastrophic, but it did leave several security people nearly catatonic.).

But growth and prosperity are in evidence all over town, even though the most recent councilmanic election makes it plain that the city's voters want to slow the pace, while consolidating Torrance's impressive claims to the title "Headquarters City," now superseded by the slogan "The Balanced City."

Honda's 1.2-million-square-foot headquarters on the former Llewellyn Iron Works/U.S. Steel property will revitalize the eastern edge of old downtown Torrance. Old Towne Place is growing; the nearby South Bay Center in Redondo Beach is being developed into a dazzling South Bay Galleria. And Torrance has more than

a dozen first run movie theatres, making it potentially a Westwood South from the film industry's point of view. (Much of this data was presented in "The Wealth of Torrance," an August 8, 1983 article written by John A. Jackson in the *Easy Reader*.)

Torrance, historically a center of heavy manufacturing, particularly in steel and aluminum, in the past ten years has undergone a transition to white-collar employment. And the trend continues.

The American Standard/Pacific Electric site, 47 acres at the southeast corner of Crenshaw and Del Amo, is under redevelopment as the Torrance Business/Industrial Center, an industrial park. A Bethlehem Steel plant at 2000 W. 190th Street has been displaced by Bridgestone Tire Co.'s corporate headquarters and facilities of several other companies in the high-technology field, including TRW and Northrop.

To get an idea of where Torrance may be going in the next 28 years — a period that will bring us up to our city's centennial — it helps to look at where we are today, 200 years after Juan Dominguez took his retirement, 72 years after the city was laid out, and 63 years after it was incorporated.

The city has grown 525 percent in area since incorporation, from 3.8 to 20

Technically in unincorporated territory north of Torrance, El Camino College is a two-year community college offering Associate in Arts degrees. This 1947 photo looking east on Redondo Beach Boulevard at Crenshaw Boulevard shows the campus' first buildings, old barracks that were hauled down the highway from the old Santa Ana Air Base, which had been declared surplus. Forrest Murdock, founding president of El Camino, drove one of the trucks that pulled one of the buildings. In 1948, construction on the college's first permanent buildings was begun. El Camino today serves 30,000 students and helps them prepare for the future with courses in traditional liberal arts and sciences, and occupations as varied as nursing, air conditioning, recreation and real estate. El Camino is the largest single-campus college in the United States and serves not only Torrance, but residents of Inglewood, Lennox, Hawthorne, Lawndale, El Segundo, Manhattan Beach, Hermosa Beach and Redondo Beach.

COURTESY OF EL CAMINO COLLEGE

Bo Derek, who claims Torrance as her hometown, actually was born and raised in that fascinating and frustrating adjacent anomaly, "the city strip." This long narrow stretch of Los Angeles City connects downtown with San Pedro Harbor, and runs just east of Torrance. Many homes have Torrance mailing addresses. She attended Narbonne High, but was off to Europe with actor and photographer John Derek at an early age. There followed *10* and then *Tarzan the Ape Man,* which this strong-willed lady produced and starred in. If anyone remembers an occasion about 1972 when the fountain at the *Daily Breeze* suddenly spouted and spewed soap bubbles, the culprits have been discovered. Bo and her friends did it.

COURTESY OF MGM

square miles. That can't be considered inevitable; parts of the city, like the Hollywood Riviera or the section north of Lomita, might have easily wound up outside Torrance. From the 1920s through the 1950s, Torrance was an aggressively expanding city, spurred on by an annexationist Chamber of Commerce. There were some lost opportunities, including a failure to annex a significant part of the Peninsula. But on balance, annexation served Torrance well.

Less than seven percent of the land remains undeveloped. Most of that is zoned for industrial development. Effectively, all of the residentially zoned property, about half of the entire city, has been developed.

Population appears to have topped out in 1970 at 134,000 and is about 130,000 now, making Torrance about the sixteenth largest city in the state. That population is aging, but not rapidly. One resident in eleven is over 65.

School enrollment in grades one through six fell precipitously from 1970 until now, from 14,500 to about 8,000. It had in fact peaked in 1960, and then leveled off for ten years before the steady fall of the last decade caused so many schools to close.

Counting mobile homes, there are about 51,000 housing units. As elsewhere in Southern California, the ratio between average income and median housing costs for non-condo homes (about 1:4.3) dramatizes the difficulties of starting off "by buying a little home in Torrance."

"Jose Cuervo, you are a friend of mine" sang Torrance resident Cindy Jordan five years ago — and since then, the tequila has had a 30 percent sales increase, substantially attributable to Cindy's uninhibited song about a lady who drinks tequila "with a little salt and lime" and then kisses all the cowboys and takes one home with her. First recorded at Piper Records in Torrance, it became No. 1 nationally last year on country music charts, and was "covered" by Shelley West and Lacey Dalton. It's been described as "a classically well-written tune with a hook, and all the lines go back to the hook." Jordan sings regularly at the Blue Moon Saloon in nearby Redondo Beach.

Some interesting things have been happening in Torrance in terms of racial diversity. A city which in 1912 had racial covenants written into its founding mandate, and which in 1960 was 98.6 percent white, is now more than 20 percent Asian and Hispanic, though the black population is still less than one percent.

In the past quarter century, our percentage of "singles" has increased from 16 to 27, while those married have dropped from 77 to 55 percent. Those "divorced or separated" have tripled; widows and widowers have increased 50 percent.

Household size has dropped dramatically. Three and four person households were the norm in 1960; it's two or three today. Folks have more space to themselves too, because there are still, as in 1960, about five rooms to a dwelling unit.

Housing values didn't even double between 1960 and 1970. Then they took off and more than quadrupled in the 1970s. At the same time, rents only doubled, and generally Torrance rents in 1984 seem reasonable, especially in comparison with nearby beach cities and the Peninsula.

The median years of school completed by Torrance residents is over 13, which may be why a high school diploma no longer impresses local employers. About 85 percent of Torrance residents have such a diploma.

More than half the local population is employed. In spite of a 50 percent growth in female employment, 11 out of 20 workers are still men. About one employee in eight works directly for government, though a large portion of the private employers are heavily dependent upon government contracts, particularly in the aerospace field.

In 1980, 32,500 Torrance residents lived north of 190th Street. Another 10,000 lived just north of Lomita. The Riviera and Walteria accounted for another 20,000.

Joe Quinones, a city of Torrance employee, raised more than $6,000 through donations to carry the Olympic Torch in 1984. He is shown here passing with the flame in front of city hall. His son also ran a kilometer with the Torch. Quinones donated his to the city of Torrance as a keepsake of the Games. The Torch passed through in the morning of July 27, 1984, entering the city traveling east on 190th Street, then south along Hawthorne Boulevard to east on Torrance Boulevard, south on Western, west on Pacific Coast Highway, and south on Crenshaw Boulevard. Thousands of cheering, flag-waving residents of all ages lined the route.

COURTESY OF JOE QUINONES

Torrance has had its share of contenders for the Olympic Gold since Lou Zamperini competed in 1936 in Berlin. Mrs. Genevieve Scully Vanderpool, originally from San Diego, now lives in Torrance. She was on our 1932 Olympic swimming team. In 1972, Steve Smith, a South High graduate, competed in the pole vault. Leslie Wolfsberger, then 17, won the sixth and final place on the women's gymnastics team for the 1976 Montreal Olympics. She finished second among U.S. competitors. Paula Weishoff, from West High's renowned volleyball program, was on the 1984 team.

How do we compare with the rest of Los Angeles County, with California and the nation? We have markedly fewer children under five and more people over 18. So our median age is about 10 percent higher. In 1980, incidentally, we had 1,048 residents over 85, almost one percent of the population.

The most heterogeneous area of Torrance is north of Artesia Boulevard between Redondo Beach Boulevard and the Gardena city line. It's about one in seven Asian, one in seven Hispanic and one in forty black.

Median incomes in Torrance exceed Los Angeles, state and federal averages by substantial percentages. And they also do so within all ethnic groups; in other words, Asians, Hispanics and blacks who live here do markedly better than those who live elsewhere. Even so, in 1980, about 2,400 households were deemed to be in economic need. At any time about 2,500 people in Torrance who would otherwise be working are prevented by disability.

In 1960, 44 percent of our population was under 18, and 93 percent of them lived with their parents. By 1980, the "under 18s" were only 24 percent of the total, and only 77 percent lived with both parents. In the same period, one-person households tripled.

Clearly, one of the city's assets over the years has been an extraordinary supply of formidable women, though as yet there has not been a female mayor.

The story of women and Torrance could begin with those redoubtable ladies, the Dominguez sisters. Inheriting from their father, the six sisters nurtured their South Bay legacy and passed it on, enhanced, to their descendants.

Women like Karmee Dolley, standing and working beside their hard-working husbands in the early days of a new town, are important to our story. So are women like Isabel Henderson, who founded the public library and guided much of the philanthropic work of the town through her activities on the Torrance Memorial Hospital board and Torrance Relief; her daughter, Dorothy Jamieson, who carried on her tradition grandly; Helena Torrance, who helped carry out her husband's vision of a hospital in his new city after his death; and Phoebe Sykes, who ran the newsstand at the Pacific Electric depot.

Also essential to the story of Torrance

are self-reliant and resourceful performing artists like Wanda Stacowitz, the blacksmith's daughter who rode on the first Torrance Rose Float and later became a heralded opera singer and teacher of that art.

And Torrance had women serving as city treasurer for 26 straight years, 1938-1964. First it was Harriet Leech until 1946, then Margaret Fordice until 1951. Then Leech returned to office and served until 1964.

And Torrance has had two female city clerks, including the incumbent, Donna Babb.

Council member Katy Geissert, first elected in 1974, is considered by many to be the most likely prospect for the title of first woman mayor of Torrance sometime in the future.

And actress Rosemary De Camp has long been a resident of Torrance, deeply committed to the furtherance of the civic welfare.

Add to these the talented, hard-driving singer-songwriter Cindy Jordan, who immortalized tequila with "Jose Cuervo, you are a friend of mine."

And actress-producer Bo Derek claims Torrance as her hometown.

Not to mention Theresa Raymer, a Torrance businesswoman who in 1984 was crowned Ms. Nude California at the Treehouse Fun Ranch nudist resort in Devore.

The diversity of Torrance women and of the fields in which they have achieved success is clear. And the women of the Torrance Woman's Club, the PTAs, the League of Women Voters and all those who provide time, intelligence and muscle to organize other community groups, activities for children and annual activities for the entire community remain vital to volunteerism in Torrance.

Many women are active in Torrance's lively homeowners organizations as well. Homeowners associations play an important role in keeping city hall responsive to the citizenry. (In 1980, 56 percent of housing units in Torrance were owner-occupied, though the trend was downward.) Homeowners often have felt that they best get the attention of elected officials by speaking through groups like the Riviera, Southwood or Southeast Torrance Homeowners

In November, 1979, Del Amo Center, with Sears, Penneys and Broadway, looked like this. The street in the foreground is Sepulveda Boulevard. Hawthorne Boulevard is to the left. Carson Street separated Del Amo — which was begun in 1958 — from the separately owned Bullock's Fashion Square, which was only three years old and included I. Magnin and a men's store, Desmond's. The supermarket in the Del Amo parking lot, right, was Magic Chef in 1970. The same location, formerly a Ralph's, is empty now.

COURTESY OF DEL AMO FASHION CENTER

This 1984 view looking north on Hawthorne Boulevard from Sepulveda Boulevard shows the modern commercial and financial center not only of Torrance, but the entire South Bay. In the left foreground are Toys R Us and Mervyn's. In the distance behind them is the Del Amo Financial Center, once envisioned as "Wall Street West" with a series of highrise office towers catering to the financial trade. On the other side of Hawthorne is the sprawling Del Amo Fashion Center, the world's largest shopping mall. The mall achieved that status in 1981, when portions of the mall north and south of Carson Street were bridged and Robinson's department store was added. Roofing the formerly open-air south side of the mall was begun in 1979 and completed by the much-heralded "Marriage of the Malls." With a Marriott Hotel rising to the north in 1984, informal discussions were beginning on the possibility of expanding the mall even further with shops that would extend north to the hotel.

PHOTO BY ROBI HUTAS

Association (SETHA).

SETHA, for example, with a membership area between Crenshaw and Western avenues, and Sepulveda Boulevard and the city boundary with Lomita, publishes a quarterly newsletter with a circulation of 3,000. They set up Neighborhood Watch programs. They ride herd on oil sites in their area to press for curbs, sidewalks and camouflaging landscape, and to have noise abated.

In June, 1984, they finally witnessed the dedication of Sur La Brea Park at 236th Street and Cabrillo Avenue, something for which they long campaigned.

The association is in an area where some residents of Torrance have Lomita addresses, so this year the group is pressing the U.S. Postal Service for Torrance addresses instead.

No description of Torrance yesterday and today would be complete without reference to restaurants, eating places, bars and lounges. In the earliest days of the city, from the cookshack that became a fire department hose cart shed, these were severely utilitarian, designed to meet the immediate requirements of hard-working oil field hands, local merchants and shoppers, and commercial travelers.

Carson Street near Madrona Avenue just prior to the joining of the malls in May, 1980. There were some who believed that putting a bridge over a major artery would be opposed more strongly than it was. But the city's attitude seemed to be that, within reason, what was good for the mall was good for Torrance. Guilford Glazer got his "bridge," and today thousands of cars daily pass beneath some of the shops which have helped swell Torrance's retail sales close to $1,000,000 a day. Back in 1914, Hurum Reeve won a "low ball pot" among Torrance merchants affected by the recent panic, with a full day's receipts at his hardware store coming to 35 cents.

In the 1950s and 1960s, Smith Brothers Fish Shanty and the Polynesian on Pacific Coast Highway in Walteria became the sort of lavish eateries that tourists literally sent post cards home about.

And now there are so many eating places that new ones sometimes find it hard to cut the mustard. Choices are so wide that even someone who dines out every night need never return to any place that does not please on first impression.

All the major fast food chains are here including McDonald's, Burger King, Bob's Big Boy, Denny's, Carl's Junior, Weinerschnitzel, Taco Bell, Jack in the Box, and Kentucky Fried Chicken. Which will still be here in 2001 A.D.?

Distinctive cuisines abound, like those of Cafe Toulouse Street, Il Cappuccino and the Main Event. Watering places like Del Conte's and Houlihan's, where community leaders gather and the proprietors take a lively and appreciative interest in the history and current activities of the town, also flourish.

Torrance has an official tree: the cork oak. There are two on Torrance Boulevard at Sartori Avenue. They were planted in 1912, and qualify as our oldest living residents.

The city flower is the hybrid delphinium or ajacis, grown by T. Muto 1928-41 on the present Civic Center site. Muto's hybrids soon took Eastern markets by storm because they withstood the rigors of shipment.

Torrance has had 18 mayors. George Proctor, a Union Tool superintendent, was the first. William H. Tolson was elected twice, 1937-40 and 1944-46.

Torrance has had a Sister City program since 1973 with Kashiwa, Japan, a suburb of Tokyo on the island of Honshu. Seven or eight Torrance students spend a few weeks every year in Kashiwa, and Japanese students come here. The Sister City Association sponsors the Bunka-Sai Festival in Torrance every year also.

Long-time residents who signed the Charter Citizen roll at Torrance's 50th anniversary party were Mrs. DeDe Sparks, Mrs. A.D. Bernard, Dan Bernard, Mr. and Mrs. Harvel Guttenfelder, Mr. and Mrs. Robert Tolson, Mr. and Mrs. Charles A. Curtiss, Florence Anderson, Mr. and Mrs. Edgar Dumont, Mr. and Mrs. Paul Rissing and son, Mr. and Mrs. Newell E. Wayt, Minni Smith, Mrs. Sam Levy, Mr. and Mrs. Albert M. Dumont, Mr. and Mrs. George L. Probert, Mr. and Mrs. Edward Schwartz, Bob McMasky, Rose Candley, Mr. and Mrs. David Sackenhoff, Mrs. Margaret J. Neff, Casper Clemmer, Mr. and Mrs. Joseph Useldinger, Mr. and Mrs. Thomas G.

Wilkes, Fay Parks, Ruth Hardin, Melvina Beckwith, Vivian Cook, Sam Boise, Myrtle Boise, Irene Vincent, Nina Adamson, John W. McKown, Glady A. McKown, Mrs. F.A. Lincoln, Sr., Fred A. Lincoln, Sr., Mrs. Clara Dunbar, Corlista Ann Reeve, Mrs. Celina Dean, Corwin Dean, Marie B. Bezich, Mrs. Otto J. Batsch, A.J. Fitzgerald, Margaret Fitzgerald, Mary Hoover, Mrs. Charles Ashley, Thomas J. Wilkes, D.W. Barnard, Rose Schmidt, Robert H. Hannan, Rosalind King, John G. Guyan, Leonard D. Babcock, F.W. Sandstrom, Mabel Webb, Catherine Mullen, Mary Mullen, Dorothy H. Jamieson, Katherine Kray, Mary Haas, Esther C. Carlson, Dewey W. Quigley, Marie P. Quigley, Damianos Merzakis, Martha L. Riggle, Mrs. Louis J. Smith, Betty Neelands Woodman, Thomas J. Bray, David R. Jones, Ola R. Laurent, Marie Taylor, Percy Bennett, Alice Koutny, William H. Sykes, Mr. and Mrs. A.E. Younghan, Milton H. Carson, Mr. and Mrs. Anthony Zamperini, Pete and Dora Zamperini, John A. Hall, Flory Cook, Mary Peckham Clark, Betty M. Yates and Jess Yates.

Because they are often those who take the liveliest interest in our city's history, it seems appropriate to note that

A far cry from Captain Walter's lodging house in old Walteria or the Murray Hotel downtown, the Torrance Marriott will open next year adjacent to Del Amo Fashion Center. There will be 478 guest rooms and eleven suites, a ballroom which will accommodate 1,600 people, lounges, pools, a sauna and a health club. According to one story about the venture, city government made it clear to Marriott representatives that the path to approval for the project would be smoother if they agreed from the beginning to name their South Bay hotel the *Torrance* Marriott. A block away on Hawthorne Boulevard is the handsome Torrance Holiday Inn, which recently built another addition, and across the street a new Brock Residence Inn was constructed for opening this year. All together, these hotels will offer housing for more people than resided in Torrance until a dozen years after the city's founding.

The look of future Torrance — a rendering of the headquarters of American Honda Motor Co. Inc., now planned for 76 acres of the old Columbia Steel site. The first phase, scheduled for completion in late 1985, includes a 250,000-square-foot parts distribution center with an additional 63,000-square-foot mezzanine, a 78,000-square-foot regional center, and a 177,000-square-foot research center. To come later are an administration center (441,000 square feet), a technical center (202,000 square feet) and a 50,000-square-foot central services area. (About 1,300,000 square feet in all, the equivalent of two dozen football fields.) Honda, the Torrance Marriott, the new parks, the revitalization of downtown ... Torrance, proud of its past, looks to its future confidently.

Torrance senior citizens have had their own council since 1973. Working with Parks and Recreation Director Gene Barnett, they enjoy a formal liason function with the city council. Recent members have included Ursel Nolte, "Doc" Gregg, Etta Morgan, Larry Gitschier, Velma Harber, Charles Hosler, Howard Gendall, Helen Parrish and Mary Locke, with Lael Walz as liason.

At the other end of the demographic spectrum, Torrance has also had a Youth Council since 1976. There are two members from each of the high schools, two from El Camino College and two appointed at large. Recent members have included Madelon Ries, Hyonju Paik, David Chung, Lisa Van Kreuningen, Craig Carlson, Mona Castillo, Sherry Chappell, Catheline Chong, Linda Chung, Paul Hendriks, Joo (Laurie) Kim and Sandy Mora, with Gary Schmidt as advisor.

Torrance has a long history of association with Pasadena's Tournament of Roses. After all, Sidney Torrance was a leader of the prestigious Valley Hunt Club in the 1890s when they launched the parade. Because of that, his new city had an entry in 1914. And Torrance's annual float became a tradition in the late 1950s. Any city resident 13 or older can decorate the float.

Recent Torrance Rose Float Association members have included president Georgean Griswold, past president Thelma Carr and Millie Blazejack,

Michelle Griswold, Sue Lions, Doris Greene, Wil and Linda Lemley, Nichelle Marks, Robert De Armond, Sally Duncan, Donna Johnson, Maureen La Tendresse, Rob Katherman and Kathy Dragoo. (Ms. Dragoo is a third generation float building volunteer; her grandmother, Rosalie Boyko, notes that every year on her birthday she works on the Torrance float, too.)

Alondra Park, 319 acres in unincorporated county territory ten minutes north of downtown Torrance, is said to be the coolest spot in Los Angeles County in the summer.

Mayor Bill Klusman, whose trademark was his top hat, was responsible for its development. Klusman, incidentally, was a great-uncle by marriage to Bob Wade, a dedicated volunteer at the Torrance Historical Museum and the creator of many of its most interesting exhibits until his death recently. Bob's wife, Addie, carries on his work at the museum.

In recent years, Torrance also is the annual scene of the Torrance Mounted Posse Rodeo.

On a even more unusual note, Torrance also has been the site of the South Bay Ground Hog Society's annual February 2 observance of Ground Hog Day, a light-hearted tribute to Southern California's status as the fair weather capital of the nation and a fund-raiser for local charities.

Karate champion and film star Chuck

Norris is a North High School graduate, who took up karate in Torrance, achieved the Black Belt, and was seven times world champion in the sport. Norris, now a resident of Rolling Hills Estates, also founded Chuck Norris Karate Studios and takes a strong public stand against drug abuse by young people.

Another long-time Torrance resident is Roger Owens, the renowned Dodger Stadium peanut vendor who has appeared on talk shows and made a national tour demonstrating his fancy style, pitching peanut bags to the fans.

Some indication of the changing emphasis in Torrance may by indicated by modifications made in the 17-year-old city logo as this book went to press. The words on the logo formerly were "Headquarters City: Industry, Finance, Business," designed to attract corporate headquarters and spur industrial parks, a financial center and other businesses to locate and expand here.

The new words are "A Balanced City: Industrial, Residential, Commercial."

Torrance today is virtually without sexually oriented businesses, unlike many neighboring cities. A Pussycat Theatre that shows X-rated films is probably the chief exception. It was established 15 years ago, before Torrance adopted a licensing review procedure for sexually oriented businesses that makes them virtually impossible to start here.

An embarrassment in a city where religious harmony has been the rule, is the fact that Torrance is headquarters to Willis Carto's Institute for Historical Review, an organization that claims Nazi atrocities are a myth and in 1979 offered $50,000 to anyone who could prove that Jews were murdered in Nazi gas chambers. In 1981, a Superior Court judge declared the Holocaust, contrary to Carto's contention, was a fact "not reasonably subject to dispute." A suit to enforce payment of the $50,000 was then referred for a jury trial, a process which can take many years. Meanwhile, in early July, 1984, the Institute's office in Torrance was hit with a midnight firebombing.

The oldest building in Torrance arguably is not any structure in the downtown, which began springing up in 1912, or anything in the vicinity of Perry School or the Weston Ranch.

Instead, it's the solid, all-American looking office building owned by local attorney Dudley Gray on Crenshaw Boulevard, just south of the San Diego Freeway. It goes back 96 years — and about 1,500 miles to Pottawattamie County, Iowa.

At least a great deal of it does, especially many authentic interior furnishings and most of the stone block facing. Gray bought them in 1976 when the old Council Bluffs courthouse was to be demolished. He's from Iowa and it had always been his dream to transplant an Iowa courthouse to Southern California. So now it sits here, home for Gray's legal practice and the practices and businesses of his tenants.

One tenant, by the way, is a man whose far-flung religious empire stretches from India through East Africa and into Torrance. It's the western regional office of the Aga Khan, the man whose father was married to Rita Hayworth and whose grandfather periodically was presented by his faithful followers with his own weight in gold, determined at a public weighing. What an incentive for going off a diet!

In the only instance in which city government has used urban renewal to demolish a residential neighborhood, the Meadow Park section at the west end of Torrance Municipal Airport was razed to make way for this industrial park. The Skypark development includes a branch of Mechanics National Bank; the U.S. headquarters of Epson, a Japanese computer and printer manufacturer; and the Good Earth restaurant, among other uses considered more compatible with the adjacent airport.
PHOTO BY ROBI HUTAS

In a sense, though it was only erected here in 1980, attorney Dudley Gray's office building on the west side of Crenshaw Boulevard just south of the San Diego Freeway is the oldest building in Torrance. Major portions of the building, which had to be modified to meet modern fire codes and to suit new uses, were part of the 1888 Council Bluffs, Iowa county courthouse. An Iowa transplant himself, Gray bought the stone block facing and other materials from the Iowa courthouse in 1976 because he'd always dreamed of transplanting an Iowa courthouse to Southern California.
PHOTO BY ROBI HUTAS

But if Torrance is doing an admirable job of preserving at least a portion of an Iowa courthouse, it is not doing as well with its own historic buildings.

In 1978, the old Belvedere (later El Nido) substation and depot of the Los Angeles & Redondo Railway (later Pacific Electric) at 182nd Street and Kingsdale Avenue was razed. It was then the oldest building on its original site in Torrance.

Constructed in 1902, it served as an electricity generation station, a passenger depot and freight office on the electric line until 1940, and thereafter as a church building. A bulldozer reduced it to rubble and condominiums were built in its place.

The old Pacific Electric Co. shops in downtown Torrance, the U.S. Steel

Perhaps we should hold tighter to the best of the past here. In many ways we do. Where else do the troops still march in a local parade on Armed Forces Day? And where else could they claim to have the world's largest shopping mall? And why is Torrance about the last city in Los Angeles County — other than Pasadena itself — that still annually creates a float for the Rose Parade?

Torrance could be the corniest, most apple pie and America big little town in Los Angeles County. And that's because there is still a special spirit of fun and friendship, an atmosphere of civic pride and great enterprise.

The authors look back fondly on the many months they have spent reliving the exciting story of the birth and growth of Torrance, often talking with the very men and women (Harvel

President Calvin Coolidge later said) should be conducted.

Good factories paying decent wages, good streets and parks as part of the initial plan, an opportunity for resident workers to own their own homes and build their churches and community institutions; that was his plan, which also included a public library and a modern hospital. And it might have been carried to quicker completion had death not claimed him in 1921. The plan was marred by racism, of course; seventy years ago in America, our vision was still as much defined by whom we excluded as by whom we included. So we cannot make the claim for Sidney Torrance that he transcended his time. But it is certainly just to avow that he fulfilled the generous instincts of a visionary man of affairs better than most other entrepreneurs of

plant and other historical industrial buildings have fallen to the wrecking ball in recent years.

And the Pacific Electric depot, the centerpiece of downtown Torrance, has been closed and is in danger of a similar fate. So are other downtown structures created by architect Irving Gill, the in-house architect of the Dominguez Land Corp. during the earliest days of the Torrance development.

Perhaps, despite "Old Main" at Torrance High School — a structure on the National Register of Historic Buildings — Torrance has been too eager to sacrifice the old buildings to make way for "progress."

But old, distinctive architecture does not necessarily make a city, and is not the thing that turns out soccer teams with youthful enthusiasm, or veterans groups with their flags, or the Torrance Youth Band with its stirring music.

Guttenfelder, Dorothy Jamieson, Chuck and Katherine Curtiss) who played roles in that story.

What makes Torrance work as a city — a place to live and work, to raise a family, to retire — a place, in fact, to complete every act in the human drama except the final one? You can be born here — at home or at Little Company of Mary or Torrance Memorial — but you can't be buried here. There are still no cemeteries.

For one thing, Jared Sidney Torrance made Torrance work. Thomas Carlyle, writing in *The Hero in History*, made the most eloquent case for the theory that great men create great events, rather than merely respond to vast, inexorable social and economic forces.

Sidney Torrance was an entrepreneur and a capitalist, and he was certainly shaped by his times. But he had a vision of the ideal climate in which the business of America (which is business,

his generation.

In an age when we are feverishly at the business of knocking holes in myths and legends, Sidney Torrance's life and accomplishments still hold up well under the test of time; he is a founding father of whom any city might be proud. No wonder the Torrance Historical Society is planning to erect, in cooperation with Olde Torrance Neighbors, a bust of Sidney Torrance in a place of honor in the city which his vision created.

As this book should have made clear, however, the living city of Torrance today is a work in progress, a continuing monument not only to Sidney Torrance, but to many dedicated men and women who amplify and improve upon Torrance's original dream of a place in which industry, commerce and residential interests can live in harmony.

What Torrance can yet become, only time — and history — will tell.

Acknowledgments

The authors owe more than the usual debt of gratitude to dozens of people, both those who are Torrance residents and others in places as near as Lomita, Los Angeles, Pasadena and South Pasadena and as far away as Gowanda, New York; York, Nebraska; and New Haven, Connecticut. Their unfailing helpfulness and enthusiasm made our task while researching this book more of a pleasure than a chore.

Our first such debt is to Jim Graham, our partner in this enterprise, who managed the critical financial aspects of this project in a firm but understanding way, keeping us all out of the perils posed by overdrafts and interceding to keep us away from one another's throats during the most difficult days.

Our second debt is to Debbie Graham, who maintained our subscription roster with the same efficient touch.

The painstaking and precise job of indexing *Historic Torrance* was done almost entirely by Jodi Graham.

Our capable typists were Patti Day, Linda Skaggs, Bonnie Prickett and Dorothy Adland.

A major role was played by Grace Elgin and Gertrude Mullen of the Torrance Historical Museum. They were always helpful and frequently suggested fruitful avenues of research. Grace also supplied energy for this project in another form — a bowlful of jelly beans that was always on hand, constantly refilled and always within reach at the museum. Addie Wade, director of displays at the museum, also was a great help.

George Post of the Torrance National Bank was a real friend when it came to telling people — in this case, all his depositors — about our book. His nephew, Dan Post of James Post Insurance, also helped to spread the word.

Our debt to three consecutive presidents of the Torrance Historical Society is acknowledged elsewhere. One of the authors is also a past president of the society, and another past president — Stanley Remelmeyer — also was involved in conceiving this book and taking the initiative to get the project under way. Special thanks to him, long-time city attorney and advocate of local history.

Those we interviewed and those who made old photographs and memorabilia available are acknowledged elsewhere and usually in the text as well. But we want to mention again our thanks to Professor Judson Grenier of California State University Dominguez Hills and his colleagues at Dominguez, Drs. Philip Wesley and Ken Bennett. Also thanks to Dr. Robert Gillingham, Judge John Shidler, Rosemary De Camp, Jerry Alter, William Deane, Gloria Snyder, David Geier and Karmee Dolley.

Others who were particularly helpful in the preparation of this volume include Elizabeth Winter, who opened her home — the former home of Jared Sidney Torrance — to us; Torrance City Clerk Donna Babb; Don Gillen, publisher of the *York News-Times* of York, Nebraska; Lorraine Marvin of the historical society in Gowanda, New York; and Reverend Patrick J. McPolin, C.M.F., of the Dominguez Ranch Adobe.

Mary Cooper of the Torrance Library Commission, Hannah Saville at the Torrance Civic Center Library and others on the staff there under city librarian Jim Buckley, and Buckley himself, helped to fill in many areas of research. Other librarians whose assistance was invaluable include Tom Owen at the Los Angeles Public Library, Carolyn Garner at the Pasadena Public Library, and Patricia Stark at Yale University. Also helpful were staffers at the Lomita library, South Pasadena library and the Southwest Museum.

H.H. Hardacre at the Pasadena Historical Society's impressive archive and museum also provided a treasure-trove of information, as did Otis Tobey of Union Oil Company, and the Los Angeles County Clerk's office.

An education in other areas of inquiry was provided by Ann Gallagher of the Torrance Council of PTAs, Mary Ann Keating of El Camino College, and Wesley H. Poling, director of alumni records at Yale.

Our heartiest thanks, too, go to Torrance's airborne friend and frequent visitor, the Goodyear Blimp, and to its amiable liason on *terra firma*, Bob Urhausen. All of the authors have had the pleasure of the Blimp's company; it was especially valuable in providing us with bird-eye views of modern Torrance.

There remain Marsha McKee and Ellen Jaklitsch, whose vital contributions are cheerfully stated on the jacket copy. They cared; they experimented with layout and style; they held the three of us to a high standard of performance. We hope that readers who are pleased with our book will consider them, in many vital respects, our co-authors.

Torrance
from 1492 through 1984

1492	Columbus "discovers" America by landing in the Bahamas.
1519	Cortes lands in Mexico and the Great Conquest begins.
1536	Cabeza de Vaca, perhaps the first "boomer," returns to the Valley of Mexico from the north with his yarn of the Seven Cities of Cibola.
1542	Cabrillo lands on Catalina and visits the "Bay of Smokes," San Pedro Bay.
November 25, 1602	Sebastian Viscaino anchors in the same bay which he names after St. Peter.
April 11, 1769	"San Carlos" sails into San Diego from Baja California with 200 aboard, including Juan Jose Dominguez.
1782	Dominguez retires with the rank of corporal, aged 59, after 34 years as a soldier; goes into stock-raising.
Fall, 1784	Dominguez receives provisional grant from his former commander, Pedro Fages, now Governor, and drives 200 head of cattle and 50 horses north to occupy his land. Dominguez builds his home on the northeast slope of Dominguez Hill, near Del Amo and Alameda.
1795	He has "over 1,000 head of cattle and many horses and mares" on his land, worked by Indians from Suegna, west of Wilmington and the inner bay, where tank farms are now.
1800	"Major Domo" Manuel Gutierrez runs the Rancho. Juan Jose, in failing health, spends much time at Mission San Gabriel and in San Diego.
1801-1830	Gutierrez allows his friend, Jose Dolores Sepulveda, to graze his cattle on the west side of the Rancho in Palos Verdes. Juan Jose protests, but does nothing. This forms the basis for the Sepulvedas' later successful claim to Rancho Palos Verdes through adverse possession.
1809	Juan Jose, blind and enfeebled, dies at Mission San Juan Capistrano, cared for by his nephew Cristobal Dominguez, sergeant in charge of the Mission guard. He lived 86 years. Rancho San Pedro is bequeathed to Cristobal with Major Domo Gutierrez receiving a lifetime tenure.
1809-1817	Cristobal, on active military service, never visits the Rancho. Gutierrez and many of his neighbors assume that the old Major Domo is now the owner.
1817	Alarmed at possible loss of his inheritance, Cristobal petitions for a regranting of title, and removal of all interlopers (but not Gutierrez) from the ranch.
1820	Cristobal, 64, retires from the army while his petition is still being considered.
1822	Mexico proclaims independence. All land titles must be reconfirmed. Cristobal re-petitions and Governor Sola acts just before leaving office (December 31, 1822). The South Bay is confirmed as the Rancho Dominguez or Rancho San Pedro.

January 6, 1825	Cristobal dies, bequeathing the Rancho to his wife, Maria de los Reyes Ybanez. He leaves four sons (Manuel, the oldest) and two daughters. Manuel, only 22, sees the urgency of action if the great inheritance is to be saved. He moves the family north at once.
1826	Governor Jose Echeandia confirms the Dominguez title. But when Jose Dolores Sepulveda is killed in an Indian attack near Monterey, his widow and five small children are allowed to remain on Rancho Palos Verdes.
1826-1858	Manuel Dominguez fights and mostly wins 22 separate legal actions to protect his title to Rancho San Pedro. (In one, a group of U.S. citizens claimed that his great-uncle Juan Jose had married an Indian woman, and that her children had sold them the Rancho. The courts found this scenario unbelievable.)
1827-1854	Manuel leads an active public life as council member, alcalde and legislator. He was a delegate to the constitutional convention in 1849 after the war. He was a County Supervisor, 1854-58, after California became part of the Union.
1834	Governor Jose Figueroa awards the Sepulveda heirs the 31,000 acres of Palos Verdes. The remaining 44,000 acres is now confirmed in undivided ownership by Cristobal and Maria's five surviving children: Manuel, Victoria, Pedro, Nasario and Elena.
1835	Nasario sells his interest to Manuel.
1846	Battle of Dominguez ranch, a running skirmish, inconclusive but bloody, considering how few men were involved. The United States wins the Mexican-American War.
1850	Pedro sells his interest to Manuel.
August 3, 1852	J.S. Torrance is born in Gowanda, New York.
1852	Manuel acquires some of his sisters' land. (July 1, 1852, sister Maria Victoria sold him, for $8,000, the tract from Dominguez Hill to the sea which now includes the city of Torrance.)
December 22, 1854	2,400-acre Wilmington Tract is sold to Phineas Banning for $20,000.
October 21, 1855	Sidney Torrance's brother Lewis is born.
1855	Legal partition and survey, first under American law, shows Manuel Dominguez personally holding 63 percent of the Rancho. Remaining portion held by his siblings was sold to Americans over the next generation. Manuel retained and improved his share.
December 18, 1858	President James Buchanan signs the Patent of Title for the Dominguez Rancho. It was the first Spanish land grant in 1784, and 74 years later, it was the first to be confirmed under United States law.
1861-1864	Torrance clerks in his father's Buffalo law office and meets his father's young assistant, Grover Cleveland, later twice President of the United States.
February 14, 1865	Sidney Torrance's older brother Clarence, 14, dies of diptheria.
June 1, 1866	His sister Jennie is born.
1868	Sidney runs away from home; finds work in Chicago.
1869	Manuel Dominguez allocates a strip of land from Los Angeles to the Harbor for a railroad right of way. Until then, travelers between the Pueblo and the Harbor regularly stopped at the Rancho for hospitality.
1870	Sidney Torrance's mother persuades him to return home from Chicago.
1871	Sidney enters Yale University.
1875	Sidney graduates.
1876	Sidney goes to East Prussia as a tutor.
1878	Visits Paris Exposition; returns to Gowanda.
1879-1882	J.S. Torrance incorporates the Bank of Gowanda, becomes a developer, builds an opera house, and wins a fire hydrant pumping competition.
October 11, 1882	Manuel Dominguez dies. His wife dies a few months later. He leaves 25,000 acres valued in probate at $16 an acre.
June 15, 1885	Formal partition of the Rancho into nine tracts. Torrance's site-to-be was the Prairie Tract.
July 4, 1887	J.S. Torrance arrives in California from Gowanda.
1887	The Dominguez sisters sell the two-mile strip along the ocean (Redondo Beach) to Vail and Freeman for $12,000. A few years later, in straitened circumstances, Vail and Freeman sell to Captains Ainsworth and Thompson.
April 1, 1888	Cyrenius Torrance, 62, dies of tuberculosis.
1888	With brother, Sidney Torrance buys controlling interest in Pasadena Electric Light & Power Co. They sell out to Southern California Edison ten years later.
February 13, 1889	J.S. Torrance, 37, marries Annie Laurie Fowler, 23.
1890	Sidney forms partnership with W.D. McGilvray. His son, J.S. Torrance, Jr., is born and dies.

1891	His son, John Fowler Torrance, is born.
1892	J.S. Torrance becomes director of Rubio Canyon Land & Water Co. A large portion of the Estuary Tract in the Harbor area is sold. This tract had been held in common by all the sisters. In April, Redondo Beach is incorporated.
April 12, 1893	Sidney Torrance's wife dies.
1895-1896	Sidney Torrance is president of the Valley Hunt Club, original sponsors of the Rose Parade. Lays out first golf course in Pasadena.
1897	Appointed receiver in bankruptcy for Mt. Lowe scenic railroad and resort.
1899	Is founding member of the Los Angeles Stock Exchange.
1900	J.S. Torrance becomes active in Union Oil Company; is in charge of their finances. His son, John Torrance, dies in elevator accident.
1907	Torrrance becomes a business partner of Joseph F. Sartori. Ana Josefa Dominguez Guyer dies (she was 79), oldest of the six daughters who survived their parents' death. Her husband is left $20,000; she leaves her five sisters 3,400 acres, spread among five of the nine tracts.
1908	J.S. Torrance reluctantly agrees to become active in Charles Lummis' Southwest Museum. By 1917, he is president of the board of directors and donates an elevator and tower to this center of American Indian studies.
1910	He moves to South Pasadena. On the advice of family attorney Henry O'Melveny, who feared another partition battle would end all amity between the strong-willed sisters, the Dominguez Estate Company is formed to adminster Ana Josefa's lands.
December 26, 1911	Pacific Electric agrees to build a line to Torrance and move their shops here. They are given a 125-acre site as an inducement.
1911	Dominguez Water Company is founded to supply water to Rancho lands and to the new city of Torrance. Eventually three sisters deed or sell land to the Estate Company, which thus controls 12,000 acres. Union Tool, thanks to J.S. Torrance's persuasions, buys a 25-acre site in the soon-to-be town, and helps Dr. Henry B. Slehman move his La Vina Sanitarium to Altadena. Dominguez Estate Company sells 2,791 acres to Jared Sidney Torrance & Associates. At $350 an acre, the price was $976,850. At the same time, at the same rate, Torrance buys 730 adjoining acres from Del Amo interests.
March 16, 1912	The founding of Torrance is announced publicly.
September 14, 1912	Herman Burmaster opens the first Torrance Post Office.
1912	Harry Dolley visits Torrance on "Grand Opening Day," and moves here shortly thereafter from Azusa. The Dominguez Land Co. hires John C. and Frederick Law Olmstead, Jr., to design the townsite, Irving Gill as in-house architect, and J.F. Rupprecht as horticulturist. Judge George W. Post moves to Torrance, at Sidney Torrance's urging, from York, Nebraska, then and now a charming town of 8,000 near Lincoln.
May 1, 1913	Torrance Athletic Club is formed with 70 members and "two pool tables in the Murray Hotel." The Gun Club is formed about the same time. The First National Bank of Torrance is founded.
January, 1914	The first issue of the *Torrance Herald* is released.
June 6, 1914	Sidney Torrance marries Helena Childs, 47. They sail to Europe on their honeymoon as war breaks out.
1914	Wanda Stacowitz, daughter of a Torrance blacksmith, rides the city's first Rose Parade float. Later she becomes an opera singer.
1915	Llewellyn Iron Works moves here.
February 11, 1916	Sidney Torrance's mother, 84, dies in Pasadena.
1917	"Old Main" is built at Torrance High School. Torrance Relief Society founded and is active through the 1930s. Diatomaceous earth mine begins operations in Walteria. (Diatoms were tiny sea animals; their fossilized shells made a fine powder with wide industrial use as filtering agent, clarifier and insulator.)
November 1, 1918	Bert Crossland is killed in action at Waagerhem, Belgium, the only Torrance man to die in World War One.
July, 1920	Torrance, fearful of land-hungry Los Angeles, petitions for incorporation election. J.S. Torrance supports it; the Del Amos don't. After months of manuevering, it passes in April, 1921, three weeks after the founder dies.
March 29, 1921	Sidney Torrance dies at the age of 68 and is buried in Gowanda.
June, 1921	The Torrance Woman's Club is formed.
December, 1921	The first gusher in the Torrance field is brought in on Del Amo property.

1921	M.R. Osburn succeeds Torrance as president of Dominguez Land Co. and on May 21, the first meeting of the board of trustees is held. George Proctor is elected president (mayor). The first Fiesta is held; Judge Post is pleased to announce he found just one crooked concession!
1923	Fire station/police station/jail is built on Cravens Avenue. Guadaloupe Avenue is changed to Post Avenue to honor recently deceased Judge Wallace Post.
July, 1924	Scandal rocks the city as police chief and local attorney are convicted of extortion. (See Chapter VI.) The Klu Klux Klan is active in Torrance; a Klan wedding is held at Legion Hall.
November 24, 1924	Torrance Rotary holds its first meeting.
1924	Dolores Dominguez Watson dies in the old family homestead. She had been a widow for 55 years. The family transfers the house and 17 acres to the Order of Immaculate Heart of Mary, more usually called the Claretian Fathers. Postal home delivery begins in Torrance.
1925	Universal's *Bob Hill* film series is shot in Torrance at Hendrie Tire Co.
1926-1931	"Imperial Torrance" takes shape as annexations increase city's size fivefold.
1927	A seminary is built at Rancho Dominguez. Later Susana Del Amo and her Spanish physician husband, Dr. Gregorio Del Amo, are buried in this chapel. The original adobe is restored and decorated with authentic furnishings donated by family members.
1928	Eberle & Riggleman report on Torrance's industrial potential stimulates a wave of investment by Santa Fe Railroad, General Petroleum (now Mobil) and others. Opening of sales activities in the Hollywood Riviera.
April 18, 1929	Possible consolidation of four cities — Redondo Beach, Hermosa Beach, Manhattan Beach and Torrance — is discussed at high levels.
1929	Cornerstone is laid for Riviera Beach Club.
1932-1933	William Klusman, socialist and chicken rancher, is mayor of Torrance.
March 10, 1933	Long Beach earthquake shakes Torrance too; many buildings are damaged. American Legion mounts relief expedition to Long Beach.
1934	Louis Zamperini sets interscholastic mile record (4:21:2) at Torrance High; it stands for 20 years.
July 22, 1936	A deeper oil zone (4,887 feet) is found in Torrance field. But by 1943 the great days of the Torrance field are over.
1936	Isabel Henderson dies and is succeeded as city librarian by her daughter, Dorothy Jamieson.
1936-1937	Silver anniversary of the founding of Torrarnce. New city hall, library, and civic auditorium built with federal funds.
1938	Columbia Pacific builds 490-foot tower east of Hawthorne and north of 190th Street. It broadcasts KNX "clear channel" with 50,000 watts of power.
1940	Helena Childs Torrance dies at the age of 72.
November 14, 1941	Earthquake in Torrance.
December 12, 1941	Resolution of city council expressing confidence in loyalty of Torrance's Japanese-American citizens.
1941	Torrance Municipal Bus Lines is founded.
February 15, 1942	"Battle of Los Angeles" as anti-aircraft fire fills the skies, but firing at what? Local 1414, U.S.W.A. chartered at Columbia Steel.
1946	Torrance airfield (Zamperini Field) is dedicated. Torrance forms a separate school district; soon thereafter forms Council of Parent-Teacher Associations (July 18, 1947).
1949	Eighteen-week wildcat strike at Columbia Steel.
1957	Clifford Reid dies.
1964	Descendants of Manuel Dominguez now number more than 100, even though only five of six daughters married and only three had children. They still own 6,000 acres of the original Rancho.
1965	Local 6500 organizes Harvey Aluminum and they call their first strike.
1967	Del Amo Rotary Club is formed. City passes $2.5 million bond issue to support independent library system; builds new library.
1968	Second Harvey Aluminum strike.
1969	Harvey Aluminum sells Torrance plant to Martin-Marietta.
1976	The Dominguez house and grounds are enrolled in the National Register of Historical Places.
September 22, 1980	President Jimmy Carter comes to North High School for a nationally televised campaign visit.
1983	Father Patrick McPolin orchestrates a multifaceted tribute to the Rancho and the Dominguez family. Participants include high-ranking Spanish and Mexican officials, Ricardo Montalban, Lorne Green, the Roger Wagner Chorale and dozens of Dominguez descendants.
1984	*Historic Torrance* is published!

Bibliography

We hope that this book will not be viewed as the definitive study of the history of Torrance, but as a sampler to stir the palate of the local history buff, or even the resident or visitor who until now may not have been sure Torrance *had* any history at all.

The authors have found fascinating contemporary accounts of Torrance people and events in the *Daily Breeze*, the *Torrance Herald* and in other newspapers in Los Angeles, Pasadena, South Pasadena and Lomita. They were invaluable to our beginning study. So were city directories from 1880 to the present for Torrance, Pasadena, South Pasadena and Los Angeles, and public records in the Los Angeles County archives and the office of the Torrance City Clerk.

Many quotations have been drawn from taped interviews and other material on file at the Torrance Historical Museum, 1345 Post Avenue, Torrance, or from interviews we ourselves did. Many of the pamphlets, maps, biographies and other new material gathered during the course of writing this book also are now on file at the Torrance Historical Museum.

Here are a few of the sources we found useful:

The Arrowhead Magazine. (Distributed free on trains L.A. & S.L.R.R.) Union Pacific, 1923.

Bartlett, Dana W. "An Industrial Garden City, Torrance." *American City*, October 1913, pp. 310-314.

Chase, John and Roger Hatheway. *Torrance Historical Resources Survey.* Torrrance, Ca.: City of Torrance, 1978.

Coil, Vernon W. *History of Torrance.* Torrance, Ca.: City of Torrance, 1967.

"Columbia Becomes Part of U.S. Steel." *Southern California Business*, December 1929, pp. 16-17.

Crain, Claire V. "Early Days of Torrance." Unpublished, 1979.

Crawford, C.M., General Manager. *A Short History of the Dominguez Family.* Dominguez Estate Company, 1955.

Crump, Spencer. *Henry Huntington and the Pacific Electric.* Trans-Anglo Books, 1970.

Crump, Spencer. *Ride the Big Red Cars: How Trolleys Helped Build Southern California.* Trans-Anglo Books, 1962, 1965.

DeMoss, Virginia. "Dominguez Domain." *Westways*, July 1981.

Devon, Duncan Gleason. *The Islands and Ports of California.* Adair, 1958.

Fink, Augusta. *Time and the Terraced Land.* Howell-North Books, 1966.

Gillingham, Robert Cameron, Ph.D. *The History of the Rancho San Pedro.* Los Angeles, Ca.: Cole-Holmquist Co. Copyright 1961 by the Dominguez Estate Company.

Grenier, Dr. Judson. *Reminiscences of the Dominguez Ranch.* Compton, Ca.: California State University Dominguez Hills, 1976, 1981.

History of the Los Angeles Country Club, 1898-1973. Los Angeles, Ca.: 1973.

History of Torrance. Torrance Unified School District Publication No. 34. (A teacher's guide for 3rd grade teachers, prepared under the direction of Mrs. Gertrude Aldershof.) Torrance, Ca.: September 1964.

Johnston, Bernice Eastman. *California's Gabrielino Indians.* Los Angeles, Ca.: Southwest Museum, 1962.

Lemler, Jon, Dave Murray and Jim Perez. "Earthquake 1933." (A high school project.)

The Life and Times of the Pacific Electric (The World's Greatest Interurban). Orange Empire Railway Museum, 1983.

McCarthy, John Russell. *Joseph Francis Sartori, 1859-1946.* Los Angeles, Ca.: The Ward Ritchie Press, 1948.

McGroarty, John Steven. *History of Los Angeles County.* Chicago, Il.: The American Historical Society, 1923.

"Moving the Factory Back to the Land." *Sunset*, March 30, 1913, pp. 299-304.

Myers, Wm. A. and Ira L. Swett. "Trolleys to the Surf." *Interurban Special* 63, 1976.

National Cyclopedia of Biography. New York: James T. White & Co., 1926.

Perry, Pineda and E. Caswell. *Pasadena Area History.* Pasadena, Ca.: James W. Anderson, 1972.

"Record of the Class of 1875." New Haven, Conn.: Sheffield Scientific School, Yale University, undated.

Robinson, W.W. *The Story of the Southwest Museum.* Los Angeles, Ca.: Southwest Museum, undated.

"Romance of the Ranchos." National Public Radio series aired in 1984.

Seims, Charles. *Mount Lowe.* San Marino, Ca.: Golden West Books, 1976.

Six Collegiate Decades. Los Angeles, Ca.: Security First National Bank, 1929.

Spalding, William A. *History and Reminiscences: Los Angeles City and County.* Los Angeles, Ca.: 1932.

Spalding, William A. *History of Los Angeles.* Los Angeles, Ca.: J.R. Finnell & Sons, 1931.

Stork, Willis. *History of the Valley Hunt Club.* Pasadena, Ca.: Valley Hunt Club, 1978.

Tateishi, John. *And Justice for All.* Random House, 1982.

Torrance, A Bicentennial Community. Torrance Chamber of Commerce, 1976.

Torrance, California, Fifty Years. Torrance Chamber of Commerce, 1971.

Torrance, Jared Sidney. "Autobiography." Unpublished, 1916.

Torrance, Jared Sidney. *The Descendants of Lewis Hart and Anne Elliott.* Privately published by Mrs. J.S. Torrance, 1923.

"Torrance on Review." *Torrance Herald,* June 1936.

Torrance: The Modern Industrial City. Los Angeles, Ca.: Thomas D. Campbell & Co., 1913.

Waddell, Paul R. and Robert F. Niven. *The Sign of the 76.* Los Angeles, Ca.: Union Oil Co., 1977.

"Walteria Decides to Annex to Torrance." *Redondo Reflex,* March 16, 1928, p. 1.

Watkins, T.H. *California, An Illustrated History.* Updated. American Legacy Press, 1973.

Weyant, James M. "Torrance Police Department History." (With assistance from Cadet Mark Sims.) May 1983.

Who's Who in Los Angeles, 1924. Los Angeles, Ca.: C.J. Lang, 1924.

Wilson, Carol Green. *California Yankee: William R. Staats, Business Pioneer.* Claremont, Ca.: The Saunders Press, 1946.

Wood, J.W. *Pasadena, California Historical and Personal.* Pasadena, Ca.: Wood, 1917.

"Yale University Obituary Record, 1920-25." New Haven, Conn.: Yale University, 1926.

Zamperini, Louis, with Helen Itria. *Devil at My Heels.* New York: E.P. Dalton Co., 1956.

Index   Numerals in **boldface** indicate an entry in a photo caption on that page. The acknowledgments, bibliography and chronology have not been indexed.